QUALIFIED TYPES: THEORY AND PRACTICE

Distinguished Dissertations in Computer Science

Edited by C.J. van Rijsbergen, University of Glasgow

The Conference of Professors of Computer Science (CPCS), in conjunction with the British Computer Society (BCS), selects annually for publication up to four of the best British PhD dissertations in computer science. The scheme began in 1990. Its aim is to make more visible the significant contribution made by Britain in particular by students to computer science, and to provide a model for future students. Dissertations are selected on behalf of CPCS by a panel whose members are:

M. Clint, Queen's University, Belfast (Chairman)

R. Milner, University of Edinburgh

K. Moody, University of Cambridge

M.S. Paterson, University of Warwick

S. Shrivastava, University of Newcastle upon Tyne

A. Sloman, University of Birmingham

F. Sumner, University of Manchester

Qualified Types:

Theory and Practice

Mark. P. Jones

University of Nottingham

CAMBRIDGE
UNIVERSITY PRESS

PUBLISHED BY THE PRESS SYNDICATE OF THE UNIVERSITY OF CAMBRIDGE
The Pitt Building, Trumpington Street, Cambridge, United Kingdom

CAMBRIDGE UNIVERSITY PRESS

The Edinburgh Building, Cambridge CB2 2RU, UK
40 West 20th Street, New York NY 10011–4211, USA
477 Williamstown Road, Port Melbourne, VIC 3207, Australia
Ruiz de Alarcón 13, 28014 Madrid, Spain
Dock House, The Waterfront, Cape Town 8001, South Africa

http://www.cambridge.org

First published 1994
First paperback edition 2003

A catalogue record for this book is available from the British Library

Library of Congress cataloguing in publication data available

ISBN 0 521 47253 9 hardback
ISBN 0 521 54326 6 paperback

Contents

Summary of notation

Substitutions

R, S, T, U,...	Substitutions (capture avoiding) of types for type variables.
id	The identity substitution.
RS	Composition of substitutions R and S.
$S[\tau_1/t_1, \ldots, \tau_n/t_n]$	Substitution mapping each t_i to τ_i, and any other variable t to St.
$[\tau_1/t_1, \ldots, \tau_n/t_n]$	Abbreviation for $id[\tau_1/t_1, \ldots, \tau_n/t_n]$.
$S[\tau_i/t_i]$	Substitution mapping each t_i to τ_i as i ranges over some (implicit) set of index values, and any other variable t to St.
$[\tau_i/t_i]$	Abbreviation for $id[\tau_i/t_i]$.
$R \approx S$	Equality of substitutions, ignoring 'new' variables, Section 3.4.2, page 26.

Terms

E, F,...	Term expressions.
x, y,...	Term variables, Section 3.1.2, page 18.
EF	Application of E to F, Section 3.1.2, page 18.
$\lambda x.E$	λ-abstraction, Section 3.1.2, page 18.
let $x = E$ **in** F	Local definition of x in F, Section 3.1.2, page 18.
$\lambda v.E$	Evidence abstraction, Section 4.2, page 34. If $v = v_1, \ldots, v_n$ is a list of evidence variables, then $\lambda v.E$ is used as an abbreviation for $\lambda v_1 \ldots . \lambda v_n.E$, Section 4.2, page 35.
Ee	Evidence application, Section 4.2, page 34. If $e = e_1, \ldots, e_n$ is a list of evidence expressions, then Ee is used as an abbreviation for $(\ldots(Ee_1)\ldots)e_n$, Section 4.2, page 35.
$FV(E)$	Term variables appearing free in E, Section 3.1.2, page 18.

$[E/x]F$	Capture free substitution of E for each free occurrence of x in F, Section 3.1.2, page 18.
id	The identity term $\lambda x.x$.
Erase E	Erasure of E, Section 5.2, page 47.

Predicates and evidence

π, π', ...	Predicates.
P, Q, R, ...	Predicate sets/assignments.
e, f, g, ...	Evidence expressions (also used to represent lists of evidence expressions), Section 4.2, page 34.
u, v, w, ...	Evidence variables (also used to represent lists of evidence variables), Section 4.2, page 34.
$v : P$	Predicate assignment. If $v = v_1, \ldots, v_n$ is a list of evidence variables and $P = \pi_1, \ldots, \pi_n$ is a list of predicates, then $v : P$ is used as an abbreviation for the predicate assignment $v_1 : \pi_1, \ldots, v_n : \pi_n$, Section 4.2, page 35.
$EV(e)$	Type variables appearing free in σ, Section 4.2, page 34.
$\emptyset$	The empty set/predicate assignment, Section 2.1, page 7.
P, Q	Union (concatenation) of P and Q, Section 2.1, page 7.
$P \Vdash Q$	Predicate entailment, Section 2.1, page 6.
$P \Vdash e : Q$	Construction of evidence e for Q from predicate assignment P, Section 4.2, page 34.
$P \vdash e = f : Q$	Evidence equality judgement, Section 5.4.1, page 49.

Types and type schemes

σ, η, ...	OML Type schemes, Section 3.1.1, page 17.
	OP types, Section 5.1, page 45.
ρ, ρ', ...	Qualified types, Section 3.1.1, page 17.
τ, ν, μ, ...	Simple types, Section 3.1.1, page 17.
t, α, β, γ, ...	Type variables, Section 3.1.1, page 17.
$\forall T.\sigma$	Polymorphic type, Section 3.1.1, page 17.

$P \Rightarrow \sigma$	Qualified type, Section 3.1.1, page 17.
	If $\sigma = Q \Rightarrow \tau$ and P, Q are predicate sets then $P \Rightarrow \sigma$ is used as an abbreviation for $(P, Q) \Rightarrow \sigma$, Section 3.1.1, page 17.
	If $P = \pi_1, \ldots, \pi_n$ is a list of predicates, then $P \Rightarrow \sigma$ is used as an abbreviation for $\pi_1 \Rightarrow \ldots \Rightarrow \pi_n \Rightarrow \rho$, Section 4.2, page 35.
$(P \mid \sigma)$	Constrained type scheme, Section 3.2.1, page 19.
Type	The set of all simple type expressions, Section 3.1.1, page 17.
$TV(\sigma)$	Type variables appearing free in σ, Section 3.1.1, page 17.
$AV(\sigma)$	Ambiguous type variables in σ, Section 5.8.3, page 64.
$Gen(A, \rho)$	Generalisation of ρ with respect to A, Section 3.2.4, page 22.
$(P \mid \sigma) \leq (Q \mid \eta)$	Ordering on constrained type schemes, Section 3.2.1, page 20.
$C : (Q \mid \eta) \geq (P \mid \sigma)$	Conversion C from $(Q \mid \eta)$ to $(P \mid \sigma)$, Section 5.5, page 54.
$C' \circ C$	Composition of conversions, Section 5.5, page 55.
$\tau \stackrel{U}{\sim} \tau'$	Most general unifier U of τ and τ', Section 3.4.1, page 26.

Typing judgements and related notation

$A,\ A', \ldots$	Type assignments, Section 3.1.3, page 18.
dom A	Domain of type assignment A, Section 3.1.3, page 18.
$A_x, x : \sigma$	Type assignment obtained from A by adding a new binding for x, Section 3.1.3, page 18.
$A(x)$	Value assigned to x in type assignment A, Section 3.1.3, page 18.
$P \mid A \vdash E : \sigma$	Typing judgement, Section 3.1.3, page 18.
$P \mid A \stackrel{s}{\vdash} E : \sigma$	Syntax-directed typing judgement, Section 3.3.1, page 23.
$P \mid A \stackrel{W}{\vdash} E : \sigma$	Type inference algorithm judgement, Section 3.4.2, page 26.
$P \mid A \vdash E \leadsto F : \sigma$	Typed translation judgement, Section 5.2, page 47.
$P \mid A \vdash E \rhd F : \sigma$	Typed reduction judgement, Section 5.4.2, page 50.
$P \mid A \vdash E = F : \sigma$	Typed equality judgement, Section 5.4, page 49.
$\vdash E = F$	Equality of terms in all applicable contexts, Section 5.4, page 49.

Acknowledgements

One small page is not enough to do justice to the people that have helped me, either directly or indirectly, with the development and production of this thesis. In the first place, my thanks go to Keble College, Oxford, and the Programming Research Group, University of Oxford for the facilities that they have provided for my use, and to Richard Bird and Bernard Sufrin for their guidance as my supervisors during the past three years. I am also pleased to acknowledge the support of the Science and Engineering Research Council of Great Britain, without whose funding this work could never have been completed.

Particular thanks to Phil Wadler whose own work provides much of the motivation for this thesis and whose comments, during an enlightening week at the University of Glasgow in July 1990, helped me to develop the original definitions on which it is based. I am also very grateful to Simon Peyton Jones, Satish Thatte, Ignacio Trejos-Zelaya and Wayne Luk for their comments and interest in my work.

Thanks also to the ever-growing number of Gofer users for their feedback and suggestions during the past year. I am happy that this part of my work has already been useful to others and also grateful for the opportunities and contacts that it has given me in return.

On a personal note, I would like to thank my parents for their love and support. A final and special thank-you to my wife, Melanie, for reminding me of the better things in life and for believing in me when I didn't.

Chapter 1

Introduction

1.1 Type systems for programming languages

Many programming languages rely on the use of a system of *types* to distinguish between different kinds of value. This in turn is used to identify two classes of program; those which are *well-typed* and accepted by the type system, and those that it rejects. Many different kinds of type system have been considered but, in each case, the principal benefits are the same:

- **The ability to detect program errors at compile time**: A type discipline can often help to detect simple program errors such as passing an inappropriate number of parameters to a function.
- **Improved performance**: If, by means of the type system, it is possible to ensure that the result of a particular calculation will always be of a certain type, then it is possible to omit the corresponding runtime checks that would otherwise be needed before using that value. The resulting program will typically be slightly shorter and faster.
- **Documentation**: The types of the values defined in a program are often useful as a simple form of documentation. Indeed, in some situations, just knowing the type of an object can be enough to deduce properties about its behaviour (Wadler, 1989).

The main disadvantage is that no effective type system is complete; there will always be programs that are rejected by the type system, even though they would have produced well-defined results if executed without consideration of the types of the terms involved. For example, the expression:

$$1 + (\textbf{if } \textit{True} \textbf{ then } 1 \textbf{ else } \text{“str”})$$

has a well-defined numeric value, but will not be accepted in many typed languages because the values 1 and “str” in the two branches of the conditional do not have the same type. More sophisticated type systems might accept the expression above, but would reject similar expressions obtained by replacing the constant *True* with increasingly complicated boolean-valued expressions.

For most of the work in this thesis we concentrate on type systems for statically typed languages. The most important factors to be considered in the design of such systems are:

- **Flexibility**: The type system should not impose too many restrictions on the programmer and should accept a reasonably large class of programs.

- **Effective type checking**: There should be an effective process for determining whether or not a particular program is acceptable. For example, it is not usually acceptable for a compiler to enter a non-terminating computation in an attempt to determine whether a given program is acceptable.

- **Intuitive behaviour**: The programmer should be able to predict which programs will be accepted and which will not.

- **Accuracy**: The types assigned to objects should accurately reflect the properties of those objects. The desire for more detailed types (that give more information about the corresponding families of values) must be balanced with the aim of maintaining effective type checking.

1.2 Type inference and polymorphism

In his seminal paper "A Theory of Type Polymorphism in Programming" (1978), Milner observed that, in many cases, there is no need to mention the types of the objects appearing in an expression since they may be inferred from context. Using a simple implicitly typed language based on the untyped λ-calculus, he showed how a *type inference algorithm* could be used to calculate valid typings for programs without explicit type annotations. In later work (Damas and Milner, 1982) it was established that the typing that Milner's algorithm assigns to a given term (if any typing is possible) is, in a very precise sense, the most general typing that can be obtained for that term, extending an earlier result due to Hindley (1969).

Another significant feature of Milner's work was its formal treatment of *polymorphism*: The ability to treat some terms as having many different types. Opportunities for polymorphism occur when the type of a term is not completely determined by its context. For example, using the notation of a modern functional language, we can consider a function *length* that takes a list of values as its argument and returns the length of the list (an integer) as its result:

$$\begin{array}{lcl} \mathit{length}\ [\,] & = & 0 \\ \mathit{length}\ (x : xs) & = & 1 + \mathit{length}\ xs \end{array}$$

The values held in the list (represented by the variable x in the second line of the definition) are not actually used in the calculation. Hence the *length* function can be treated as having type $[a] \to \mathit{Int}$ for any type a, where Int denotes the type of integers, $[a]$ denotes the type of lists with members of type a, and $a \to b$ denotes the type of functions mapping values of type a to values of type b. Rather than picking any one particular type of this form, we say that *length* has a *type scheme* $\forall a.[a] \to \mathit{Int}$, using explicit universal quantification as in (Damas and Milner, 1982) to indicate that the choice of a is arbitrary. Following Strachey (1967), this is often described as *parametric polymorphism* since the set of types represented by a type scheme can be obtained by choosing different values for the quantified type variables (the parameters) in the type part of the type scheme.

More generally, if *Type* denotes the set of all first-order types, and $f(t)$ is an element of *Type* (possibly involving the type variable t), then an object with type scheme $\forall t.f(t)$ can be treated as having any of the types in the set

$$\{f(\tau) \mid \tau \in \mathit{Type}\},$$

where $f(\tau)$ is obtained by substituting τ for t in $f(t)$ in the obvious way. Treating the elements of *Type* as type schemes with no quantified variables, each $\tau \in \mathit{Type}$ corresponds to the singleton set of types $\{\tau\}$. With this in mind, the elements of *Type* are often referred to as *monotypes*.

1.3 The choice between 'all' and 'one'

While convenient for many programs, there are also examples that cannot be described comfortably using either parametric polymorphic types or monotypes; the choice between 'all' and 'one' is too severe. What type, for example, should be assigned to the addition function $(+)$? We would certainly hope to be able to use the same operator to add both integer and floating point numbers, but the standard Hindley/Milner type system gives only two options:

- The simplest solution is to use distinct monotyped function symbols for each variant of the addition function that is required. However, the use of several different symbols describing a single concept seems unnatural and may not be practical in situations where any significant number of variations is required. Furthermore, we will typically need to repeat the definitions of any values defined, either directly or indirectly, in terms of addition for each different choice of that function.

- An alternative approach would be to treat addition as having a polymorphic type – for example, $(\forall a.a \to a \to a)$ – but this makes the type system unsound, or at least, reduces its ability to detect type errors involving the use of addition since there are types a on which the addition operator is undefined. As a result, there are programs that will be accepted by the type system, and yet result in a run-time type error. Note that the implementation of addition will typically involve the use of distinct sections of code for each different type for which the function is defined. This is in stark contrast to the *length* function described above where the same code can be used for every different choice of type, and is an example of what is commonly called *ad-hoc polymorphism*.

In the past, many language designers have side-stepped these issues; typical approaches include: treating all kinds of numeric values as the elements of a single type, relying on implicit coercions between numeric values of different kinds or using somewhat ad-hoc techniques to determine which particular version of a function is needed in a given context.

There have also been a number of attempts to solve these problems using *constrained type systems* in which the range of type variables may be restricted to particular families of types. We mention in particular the work of Kaes (1988) and Wadler and Blott (1989) on parametric overloading, of Mitchell (1984) and Fuh and Mishra (1989, 1990) on subtyping and of Harper and Pierce (1990) on extensible records. These papers provide much of the motivation for this thesis and their examples will be used to illustrate some of the applications of our work.

1.4 Qualified types

This thesis develops a general approach to constrained type systems based on the use of *qualified types* and providing an intermediate level between monomorphic and polymorphic typing disciplines. For example, if $\pi(t)$ is a predicate on types, then we can use a type scheme of the form $\forall t.\pi(t) \Rightarrow f(t)$ to represent a set of types:

$$\{ f(\tau) \mid \tau \text{ is a type such that } \pi(\tau) \text{ holds} \}.$$

For example, we might write the type of the addition function described in the previous section as $\forall t.Num\ t \Rightarrow t \to t \to t$ where $Num\ t$ is a predicate that is true exactly when t is a numeric type. Many further examples will be given in later chapters.

The use of qualified types may be thought of in two ways: Either as a restricted form of polymorphism, or as an extension of the use of monotypes, commonly described as *overloading*, in which a function may have different interpretations according to the types of its arguments.

The main benefits of using qualified types are:

- A general approach that includes familiar type systems as special cases. Results and tools developed for the general system are immediately applicable to each particular application.
- A flexible treatment of predicates on types and inferences between them that is largely independent of any single type system.
- More accurate assignment of types to objects without losing the ability to support effective type checking.
- The ability to include local constraints as part of the type of an object. This enables the definition and use of polymorphic overloaded values within a program.
- A precise treatment of the relationship between implicit and explicit overloading. This is particularly useful for describing the implementation of systems supporting qualified types.

1.5 Outline of thesis

This thesis addresses both theoretical and practical issues concerning the use and application of qualified types and we begin by summarising the contents of the following chapters.

The choice of a suitable language of predicates is clearly an important part of any application of qualified types. Chapter 2 introduces a formal framework for predicate systems and specifies some simple properties which they are expected to satisfy. We illustrate these definitions by giving systems of predicates which can be used to describe the use of type classes, subtyping and extensible records.

Chapter 3 describes an extension of Milner's type system which includes support for overloading based on the use of qualified types and parameterised by an arbitrary system of predicates. We define an ordering on the set of type schemes and show that there is a type inference algorithm which calculates *principal types*, i.e. greatest possible typings with respect to this ordering.

The next two chapters re-examine and extend the work of Chapters 2 and 3, using the concept of *evidence* introduced in Chapter 4 to give a semantic interpretation for overloading. We show how the definition of predicate systems can be extended to describe the construction of evidence and suggest suitable choices of evidence for particular applications. In the case of type classes and subtyping, these include well-known techniques which are already used in the implementation of such systems. Previous work with extensible records does not appear to have made use of analogous techniques, but we show how the concept of evidence leads us to a promising new implementation.

Chapter 5 shows how the semantics of programs in the language described in Chapter 3 can be captured by translating them into a language with explicit constructs for manipulating evidence values. Each source term may have many different translations and it is necessary to show that these are semantically equivalent in order to prove that the meaning of the original term is well-defined. We accomplish this by identifying a particular *principal translation* and showing how any other translation can be expressed in terms of this. These results depend on a notion of *uniqueness of evidence*, a property of the predicate system which must be verified independently for each application of qualified types. The most important and novel aspect of our approach is the use of *conversions* to give a semantic interpretation for the ordering relation between type schemes.

The following three chapters deal with more practical issues and we adopt a less rigourous approach with the emphasis on concrete implementation techniques rather than the formal properties of the type systems involved. Chapter 6 begins the transition from theory to practice by describing a number of extensions to the type systems presented in the previous chapters. Each of these might potentially be used to provide more accurate type checking, simplified principal types or more efficient implementations.

In Chapter 7 we focus on the system of type classes used in the functional programming language Haskell and describe some useful optimisations to the original implementation suggested by Wadler and Blott (1989). In particular, we concentrate on the task of trying to minimise the construction of dictionary values which play the role of evidence in this particular application.

Chapter 8 outlines an alternative approach to type classes as implemented in Gofer, a small, experimental system developed by the author. We discuss the relationship between the two approaches and show how the system of type classes in Gofer lends itself to a remarkably clean and efficient implementation.

Finally, Chapter 9 outlines several ideas for further work motivated by the issues raised in the preceding chapters.

Chapter 2

Predicates

The key feature of a system of qualified types that distinguishes it from other systems based solely on parametric polymorphism is the use of a language of *predicates* to describe sets of types (or more generally, relations between types). Exactly which sets of types and relations are useful will (of course) vary from one application to another and it does not seem appropriate to base a general theory on any particular choice. Our solution, outlined in this chapter, is to work in a framework where the properties of a (largely unspecified) language of predicates are described in terms of an entailment relation that is expected to satisfy a few simple laws. In this way, we are able to treat the choice of a language of predicates as a parameter for each of the type systems described in subsequent chapters. This approach also has the advantage that it enables us to investigate how the properties of particular type systems are affected by properties of the underlying systems of predicates.

The basic notation for predicates and entailment is outlined in Section 2.1. The remaining sections illustrate this general framework with applications to: Haskell-style type classes (Section 2.2), subtyping (Section 2.3) and extensible records (Section 2.4). Although we consider each of these examples independently, this work opens up the possibility of combining elements of each in a single concrete programming language.

2.1 Basic definitions

For much of this thesis we deal with an abstract language of predicates on types. The exact form of individual predicates is not significant but, in practical applications, they are often written using expressions of the form $\pi = p\ \tau_1\ \ldots\ \tau_n$ where p is a predicate symbol corresponding to an n-place relation between types: The predicate π represents the assertion that the types denoted by the type expressions $\tau_1,\ldots,\tau_n$ are in this relation. The only condition imposed on the set of predicates is that it be closed under substitutions mapping type variables (and hence type expressions) to type expressions, i.e. for any such substitution S and any predicate π as above, the expression:

$$S\pi = p\ (S\tau_1)\ \ldots\ (S\tau_n)$$

should also be a predicate.

Properties of predicates are captured by an entailment relation $\Vdash$ between (finite) sets of predicates. An entailment of the form $P \Vdash \{\pi\}$ indicates that the predicate π can be inferred from the predicates in P. In practice, we often write π as an abbreviation for the singleton predicate set $\{\pi\}$ and hence write this entailment as $P \Vdash \pi$. More generally, we expect the entailment relation between arbitrary finite sets of predicates to satisfy:

$$P \Vdash Q \quad \Leftrightarrow \quad \forall \pi \in Q.\, P \Vdash \pi. \qquad (\textit{set-entail})$$

This is often used implicitly in the definition of entailment for particular applications of qualified types. Thus we describe only the rules for entailments of the form $P \Vdash \pi$ and use (*set-entail*) to extend this to the desired relation between predicate sets.

The only other properties that we assume about entailment are as follows:

- **Monotonicity**. $P \Vdash P'$ whenever $P \supseteq P'$. By (*set-entail*), this is equivalent to saying that $P \Vdash \pi$ for each $\pi \in P$.
- **Transitivity**. If $P \Vdash Q$ and $Q \Vdash R$, then $P \Vdash R$.
- **Closure property**. If $P \Vdash Q$, then $SP \Vdash SQ$ for any substitution S. This condition is needed to ensure that the system of predicates is compatible with the use of parametric polymorphism.

A number of other useful properties of $\Vdash$ follow directly from these laws. For example, taking $P' = P$ in the definition of monotonicity gives $P \Vdash P$, showing that $\Vdash$ is reflexive. Furthermore, taking $P' = \emptyset$ we find that $P \Vdash \emptyset$ for all P. Some additional derived properties are given below.

In the following, we write P, Q for the union of predicate sets P and Q and use P, π as an abbreviation for $P, \{\pi\}$. The principal reason for this choice of notation (rather than the conventional $P \cup Q$) is to avoid any preconceptions about the properties of the $(\_,\_)$ operator. This will be convenient in later work (Chapters 4 and 5 in particular) where we consider entailments between ordered collections of predicates.

With this in mind, we reformulate the properties of predicate entailment given above so that we do not need to rely on any particular interpretation of $\emptyset$ and $(\_,\_)$ in formal proofs. A suitable collection of rules is given in Figure 2.1 and these are usually taken used as part of definition of entailment in specific applications.

Notice the law (*univ*) which is needed to establish the derived rules of distributivity (*dist*) and the cut rule (*cut*). For the special case of predicate sets, all three of these rules can be proved using monotonicity, transitivity and (*set-entail*) and hence the rules in Figure 2.1 may seem unnecessarily complicated. However, the benefits of this approach will become more apparent in later chapters.

For the purposes of entailment, we can treat $(\_,\_)$ as an associative operator: It is a simple exercise to show that $P, (Q, R) \Vdash (P, Q), R$ and $(P, Q), R \Vdash P, (Q, R)$ for any P, Q and R. By (*trans*), it follows that $(P, Q), R$ and $P, (Q, R)$ are equivalent in the sense that:

$$P' \Vdash P, (Q, R) \Leftrightarrow P' \Vdash (P, Q), R \quad \text{and} \quad P, (Q, R) \Vdash P' \Leftrightarrow (P, Q), R \Vdash P'.$$

The equivalence of $P, \emptyset$ and $\emptyset, P$ to P can be established in a similar way, so that $\emptyset$ can be treated as an identity for $(\_,\_)$.

Monotonicity:	(id)	$P \Vdash P$
	$(term)$	$P \Vdash \emptyset$
	(fst)	$P, Q \Vdash P$
	(snd)	$P, Q \Vdash Q$
	$(univ)$	$\dfrac{P \Vdash Q \quad P \Vdash R}{P \Vdash Q, R}$
Transitivity:	$(trans)$	$\dfrac{P \Vdash Q \quad Q \Vdash R}{P \Vdash R}$
Closure property:	$(close)$	$\dfrac{P \Vdash Q}{SP \Vdash SQ}$
Derived rules:	$(dist)$	$\dfrac{P \Vdash Q \quad P' \Vdash Q'}{P, P' \Vdash Q, Q'}$
	(cut)	$\dfrac{P \Vdash Q \quad P, Q \Vdash R}{P \Vdash R}$

Figure 2.1: Rules for predicate entailment.

2.2 Type classes

Much of the original motivation for qualified types came from the study of *type classes*, introduced by Wadler and Blott (1989) and adopted as part of the standard for the programming language Haskell (Hudak et al., 1992). Type classes are particularly useful for describing the implementation of standard polymorphic operators (such as computable equality), but they can also be used as a more general tool for the development of clear, modular programs (Jones, 1990).

In this section we sketch the principal components of a system of type classes and describe the corresponding system of predicates. The use and implementation of type classes is considered in more depth in Chapters 4, 7 and 8.

2.2.1 Class declarations

Broadly speaking, a *type class* represents a family of types (the *instances* of the class) together with an associated set of *member functions* defined for each instance of the class. For each class C and type τ, a predicate of the form $C\ \tau$ represents the assertion that τ is an instance of the class C. This notation follows the concrete syntax of Haskell (were it not for the use of a limited character set, these predicates might well have been written in the form $\tau \in C$). A standard example is the set of types whose elements may be tested for equality. The following *class declaration* illustrates how this can be defined in the concrete syntax of Haskell:

```
class Eq a where
    (==)  ::  a -> a -> Bool
```

The definition is in two parts:

- The expression Eq a in the first line introduces a name Eq for the class and indicates that the type variable a will be used to represent an arbitrary instance of the class in the following part of the definition.
- The second line gives the names of the member functions of the class. In this case we have a single member function, represented by the infix operator symbol (==). The type signature a -> a -> Bool indicates that, for each instance a of Eq, the equality operator is defined as a function taking two arguments of type a and returning a boolean value of type Bool.

The equality operator (==) will now be treated as having the (qualified) type:

```
(==)  ::  Eq a => a -> a -> Bool
```

Note the convention that all free variables in a type expression are implicitly bound by a universal quantifier at the outermost level. Thus (==) is 'polymorphic' in a, but the choice of types for a is restricted to instances of Eq.

Even before we have defined a single instance of the class, we can use the (==) operator, either directly or indirectly, in the definition of other values. For example:

```
member x []        =  False
member x (y:ys)    =  x==y || member x ys

xs `subset` ys     =  all (\x -> member x ys) xs
```

The restriction to lists of values whose type is an instance of Eq is reflected by the types assigned to these functions:

```
member  ::  Eq a => a -> [a] -> Bool
subset  ::  Eq a => [a] -> [a] -> Bool
```

2.2.2 Instance declarations

The instances of a class are defined by a collection of *instance declarations* as illustrated by the following examples. An implementation of the equality function on integers, supplied by a built-in primitive primEqInt with monomorphic type Int -> Int -> Bool, can be included as part of the definition of (==) using the declaration:

```
instance Eq Int where
    (==)  =  primEqInt
```

The same function might also be used, indirectly, to define an equality operation on values of type Char representing characters:

```
instance Eq Char where
    c == c'  =  ord c == ord c'
```

(`ord c` gives the integer code corresponding to the character `c`.)

Instances of a class may also be given for standard and user-defined algebraic data types as in the following definition of equality on lists:

```
instance Eq a => Eq [a] where
    []     == []     =  True
    []     == (y:ys) =  False
    (x:xs) == []     =  False
    (x:xs) == (y:ys) =  x==y && xs==ys
```

The expression `Eq a => Eq [a]` in the first line indicates that the definition of equality on lists depends on the definition of equality on the elements held in the lists: If `a` is an instance of `Eq`, then so is `[a]`.

Note that the set of types defined by a finite collection of instance declarations may be infinite (but recursively enumerable).

2.2.3 Superclasses

The system of type classes used in Haskell also supports a mechanism for defining hierarchies of classes using a notion of *superclasses*. For example, a simple declaration for the class `Ord` (whose instances are those types with elements ordered using the `(<=)` operator) might be:

```
class Eq a => Ord a where
    (<=)  ::  a -> a -> Bool
```

indicating that every instance of `Ord` should also be an instance of `Eq`. (Note that, in this situation, the `=>` symbol should be read as $\supseteq$ not implication; to say that `Eq` is a superclass of `Ord` means that `t`∈`Ord` implies `t`∈`Eq` and not the converse.)

2.2.4 The entailment relation for type classes

The definition of the predicate entailment relation $\Vdash$ depends on the information provided by the class and instance declarations appearing in a program. The relevant details can be represented by a set Γ which we call a *type class environment* containing two kinds of term:

Class $P \Rightarrow \pi$	corresponding to the first line of a class declaration; each of the classes in P is a superclass of the class named by π.
Inst $P \Rightarrow \pi$	corresponding to the first line of an instance declaration; if there is an instance for each predicate in P, then there is an instance for π.

For example, the type class environment for the declarations above is:

$$\begin{array}{l}\{\mathit{Class}\ \{\} \Rightarrow \mathit{Eq}\ a, \\ \ \mathit{Class}\ \{\mathit{Eq}\ a\} \Rightarrow \mathit{Ord}\ a, \\ \ \mathit{Inst}\ \{\} \Rightarrow \mathit{Eq}\ \mathit{Int}, \\ \ \mathit{Inst}\ \{\} \Rightarrow \mathit{Eq}\ \mathit{Char}, \\ \ \mathit{Inst}\ \{\mathit{Eq}\ a\} \Rightarrow \mathit{Eq}\ [a]\,\}\end{array}$$

The definition of predicate entailment for type classes is given by the rules in Figure 2.2, combined with the general rules in Figure 2.2. These rules are parameterised by the choice of a fixed type class environment Γ (with type variables in Γ interpreted as meta-variables of the inference rules).

$$(\mathit{super})\quad \frac{P \Vdash \pi \quad (\mathit{Class}\ P' \Rightarrow \pi) \in \Gamma \quad \pi' \in P'}{P \Vdash \pi'}$$

$$(\mathit{inst})\quad \frac{P \Vdash P' \quad (\mathit{Inst}\ P' \Rightarrow \pi) \in \Gamma}{P \Vdash \pi}$$

Figure 2.2: Rules for type class entailment

The main advantages of this treatment of type classes are:

- The current version of Haskell makes a number of (largely syntactic) restrictions on the form of class and instance declarations and limits type classes to a single parameter. On the other hand, the framework described here makes no assumptions about the elements of a type class environment and can be used to reason about 'multiple parameter classes' with predicates of the form $C\ \tau_1\ \ldots\ \tau_n$.
- The same ideas can be used to describe alternatives to the Haskell approach to type classes. Chapter 8 deals with one interesting example of this.
- There is a natural and direct treatment of superclasses as part of the definition of $\Vdash$. This is in contrast with the approach described in (Chen, Hudak and Odersky, 1992) where superclasses are encoded using *class sets*, and with other proposals, for example (Blott, 1991), that do not formalise the use of superclasses. One notable exception is the paper by Nipkow and Snelting (1991) that uses a sort hierarchy to model superclasses.

2.3 Subtyping

In many programming languages, it is possible for functions expecting real number arguments to be applied to integer values, even though the two kinds of number may have different representations. This is often dealt with by considering the type of integers *Int* to be a *subtype* of the type of real numbers *Real*, written $\mathit{Int} \subseteq \mathit{Real}$, indicating that every integer can be treated as a real number by applying a suitable *coercion function*.

In this section we outline a simple approach to subtyping using predicates of the form $\sigma \subseteq \tau$ to represent the assertion that σ is a subtype of τ. A simple definition of entailments between such predicates might be based on the rulesin Figure 2.3 as in (Mitchell, 1984) and later extended in (Jategaonkar and Mitchell, 1988; Fuh and Mishra, 1989, 1990; Mitchell, 1991). Notice the rule (*arrow*) that describes the way in which inclusions between function types

$$(\mathit{refl}) \qquad P \Vdash \sigma \subseteq \sigma$$

$$(\mathit{trans}\text{-}\subseteq) \qquad \frac{P \Vdash \sigma \subseteq \rho \quad P \Vdash \rho \subseteq \tau}{P \Vdash \sigma \subseteq \tau}$$

$$(\mathit{arrow}) \qquad \frac{P \Vdash \sigma \subseteq \sigma' \quad P \Vdash \tau' \subseteq \tau}{P \Vdash (\sigma' \to \tau') \subseteq (\sigma \to \tau)}$$

Figure 2.3: Rules for structural subtyping

are determined by inclusions between their component types. For example, if $\mathit{Int} \subseteq \mathit{Real}$, we can deduce:

$$(\mathit{Real} \to \mathit{Int}) \subseteq (\mathit{Int} \to \mathit{Int}) \quad \text{and} \quad (\mathit{Int} \to \mathit{Int}) \subseteq (\mathit{Int} \to \mathit{Real}),$$

corresponding to the coercions obtained by composing on the right or left respectively with a coercion from *Int* to *Real*.

The system of predicates described above can be used both in languages that allow only explicit coercions and in those which allow implicit coercions. A simple application of the former might be to use an addition function:

$$\mathit{add} :: \forall a.a \subseteq \mathit{Real} \Rightarrow a \to a \to \mathit{Real}$$

to add two integers together, obtaining a real number as the result. In simple languages, functions like *add* might be provided as built-in primitives. The benefit of using qualified types is that other functions defined in terms of these primitives may also be overloaded. For example:

$$\begin{array}{lcl} \mathit{double} & :: & \forall a.a \subseteq \mathit{Real} \Rightarrow a \to \mathit{Real} \\ \mathit{double}\ x & = & \mathit{add}\ x\ x \end{array}$$

There is nothing to prohibit the use of a primitive function:

$$\mathit{coerce} :: \forall a.\forall b.a \subseteq b \Rightarrow a \to b$$

that can be used at any point in a program where a coercion is required.

More sophisticated systems, including all of those cited above, allow the use of implicit coercions: If E is a term of type σ and $\sigma \subseteq \sigma'$, then the term E can also be treated as a term of type σ'. This is in contrast with a system that permits only explicit coercions where it might be necessary to write *coerce* E to obtain a term of type σ'. In these systems, the addition of two integers to obtain a real result can be described without explicit overloading using a function:

$$\mathit{add} :: \mathit{Real} \to \mathit{Real} \to \mathit{Real}$$

with two implicit coercions from *Int* to *Real*. As a further example, the *coerce* function described above can be implemented by the standard 'identity function', $\lambda x.x$ (but of course, there is no practical use for *coerce* in a system that already has implicit coercions!).

In this thesis we concentrate on type systems suitable for languages with explicit coercions. Section 6.3 outlines the extensions needed to support the use of implicit coercions and describes some of the problems that can occur.

2.4 Extensible records

A *record* is a collection of values (known as *fields*), possibly of different types, each of which is associated with a distinct element l drawn from some specified set of *labels*. Simple examples include the empty record $\langle\rangle$ (with no fields) and $\langle x = 1,\ y = \mathit{True}\rangle$ which has two fields labelled x and y containing an integer and a boolean value respectively.

There has been considerable interest in the use of records to model features of object oriented programming languages including inheritance and subtyping. A number of different approaches have been considered including (Wand, 1987; Cardelli, 1988; Stansifer, 1988; Rémy, 1989; Cardelli and Mitchell, 1990).

The approach described in this section is based on work described by (Harper and Pierce, 1990). This system, in common with some of the other approaches mentioned above, provides a system of *extensible records*, the key feature being that any record which does not have a field corresponding to a particular label may be extended to include such a field. This operation on record values is often described as *polymorphic extension* since it can be applied to any type of record except those which already contain a field with the particular label concerned. As such, this is a natural application for qualified types.

For reasons of space, we can only sketch the basic ideas here. Further details and a discussion of the relationship between this approach and those of other systems of extensible records are given in (Harper and Pierce, 1990).

To begin with we will assume that the language of expressions includes record expressions described by the syntax:

$$
\begin{array}{rcll}
\rho & ::= & \langle\rangle & \textit{empty record} \\
 & | & \rho \setminus l & \textit{restriction} \\
 & | & \langle \rho \mid l = e \rangle & \textit{extension} \\
 & | & \rho.l & \textit{selection}
\end{array}
$$

where $(\rho \setminus l)$ gives the result of removing the field labelled l from the record ρ, $\langle \rho \mid l = e\rangle$ gives the result of adding a field l with value e to the record ρ and $(\rho.l)$ returns the value of the field labelled l in the record ρ. Not all of the expressions permitted by this syntax are well-formed, but we will rely on the use of types and predicates to detect such errors rather than on purely syntactic conditions.

It is often convenient to use the following abbreviations for record expressions:

$$
\begin{array}{lcl}
\langle x = e \rangle & = & \langle \langle\rangle \mid x = e \rangle \\
\langle x_1 = e_1,\ \ldots,\ x_n = e_n,\ x_{n+1} = e_{n+1} \rangle & = & \langle \langle x_1 = e_1,\ \ldots,\ x_n = e_n \rangle \mid x_{n+1} = e_{n+1} \rangle
\end{array}
$$

Note that the order of fields in a record is not significant so that, for example, the expressions $\langle x = 2,\ y = 3\rangle$ and $\langle y = 3,\ x = 2\rangle$ represent the same record.

Record formation:

$$P \Vdash \mathsf{record}\ \langle\rangle$$

$$\frac{P \Vdash \mathsf{record}\ r \quad P \Vdash r\ \mathsf{lacks}\ l}{P \Vdash \mathsf{record}\ \langle r \mid l\!:\!t\rangle}$$

$$\frac{P \Vdash \mathsf{record}\ r \quad P \Vdash r\ \mathsf{has}\ l\!:\!t}{P \Vdash \mathsf{record}\ r \setminus l}$$

Absent fields:

$$P \Vdash \langle\rangle\ \mathsf{lacks}\ l$$

$$\frac{P \Vdash \mathsf{record}\ r \setminus l}{P \Vdash r \setminus l\ \mathsf{lacks}\ l}$$

$$\frac{P \Vdash r\ \mathsf{lacks}\ l}{P \Vdash r \setminus l'\ \mathsf{lacks}\ l} \quad l \neq l'$$

$$\frac{P \Vdash r\ \mathsf{lacks}\ l}{P \Vdash \langle r \mid l'\!:\!t'\rangle\ \mathsf{lacks}\ l} \quad l \neq l'$$

Present fields:

$$\frac{P \Vdash \mathsf{record}\ \langle r \mid l\!:\!t\rangle}{P \Vdash \langle r \mid l\!:\!t\rangle\ \mathsf{has}\ l\!:\!t}$$

$$\frac{P \Vdash r\ \mathsf{has}\ l\!:\!t}{P \Vdash r \setminus l'\ \mathsf{has}\ l\!:\!t} \quad l \neq l'$$

$$\frac{P \Vdash r\ \mathsf{has}\ l\!:\!t}{P \Vdash \langle r \mid l'\!:\!t'\rangle\ \mathsf{has}\ l\!:\!t} \quad l \neq l'$$

Figure 2.4: Predicate entailment for extensible records

The types of record expressions are written in a similar way:

$$\begin{array}{rcll} r & ::= & \langle\rangle & \textit{empty record} \\ & \mid & \langle r \mid l\!:\!\sigma\rangle & \textit{extension} \\ & \mid & r \setminus l & \textit{restriction} \end{array}$$

where $\langle\rangle$ is the unit type of the empty record, $r \setminus l$ is the same as the record type r but without the field labelled l and $\langle r \mid l : \sigma\rangle$ is the same as the record type r but with an additional field labelled l of type σ. As with record expressions above, not all of the type expressions permitted by this syntax are well-formed. In addition, there is a non-trivial equivalence between valid record types. For example, $\langle r \mid l : \sigma\rangle \setminus l$ is equivalent to r, and $\langle r \mid l\!:\!\sigma\rangle \setminus l'$ is equivalent to $\langle r \setminus l' \mid l\!:\!\sigma\rangle$, assuming that $l \neq l'$.

The process of determining exactly which labels are bound and which are unbound in any particular record can be described using predicates of the form:

$\mathsf{record}\ r$	indicating that r is a well-formed record type.
$r\ \mathsf{has}\ l\!:\!t$	indicating that a record of type r has a field labelled l of type t.
$r\ \mathsf{lacks}\ l$	indicating that a record of type r does not have a field labelled l.

The intuitive meanings of these predicates are formalised by the rules in Figure 2.4.

Predicates of the form (r has $l : t$) and (r lacks l) are also useful in qualified types. For example, the primitive operations of record *restriction*, *extension* and *selection* can be represented by families of functions (indexed by labels) of type:

$$\begin{array}{lcl} (\_ \setminus l) & :: & \forall r.\forall t.(r \ \textsf{has}\ l : t) \Rightarrow r \rightarrow r \setminus l \\ (\_ \mid l = \_) & :: & \forall r.\forall t.(r \ \textsf{lacks}\ l) \Rightarrow r \rightarrow t \rightarrow (r \mid l : t) \\ (\_ . l) & :: & \forall r.\forall t.(r \ \textsf{has}\ l : t) \Rightarrow r \rightarrow t \end{array}$$

The following function definition provides another simple example:

$$\begin{array}{lcl} f & :: & \forall r.\,(r \ \textsf{has}\ x : Int,\ r \ \textsf{lacks}\ y) \Rightarrow r \rightarrow \langle r \mid y : Int \rangle \\ f\ r & = & \langle r \mid y = r.x + 1 \rangle \end{array}$$

Chapter 3

Type inference for qualified types

This chapter describes an ML-like language (i.e. implicitly typed λ-calculus with local definitions) and extends the framework of (Milner, 1978; Damas and Milner, 1982) with support for overloading using qualified types and an arbitrary system of predicates of the form described in the previous chapter. The resulting system retains the flexibility of the ML type system, while allowing more accurate descriptions of the types of objects. Furthermore, we show that this approach is suitable for use in a language based on type inference, in contrast for example with more powerful languages such as the polymorphic λ-calculus that require explicit type annotations.

Section 3.1 introduces the basic type system and Section 3.2 describes an ordering on types, used to determine when one type is more general than another. This is used to investigate the properties of polymorphic types in the system.

The development of a type inference algorithm is complicated by the fact that there are many ways in which the typing rules in our original system can be applied to a single term, and it is not clear which of these (if any!) will result in an optimal typing. As an intermediate step, Section 3.3 describes a *syntax-directed* system in which the choice of typing rules is completely determined by the syntactic structure of the term involved, and investigates its relationship to the original system. Exploiting this relationship, Section 3.4 presents a type inference algorithm for the syntax-directed system which can then be used to infer typings in the original system. We show that the set of all derivable typings for a term can be characterised by a single *principal type scheme* that is calculated by this algorithm. In addition, we describe the relationship between the decidability of type checking and the decidability of a property of predicate entailment.

In subsequent chapters, we extend the results presented here to describe the relationship between implicitly overloaded terms and their translations in a language with explicit overloading. Detailed proofs for these extensions are included in Appendix A from which it is possible to derive the simpler results of this chapter. Proofs for the results of this chapter may also be found in (Jones, 1991b).

3.1 An extension of ML with qualified types

This section describes an extension of the core of the ML type system with support for overloading using qualified types. For ease of reference we will call this system OML, an abbreviation of 'Overloaded ML'.

3.1.1 Type expressions

Following the definition of types and type schemes in ML we consider a structured language of types, the principal restriction being the inability to support functions with either polymorphic or overloaded arguments:

$$\begin{array}{rcll} \tau & ::= & t & \textit{type variables} \\ & | & \tau \to \tau & \textit{function types} \\ \rho & ::= & P \Rightarrow \tau & \textit{qualified types} \\ \sigma & ::= & \forall T.\rho & \textit{type schemes} \end{array}$$

Here t ranges over a given (countably infinite) set of type variables and P and T range over finite sets of predicates and finite sets of type variables respectively. The $\to$ symbol is treated as a right associative infix binary operator. Additional type constructors such as those for lists, pairs and record types will be used as required. The set of type variables appearing (free) in an expression X is denoted $TV(X)$ and is defined in the obvious way. In particular, $TV(\forall T.\rho) = TV(\rho) \setminus T$.

It is convenient to introduce some abbreviations for qualified type and type scheme expressions. In particular, if $\rho = (P \Rightarrow \tau)$ and $\sigma = \forall T.\rho$, then we write:

Abbreviation	Qualified type	Abbreviation	Type scheme
τ	$\emptyset \Rightarrow \tau$	ρ	$\forall \emptyset.\rho$
$\pi \Rightarrow \rho$	$(\pi, P) \Rightarrow \tau$	$\forall t.\sigma$	$\forall (T \cup \{t\}).\rho$
$P' \Rightarrow \rho$	$(P', P) \Rightarrow \tau$	$\forall T'.\sigma$	$\forall (T \cup T').\rho$

With these abbreviations, we will treat the $\Rightarrow$ symbol as a right associative binary operator, with $\to$ binding more tightly than $\Rightarrow$. In addition, if $\{\alpha_i\}$ is an indexed set of type variables, then we write $\forall \alpha_i.\rho$ as an abbreviation for $\forall\{\alpha_i\}.\rho$. As usual, type schemes are regarded as equal if they are identical up to renaming of bound variables.

Using this notation, any type scheme can be written in the form $\forall \alpha_i.P \Rightarrow \tau$, representing the set of qualified types:

$$\{\, [\tau_i/\alpha_i]P \Rightarrow [\tau_i/\alpha_i]\tau \mid \tau_i \in \textit{Type} \,\}$$

where $[\tau_i/\alpha_i]$ is the substitution mapping each of the variables α_i to the corresponding type τ_i and *Type* is the set of all simple type expressions i.e. those represented by τ in the grammar above.

3.1.2 Terms

As in (Milner, 1978; Damas and Milner, 1982; Clément et al., 1986), we use a term language based on simple untyped λ-calculus with the addition of a *let* construct to enable the definition and use of polymorphic (and in this case, overloaded) terms. Specifically, the terms of OML are given by the syntax:

$$
\begin{array}{rcll}
E & ::= & x & \textit{variable} \\
 & | & EF & \textit{application} \\
 & | & \lambda x.E & \textit{abstraction} \\
 & | & \mathbf{let}\ x = E\ \mathbf{in}\ F & \textit{local definition}
\end{array}
$$

Here x ranges over some given (countably infinite) set of term variables. We write $FV(E)$ for the set of all free (term) variables appearing in the term E, and write $[E/x]F$ for the term obtained by substituting E for each free occurrence of x in F. This may involve renaming of bound variables to avoid capture problems.

Note that we do not provide constructs for the introduction of new overloadings such as **inst** and **over** in (Wadler and Blott, 1989). As a result, if none of the free variables for a given term have qualified (i.e. overloaded) types, then no overloading will be used in the expression.

3.1.3 Typing rules

A *type assignment* is a (finite) set of *typing statements* of the form $x : \sigma$ in which no term variable x appears more than once. If A is a type assignment, then we write $dom\ A = \{ x \mid (x : \sigma) \in A \}$, and if x is a term variable with $x \notin dom\ A$, then we write $A, x : \sigma$ as an abbreviation for the type assignment $A \cup \{x : \sigma\}$. The type assignment obtained from A by removing any typing statement for the variable x is denoted A_x. Any type assignment A can be interpreted as a function which assigns a type expression to each element of $dom\ A$. In particular, if $(x : \sigma) \in A$, then we write $A(x) = \sigma$.

A *typing* is an expression of the form $P \mid A \vdash E : \sigma$ representing the assertion that a term E has type σ when the predicates in P are satisfied and the types of free variables in E are as specified in the type assignment A. The typing rules for this system are given in Figure 3.1. Most of these are similar to the usual rules for the ML type system; only the rules $(\Rightarrow I)$ and $(\Rightarrow E)$ for dealing with qualified types and the $(\forall I)$ rule for polymorphic generalisation involve the predicate set. Note the use of the symbols τ, ρ and σ to restrict the application of certain rules to specific sets of type expressions.

3.2 Understanding type schemes

In order to find all of the ways in which a particular term E can be used with a given type assignment A, we need to find a representation (including a test for membership) for sets of the form:

$$\{ (P \mid \sigma) \mid P \mid A \vdash E : \sigma \},$$

where $(P \mid \sigma)$ denotes a pair consisting of a predicate set P and the type scheme σ. As a first step in this direction, we define a preorder $(\leq)$ on such pairs and investigate a number of properties of this ordering.

Our principal motivation in the definition of $(\leq)$ is that a statement of the form $(P' \mid \sigma') \leq (P \mid \sigma)$ should mean that it is possible to use an object which can be treated as having type σ in an environment satisfying the predicates in P whenever an object of type σ' is required

Standard rules:

$$(var)\quad \frac{(x\!:\!\sigma) \in A}{P\,|\,A \vdash x : \sigma}$$

$$(\rightarrow E)\quad \frac{P\,|\,A \vdash E : \tau' \rightarrow \tau \qquad P\,|\,A \vdash F : \tau'}{P\,|\,A \vdash EF : \tau}$$

$$(\rightarrow I)\quad \frac{P\,|\,A_x, x\!:\!\tau' \vdash E : \tau}{P\,|\,A \vdash \lambda x.E : \tau' \rightarrow \tau}$$

Qualified types:

$$(\Rightarrow E)\quad \frac{P\,|\,A \vdash E : \pi \Rightarrow \rho \qquad P \Vdash \pi}{P\,|\,A \vdash E : \rho}$$

$$(\Rightarrow I)\quad \frac{P, \pi\,|\,A \vdash E : \rho}{P\,|\,A \vdash E : \pi \Rightarrow \rho}$$

Polymorphism:

$$(\forall E)\quad \frac{P\,|\,A \vdash E : \forall \alpha.\sigma}{P\,|\,A \vdash E : [\tau/\alpha]\sigma}$$

$$(\forall I)\quad \frac{P\,|\,A \vdash E : \sigma \qquad \alpha \notin TV(A) \cup TV(P)}{P\,|\,A \vdash E : \forall \alpha.\sigma}$$

Local Definition:

$$(let)\quad \frac{P\,|\,A \vdash E : \sigma \qquad Q\,|\,A_x, x\!:\!\sigma \vdash F : \tau}{P, Q\,|\,A \vdash (\textbf{let}\ x = E\ \textbf{in}\ F) : \tau}$$

Figure 3.1: Typing rules for OML.

in an environment satisfying the predicates in P'. In such a case we refer to the former as being *more general* than the latter.

3.2.1 Constrained type schemes

A typing of the form $P\,|\,A \vdash E : \sigma$ assigns a type scheme σ to the term E and constrains uses of this typing to environments satisfying the predicates in P. Motivated by this observation, and by our comments in the introduction above, we introduce a convenient notation for such pairs:

Definition 3.1 *A* constrained type scheme *is an expression of the form* $(P\,|\,\sigma)$ *where* P *is a set of predicates and* σ *is a type scheme.*

Note that a type scheme σ may be treated as an abbreviation for the constrained type scheme $(\emptyset\,|\,\sigma)$.

Definition 3.2 *A qualified type* $R \Rightarrow \mu$ *is said to be a* generic instance *of the constrained type scheme* $(P\,|\,\forall \alpha_i.Q \Rightarrow \tau)$ *if there are types* τ_i *such that:*

$$R \Vdash P, [\tau_i/\alpha_i]Q \quad \textit{and} \quad \mu = [\tau_i/\alpha_i]\tau.$$

In particular, note that $P \Rightarrow \tau$ is a generic instance of $Q \Rightarrow \nu$ if and only if $P \Vdash Q$ and $\nu = \tau$.

Every constrained type scheme has at least one generic instance: Given a constrained type scheme $(P \mid \sigma)$, where $\sigma = \forall \alpha_i.P' \Rightarrow \tau$ and any types $\tau_i \in \mathit{Type}$, then $((P, [\tau_i/\alpha_i]P') \Rightarrow [\tau_i/\alpha_i]\tau)$ is a generic instance of $(P \mid \sigma)$.

The generic instance relation can be used to define a general ordering $(\leq)$ on constrained type schemes in the following manner:

Definition 3.3 *The constrained type scheme* $(Q \mid \eta)$ *is said to be* more general *than a constrained type scheme* $(P \mid \sigma)$*, written* $(P \mid \sigma) \leq (Q \mid \eta)$*, if every generic instance of* $(P \mid \sigma)$ *is a generic instance of* $(Q \mid \eta)$.

Since every type scheme σ is equivalent to a constrained type scheme of the form $(\emptyset \mid \sigma)$ and every qualified type ρ is equivalent to a type scheme of the form $\forall \emptyset.\rho$, the ordering defined above can also be used to compare type schemes and qualified types as well as constrained type schemes. For example:

- $(P \mid \sigma) \leq (Q \mid \eta)$ indicates that the type scheme η (in an environment satisfying Q) is more general than σ (in an environment satisfying P).
- $(P \mid \sigma) \leq \eta$ indicates that η is more general than σ (in an environment satisfying P).
- $\sigma \leq \eta$ indicates that η is more general than σ in any environment.

Note that Definition 3.3 is equivalent to saying that $(P \mid \sigma) \leq (Q \mid \eta)$ if and only if the set of generic instances of $(P \mid \sigma)$ is a subset of the generic instances of $(Q \mid \eta)$. With this insight, it is straightforward to show that $(\leq)$ is a preorder on constrained type schemes and that a qualified type ρ is a generic instance of the type scheme σ if and only if $\rho \leq \sigma$.

3.2.2 Examples

To illustrate the definition of $(\leq)$, consider the system of type classes described in Section 2.2 with a type class *Eq* that includes the type of integers (i.e. $\Vdash \mathit{Eq}\ \mathit{Int}$). Given this assumption, is is straightforward to show that:

$$\mathit{Int} \to \mathit{Int} \ \leq\ (\forall a.\mathit{Eq}\ a \Rightarrow a \to a) \ \leq\ (\forall a.a \to a).$$

The presence of free variables warrants careful attention. Consider the fact that:

$$(\forall a.\mathit{Eq}\ b \Rightarrow a \to a) \ \leq\ (\forall a.a \to a).$$

Both type schemes can be instantiated to any type of the form $\tau \to \tau$, but while this is possible in any environment for the right hand side, the left hand side can only be instantiated in an environment satisfying $\mathit{Eq}\ b$. On the other hand, the type schemes $(\forall a.\mathit{Eq}\ a \Rightarrow a \to a)$ and $(\forall a.\mathit{Eq}\ b \Rightarrow a \to a)$ are incomparable: The first can only be instantiated to the type $\tau \to \tau$ in an environment satisfying $\mathit{Eq}\ \tau$, but can be instantiated to $\mathit{Int} \to \mathit{Int}$ in any environment (assuming again that $\Vdash \mathit{Eq}\ \mathit{Int}$). The second can be instantiated to any type of the form $\tau \to \tau$, but only in environments satisfying $\mathit{Eq}\ b$.

3.2.3 Properties of the $(\leq)$ ordering

We begin by defining an equivalence relation on constrained type schemes:

$$(P\,|\,\sigma) \simeq (Q\,|\,\eta) \quad \Leftrightarrow \quad (P\,|\,\sigma) \leq (Q\,|\,\eta) \;\wedge\; (Q\,|\,\eta) \leq (P\,|\,\sigma).$$

Note in particular that, if $\sigma = \forall \alpha_i.P \Rightarrow \tau$, then $\sigma \simeq \forall \beta_i.[\beta_i/\alpha_i](P \Rightarrow \tau)$ for any distinct variables β_i which do not appear free in σ.

The following properties are easily established:

- If ρ is a qualified type and P is a set of predicates, then $(P\,|\,\rho) \simeq P \Rightarrow \rho$.
- If σ is a type scheme and P is a set of predicates, then $(P\,|\,\sigma) \leq \sigma$.
- If $\sigma' \leq \sigma$ and $P' \Vdash P$, then $(P'\,|\,\sigma') \leq (P\,|\,\sigma)$.
- If none of the variables α_i appear in P, then the constrained type scheme $(P\,|\,\forall\alpha_i.\rho)$ is equivalent to the type scheme $\forall\alpha_i.P \Rightarrow \rho$.

The definition of $(\leq)$ given above is an extension of the ordering relation described in (Damas and Milner, 1982). In the latter system, we find that $TV(\sigma') \subseteq TV(\sigma)$ whenever $\sigma \leq \sigma'$ and this leads to a simple syntactic characterisation of the ordering relation between type schemes. This property fails to hold in the current system. For example, given a unary predicate symbol Any such that $\Vdash Any\ a$ for any type a, we have:

$$(\forall a.a \to a) \leq (\forall a.Any\ b \Rightarrow a \to a),$$

where the type variable b appears free on the right hand side but does not appear on the left hand side. It is however possible to obtain the following syntactic characterisation of the instance ordering provided we make a simple assumption about the bound variables used in the type schemes involved:

Proposition 3.4 *Suppose that $\sigma = \forall\alpha_i.Q \Rightarrow \nu$, $\sigma' = \forall\beta_j.Q' \Rightarrow \nu'$ and that none of the variables β_j appears free in σ, P or P'. Then $(P'\,|\,\sigma') \leq (P\,|\,\sigma)$ if and only if there are types τ_i such that:*

$$\nu' = [\tau_i/\alpha_i]\nu \quad \textit{and} \quad P', Q' \Vdash P, [\tau_i/\alpha_i]Q.$$

The application of a substitution S to a constrained type scheme $(P \mid \sigma)$ is defined by $S(P \mid \sigma) = (SP \mid S\sigma)$. The next proposition shows that the ordering between constrained type schemes is preserved by substitutions; this is particularly important for our treatment of polymorphism.

Proposition 3.5 *For any substitution S and constrained type schemes $(P\,|\,\sigma)$ and $(Q\,|\,\eta)$:*

$$(P\,|\,\sigma) \leq (Q\,|\,\eta) \quad \Rightarrow \quad S(P\,|\,\sigma) \leq S(Q\,|\,\eta).$$

3.2.4 Generalisation

Given a derivation $P \mid A \vdash E : \tau$, it is useful to have a notation for the most general type scheme that can be obtained for E from this derivation using the rules $(\Rightarrow I)$ and $(\forall I)$ given in Figure 3.1:

Definition 3.6 *The* generalisation *of a qualified type ρ with respect to a type assignment A is written $Gen(A, \rho)$ and defined by:*

$$Gen(A, \rho) \quad = \quad \forall (TV(\rho) \setminus TV(A)).\rho.$$

In other words, if $\{\alpha_i\} = TV(\rho) \setminus TV(A)$, then $Gen(A, \rho) = \forall \alpha_i.\rho$. The following propositions describe the interaction of generalisation with predicate entailment and substitution.

Proposition 3.7 *Suppose that A is a type assignment, P and P' are sets of predicates and τ is a type. Then $Gen(A, P' \Rightarrow \tau) \leq Gen(A, P \Rightarrow \tau)$ whenever $P' \Vdash P$.*

Proposition 3.8 *If A is a type assignment, ρ is a qualified type and S is a substitution, then:*

$$Gen(SA, S\rho) \leq S(Gen(A, \rho)).$$

Furthermore, there is a substitution R such that:

$$RA = SA \quad \text{and} \quad SGen(A, \rho) = Gen(RA, R\rho).$$

3.2.5 Ordering of type assignments

The definition of constrained type schemes and the ordering $(\leq)$ extends naturally to an ordering on (constrained) type assignments.

Definition 3.9 *If A and A' are type assignments and P, P' are sets of predicates, then we say that $(P \mid A)$ is* more general *than $(P' \mid A')$, written $(P' \mid A') \leq (P \mid A)$, if $dom\ A = dom\ A'$ and $(P' \mid A'(x)) \leq (P \mid A(x))$ for each $x \in dom\ A$.*

For much of our work, we will only use two special cases of $(P' \mid A') \leq (P \mid A)$:

- If $P = P' = \emptyset$, then we write $A' \leq A$, indicating that the types assigned to variables in A are more general than the corresponding types in A' in any environment.
- If $P = \emptyset$, then we write $(P' \mid A') \leq A$. This is similar to $A' \leq A$, but restricted to environments which satisfy the predicates P'.

The results of Section 3.2.1 can be used to establish the following properties about the ordering on type assignments:

- The ordering on type assignments is reflexive, transitive and preserved by substitutions.
- If A is a type assignment and P is a set of predicates, then $(P \mid A) \leq A$.
- If $A' \leq A$ and $P' \Vdash P$, then $(P' \mid A') \leq (P \mid A)$.
- If $A' \leq A$, then $A'_x \leq A_x$.
- If $A' \leq A$, $\sigma' \leq \sigma$ and $x \notin dom\ A$, then $(A', x : \sigma') \leq (A, x : \sigma)$.

3.3 A syntax-directed approach

The typing rules in Figure 3.1 provide clear descriptions of the treatment of each of the syntactic constructs of the term and type languages. Unfortunately, they are not suitable for use in a type inference algorithm where it should be possible to determine an appropriate order in which to apply the typing rules by a simple analysis of the syntactic structure of the term whose type is required.

In this section, we introduce an alternative set of typing rules with a single rule for each syntactic construct in the term language. We refer to this as the *syntax-directed* system because it has the following important property:

> All typing derivations for a given term E (if there are any) have the same structure, uniquely determined by the syntactic structure of E.

We regard the syntax-directed system as a tool for exploring the type system of Section 3.1 and we establish a congruence between the two systems so that results about one can be translated into results about the other. The advantages of working with the syntax-directed system are:

- The rules are better suited to use in a type inference algorithm; having found types for each of the subterms of a given term E, there is at most one rule which can be used to obtain a type for the term E itself.
- Only type expressions are involved in the matching process. Type schemes and qualified types can only appear in type assignments.
- There are fewer rules and hence fewer cases to be considered in formal proofs.

A similar approach is described in (Clément et al., 1986) which gives a deterministic set of typing rules for ML and outlines their equivalence to the rules in (Damas and Milner 1982).

3.3.1 Syntax-directed typing rules

The typing rules for the syntax-directed system are given in Figure 3.2. Typings and derivations in this system are written with a superscript as in $P \,|\, A \overset{s}{\vdash} E : \tau$ where τ ranges over the set of type expressions rather than the set of type schemes as in the typing judgements of Section 3.1. Other than this, the main differences between the two systems are in the rules $(var)^s$ and $(let)^s$ which use the operations of instantiation and generalisation introduced in Sections 3.2.1 and 3.2.4.

3.3.2 Properties of the syntax-directed system

The following proposition illustrates the parametric polymorphism present in the syntax-directed system; instantiating the free type variables in a derivable typing with arbitrary types produces another derivable typing.

$$(var)^s \quad \frac{(x{:}\sigma) \in A \quad (P \Rightarrow \tau) \leq \sigma}{P \,|\, A \overset{s}{\vdash} x : \tau}$$

$$(\to E)^s \quad \frac{P \,|\, A \overset{s}{\vdash} E : \tau' \to \tau \quad P \,|\, A \overset{s}{\vdash} F : \tau'}{P \,|\, A \overset{s}{\vdash} EF : \tau}$$

$$(\to I)^s \quad \frac{P \,|\, A_x, x{:}\tau' \overset{s}{\vdash} E : \tau}{P \,|\, A \overset{s}{\vdash} \lambda x.E : \tau' \to \tau}$$

$$(let)^s \quad \frac{P \,|\, A \overset{s}{\vdash} E : \tau \quad P' \,|\, A_x, x{:}\sigma \overset{s}{\vdash} F : \tau' \quad \sigma = Gen(A, P \Rightarrow \tau)}{P' \,|\, A \overset{s}{\vdash} (\textbf{let } x = E \textbf{ in } F) : \tau'}$$

Figure 3.2: Syntax-directed inference system.

Proposition 3.10 *If $P \,|\, A \overset{s}{\vdash} E : \tau$ and S is a substitution, then $SP \,|\, SA \overset{s}{\vdash} E : S\tau$.*

A similar result is established in (Damas, 1985) where it is shown that for any derivation $A \vdash E : \tau$ in the usual (non-deterministic) ML type system and any substitution S, there is a derivation $SA \vdash E : S\tau$ which can be chosen in such a way that the height of the latter is bounded by the height of the former. This additional condition is needed to ensure the validity of proofs by induction on the size of a derivation. This complication is avoided by the syntax-directed system; the derivations in Proposition 3.10 are guaranteed to have the same structure because the term E is common to both.

The syntax-directed system also has a form of polymorphism over the sets of environments in which a particular typing can be used, as described by the following proposition:

Proposition 3.11 *If $P \,|\, A \overset{s}{\vdash} E : \tau$ and $Q \Vdash P$, then $Q \,|\, A \overset{s}{\vdash} E : \tau$.*

Recall that the basic intuition in the definition of the ordering on type schemes was that $\sigma' \leq \sigma$ should mean that, at least for the purposes of type inference, it is possible to use an object of type σ whenever with an object of type σ' is required. In much the same way, if the type assignments A and A' are such that $A' \leq A$ (so that the type assigned to each variable in A is more general than the corresponding type in A'), then we would expect that any typing which can be derived using A' could also be derived from A. The following proposition establishes a slightly more general form of this result:

Proposition 3.12 *If $P \,|\, A' \overset{s}{\vdash} E : \tau$ and $(P \,|\, A') \leq A$, then $P \,|\, A \overset{s}{\vdash} E : \tau$.*

The hypothesis $(P \,|\, A') \leq A$ means that the types assigned to variables in A are more general than those given by A' in any environment which satisfies the predicates in P. For example:

$$(Eq\ Int \,|\, \{(==) : Int \to Int \to Bool\}) \quad \leq \quad \{(==) : \forall a.Eq\ a \Rightarrow a \to a \to Bool\}.$$

Using the result of Proposition 3.12, we can confirm the intuition that it should be possible to replace an integer equality function of type $Int \to Int \to Bool$ with a generic equality function of type $\forall a.Eq\ a \Rightarrow a \to a \to Bool$ in any environment which satisfies $Eq\ Int$.

Corollary 3.13 *If $P \,|\, A' \overset{s}{\vdash} E : \tau$ and $A' \leq A$, then $P \,|\, A \overset{s}{\vdash} E : \tau$.*

This follows directly from Proposition 3.12; $(P \,|\, A') \leq A'$ for any type assignment A' and predicates P and hence $A' \leq A$ implies $(P \,|\, A') \leq A$.

3.3.3 Relationship with original type system

In order to use the syntax-directed system as a tool for reasoning about the type system described in Section 3.1, we need to investigate the way in which the existence of a derivation in one system determines the existence of derivations in the other.

Our first result establishes the soundness of the syntax-directed system with respect to the original typing rules, showing that any derivable typing in the former system is also derivable in the latter.

Theorem 3.14 *If* $P\,|\,A \overset{s}{\vdash} E : \tau$*, then* $P\,|\,A \vdash E : \tau$.

The translation of derivations in the original type system to those of the syntax-directed system is less obvious. For example, if $P\,|\,A \vdash E : \sigma$, then it will not in general be possible to derive the same typing in the syntax-directed system because σ is a type scheme, not a simple type. However, for any derivation $P'\,|\,A \overset{s}{\vdash} E : \tau$, theorem 3.14 guarantees the existence of a derivation $P'\,|\,A \vdash E : \tau$ and hence $\emptyset\,|\,A \vdash E : Gen(A, P' \Rightarrow \tau')$ by definition 3.6. The following theorem shows that it is always possible to find a derivation in this way such that the inferred type scheme $Gen(A, P' \Rightarrow \tau')$ is more general than the constrained type scheme $(P\,|\,\sigma)$ determined by the original derivation.

Theorem 3.15 *If* $P\,|\,A \vdash E : \sigma$*, then there is a set of predicates* P' *and a type* τ *such that* $P'\,|\,A \overset{s}{\vdash} E : \tau$ *and* $(P\,|\,\sigma) \leq Gen(A, P' \Rightarrow \tau)$.

3.4 Type inference

This section describes an algorithm which calculates a typing for a given term, using an extension of Milner's algorithm W to support qualified types. We show that the typings produced by this algorithm are derivable in the syntax-directed system and that they are, in a certain sense, the most general typings possible. Combining this with the results of the previous section, the algorithm can be used to reason about the type system in Section 3.1.

3.4.1 Unification

This section describes the unification algorithm which is a central component of the type inference algorithm. A substitution S is called a *unifier* for the type expressions τ and τ' if $S\tau = S\tau'$.

Theorem 3.16 (Robinson, 1965) *There is an algorithm whose input is a pair of type expressions* τ *and* τ' *such that either:*

> *the algorithm fails and there are no unifiers for* τ *and* τ'*,*

or

> *the algorithm succeeds with a substitution* U *as its result and the unifiers of* τ *and* τ' *are precisely those substitutions of the form* RU *for any substitution* R*. The substitution* U *is called a* most general unifier *for* τ *and* τ'*, and is denoted* $mgu(\tau, \tau')$.

In the following, we write $\tau \overset{U}{\sim} \tau'$ for the assertion that the unification algorithm succeeds by finding a most general unifier U for τ and τ'.

3.4.2 A type inference algorithm

Following the presentation of (Rémy, 1989), we describe the type inference algorithm using the inference rules in Figure 3.3. These rules use typings of the form $P \,|\, TA \overset{W}{\vdash} E : \tau$ where P is a set of predicates, T is a substitution, A is a type assignment, E is a term and τ is a simple type expression. The typing rules can be interpreted as an attribute grammar in which A and E are inherited attributes, while P, T and τ are synthesised.

$$(var)^{W} \quad \frac{(x : \forall \alpha_i . P \Rightarrow \tau) \in A \quad \beta_i \text{ new}}{[\beta_i/\alpha_i]P \,|\, A \overset{W}{\vdash} x : [\beta_i/\alpha_i]\tau}$$

$$(\rightarrow E)^{W} \quad \frac{P \,|\, TA \overset{W}{\vdash} E : \tau \quad Q \,|\, T'TA \overset{W}{\vdash} F : \tau' \quad T'\tau \overset{U}{\sim} \tau' \rightarrow \alpha \quad \alpha \text{ new}}{U(T'P, Q) \,|\, UT'TA \overset{W}{\vdash} EF : U\alpha}$$

$$(\rightarrow I)^{W} \quad \frac{P \,|\, T(A_x, x : \alpha) \overset{W}{\vdash} E : \tau \quad \alpha \text{ new}}{P \,|\, TA \overset{W}{\vdash} \lambda x . E : T\alpha \rightarrow \tau}$$

$$(let)^{W} \quad \frac{P \,|\, TA \overset{W}{\vdash} E : \tau \quad P' \,|\, T'(TA_x, x : \sigma) \overset{W}{\vdash} F : \tau' \quad \sigma = Gen(TA, P \Rightarrow \tau)}{P' \,|\, T'TA \overset{W}{\vdash} (\mathbf{let}\ x = E\ \mathbf{in}\ F) : \tau'}$$

Figure 3.3: Type inference algorithm W.

The algorithm may also be described in a more conventional style as the function W defined in Figure 3.4, the relationship between these two presentations being that $P \,|\, TA \overset{W}{\vdash} E : \tau$ if and only if $W(A, E)$ succeeds with result (P, T, ν) (note that the evaluation of $W\ A\ E$ will only terminate successfully if each unification is successful).

One of the advantages of the presentation of type inference in Figure 3.3 is that it highlights the relationship between W and the syntax-directed type system, as illustrated by the following theorem:

Theorem 3.17 *If* $P \,|\, TA \overset{W}{\vdash} E : \tau$, *then* $P \,|\, TA \overset{s}{\vdash} E : \tau$.

Combining this with the result of theorem 3.14 gives the following important corollary.

Corollary 3.18 *If* $P \,|\, TA \overset{W}{\vdash} E : \tau$, *then* $P \,|\, TA \vdash E : \tau$.

With the exception of $(let)^{W}$, each of the rules in Figure 3.3 introduces 'new' variables; i.e. variables which do not appear in the hypotheses of the rule nor in any other distinct branches of the complete derivation. Note that it is always possible to choose type variables in this way because the set of type variables is assumed to be countably infinite. In the presence of new variables, it is convenient to work with a weaker form of equality on substitutions, writing $S \approx R$ to indicate that $St = Rt$ for all but a finite number of new variables t. In most cases, we can treat $S \approx R$ as $S = R$, since the only differences between the substitutions occur at variables which are not used elsewhere in the algorithm.

$$
\begin{array}{lll}
W\ A\ x & = & ([\beta_i/\alpha_i]P, id, [\beta_i/\alpha_i]\tau) \\
 & & \textbf{where}\ \ \begin{array}{lll} (\forall \alpha_i.P \Rightarrow \tau) & = & A\ x \\ \beta_i & = & \text{new variables} \end{array} \\[2ex]
W\ A\ (EF) & = & (U(T'P, Q), UT'T, U\alpha) \\
 & & \textbf{where}\ \ \begin{array}{lll} (P, T, \tau) & = & W\ A\ E \\ (Q, T', \tau') & = & W\ (TA)\ F \\ \alpha & = & \text{new variable} \\ U & = & mgu\ (T'\tau)\ (\tau' \to \alpha) \end{array} \\[2ex]
W\ A\ (\lambda x.E) & = & (P, T, T\alpha \to \tau) \\
 & & \textbf{where}\ \ \begin{array}{lll} (P, T, \tau) & = & W\ (A_x, x\!:\!\alpha)\ E \\ \alpha & = & \text{new variable} \end{array} \\[2ex]
W\ A\ (\textbf{let}\ x = E\ \textbf{in}\ F) & = & (P', T'T, \tau') \\
 & & \textbf{where}\ \ \begin{array}{lll} (P, T, \tau) & = & W\ A\ E \\ \sigma & = & Gen(TA, P \Rightarrow \tau) \\ (P', T', \tau') & = & W\ (TA_x, x\!:\!\sigma)\ F \end{array}
\end{array}
$$

Figure 3.4: The type inference algorithm expressed as an (almost) functional program. A full functional definition would require a more formal treatment of 'new' variables.

This notation enables us to give an accurate statement of the following result which shows that the typings obtained by W are, in a precise sense, the most general derivable typings for a given term.

Theorem 3.19 *Suppose that* $P \mid SA \vdash^{s} E : \tau$. *Then* $Q \mid TA \vdash^{W} E : \nu$ *and there is a substitution* R *such that* $S \approx RT$, $\tau = R\nu$ *and* $P \Vdash RQ$.

Combining the result of theorem 3.19 with that of theorem 3.15 we obtain a similar completeness result for W with respect to the type system of Section 3.1.

Corollary 3.20 *Suppose that* $P \mid SA \vdash E : \sigma$. *Then* $Q \mid TA \vdash^{W} E : \nu$ *and there is a substitution* R *such that* $S \approx RT$ *and* $(P \mid \sigma) \leq RGen(TA, Q \Rightarrow \nu)$.

3.4.3 Principal type schemes

Extending the standard notion of well-typed terms to the current framework, we will say that a term E is *well-typed* under a given type assignment A if there is a predicate set P and a type scheme σ such that $P \,|\, A \vdash e : \sigma$. The main aim in this section is to investigate the relationship between well-typed terms and the type inference algorithm described above.

The concept of a *principal type scheme*, originally introduced in the study of combinatory logic (Curry and Feys, 1958; Hindley, 1969), is particularly useful for this work, corresponding to the most general derivable typing with respect to $(\leq)$ under a given type assignment.

Definition 3.21 *A* principal type scheme *for a term E under a type assignment A is a constrained type scheme $(P \mid \sigma)$ such that $P \mid A \vdash E : \sigma$, and $(P' \mid \sigma') \leq (P \mid \sigma)$ whenever $P' \mid A \vdash E : \sigma'$.*

The following result gives a sufficient condition for the existence of principal type schemes by showing how they can be constructed from typings produced by W.

Corollary 3.22 *If $Q \mid TA \overset{W}{\vdash} E : \nu$, then $Gen(TA, Q \Rightarrow \nu)$ is a principal type scheme for E under TA.*

Combining this with Corollary 3.20 gives a necessary condition for the existence of principal type schemes: a term is well-typed if and only if it has a principal type scheme which can be calculated using the type inference algorithm.

Corollary 3.23 (Principal type theorem) *Let E be a term and A an arbitrary type assignment. Then the following conditions are equivalent:*

(1) E is well-typed under A.

(2) $Q \mid TA \overset{W}{\vdash} E : \nu$ for some Q and ν and there is a substitution R such that $RTA = A$.

(3) E has a principal typing under A.

It is straightforward to show that *(1)* implies *(2)* and that *(3)* implies *(1)* using Corollary 3.20 and the definition of principal types respectively. Only the proof that *(2)* implies *(3)* requires a little more attention. Writing $\eta = Gen(TA, Q \Rightarrow \nu)$, the main difficulty is to establish that $R\eta \geq (P \mid \sigma)$ for any P and σ such that $P \mid A \vdash E : \sigma$. By Corollary 3.20 it follows that $R'\eta \geq (P \mid \sigma)$ for some substitution R' such that $R'TA = A$. However, the only free variables in η also appear free in TA and hence it follows that $R\eta = R'\eta \geq (P \mid \sigma)$ as required. Note that there is an important special case when $TV(A) = \emptyset$ (for example, if E is a closed term and $A = \emptyset$), when $TA = A$ and $R\eta = \eta$, and hence we can use $Gen(A, Q \Rightarrow \nu)$ as a principal type scheme for E.

Similar arguments can be used to solve the problems posed at the beginning of Section 3.2. More precisely we can show that

$$\{(P \mid \sigma) \mid P \mid A \vdash E : \sigma\} = \{(P \mid \sigma) \mid (P \mid \sigma) \leq R\eta\},$$

assuming that $Q \mid TA \overset{W}{\vdash} E : \nu$, $\eta = Gen(TA, Q \Rightarrow \nu)$ and that R is a substitution such that $RTA = A$. (Strictly speaking, our argument shows only that the left hand side is a subset of the right hand side. The reverse inclusion can be established using the definition of the ordering relation and the soundness results given above.)

On the other hand, if the type inference algorithm fails, or if there is no substitution R which satisfies $RTA = A$, then Corollary 3.20 allows us to deduce that:

$$\{(P \mid \sigma) \mid P \mid A \vdash E : \sigma\} = \emptyset.$$

(Assume that the right hand side is non-empty and argue by contradiction.)

3.4.4 Decidability of type inference problems

We are now in a position to exploit the results presented above to obtain results about the type system of OML, and its suitability for concrete implementations. Typical problems that we might have to deal with include:

- Given a particular term E and a type assignment A, determine whether E is well-typed under A. This is (essentially) the *strong type inference problem* as described by (Tiuryn, 1990).
- Given a predicate set P, a type assignment A, a term E and a type scheme σ, determine whether there is a derivation for $P \,|\, A \vdash E : \sigma$.

For practical purposes, it is essential that there is an effective algorithm which can be used to answer these questions.

From the form of the type inference algorithm described here it is clear that the process of determining whether a given term has a principal type scheme under a particular assumption is indeed decidable, given the effective algorithm guaranteed by Theorem 3.16 for calculating most general unifiers. By Corollary 3.23, this is equivalent to deciding whether a give term is well-typed and hence the strong type inference problem for OML is decidable.

There are two cases to consider for the second problem. If there is no principal type for a term E under the assignment A, then the set of derivable typings of the form $P \,|\, A \vdash E : \sigma$ is empty as above – there are no derivations of this form.

For the second case, if $Q \,|\, TA \overset{W}{\vdash} E : \nu$ for some Q, T and ν and there is a substitution R such that $RTA = A$ then the problem of discovering whether $P \,|\, A \vdash E : \sigma$ reduces to that of determining whether $(P \,|\, \sigma) \leq R\eta$. Writing $\sigma = \forall \alpha_i . Q' \Rightarrow \nu'$ and $\sigma' = R'\eta = \forall \beta_j . Q'' \Rightarrow \nu''$ where the variables α_i do not appear free in σ' or P, this is equivalent to finding types τ_j such that:

$$\nu' = [\tau_j/\beta_j]\nu'' \quad \text{and} \quad P, Q' \Vdash [\tau_j/\beta_j]Q''.$$

If we write $\{\gamma_k\} = TV(\nu') \cap \{\beta_j\}$ and $\{\delta_l\} = \{\beta_j\} \setminus TV(\nu')$, then we can solve the first equation by finding types τ'_k such that $\nu' = [\tau'_k/\gamma_k]\nu''$. Such a solution (if it exists) is uniquely determined and can be calculated using a simple matching algorithm. It remains to find types τ''_l such that $P, Q' \Vdash [\tau''_l/\delta_l, \tau'_k/\gamma_k]Q''$.

Taking a moment to reorganise the notation used here, the problem of determining whether a particular typing judgement $P \,|\, A \vdash E : \sigma$ can be derived is decidable if, for any predicate sets P_1 and P_2 and any set of variables α_i, it is decidable whether there are types τ_i such that $P_1 \Vdash [\tau_i/\alpha_i]P_2$. In fact, for reasons we describe in Section 5.8.2, we will usually only be interested in terms for which the principal type scheme $Gen(TA, Q \Rightarrow \nu)$ satisfies $TV(Q) \subseteq TV(\nu)$. In this case, we require only that determining whether $P_1 \Vdash P_2$ is decidable for any choice of P_1 and P_2.

3.5 Related work

As we have already noted, the results described in this chapter are based very firmly on the work of Milner and Damas on the development of type inference for ML. The possibility of extending their system to include support for overloading was actually suggested by Milner

(1978) but left as a topic for further research. One early approach was described by Damas (1985), allowing a single variable to be treated as having several different types in any given type assignment. The main weakness with this system is that it is no longer possible to represent all typings of a term by a single principal type scheme, leading to a potential combinatorial explosion for typing terms with local definitions.

Type inference in the presence of constraints on types (corresponding to our use of predicate sets in the typing rules for OML) has been widely studied in the particular case of subtyping (Mitchell, 1984, 1991; Fuh and Mishra, 1989, 1990). In contrast with OML, each of these systems includes support for implicit coercions, an issue we discuss further in Section 6.3. Each of these papers uses a form of untyped λ-calculus without local definitions, although the more recent papers include some comments about how these extensions might be dealt with. There is no provision for including constraints as part of the type of an object, although Fuh and Mishra (1990) certainly hint at this idea.

Other interesting examples of type inference in the presence of constraints include the work of Ohori and Buneman (1988, 1989) on type systems for object oriented programming and database applications and of Thatte (1991) on type isomorphisms. Adapting the results from earlier versions of our work presented in (Jones 1991b, 1992a), Odersky (1992) has described another example which uses type constraints to record information about sharing, motivated by insights from the study of linear logic. Systems of type inference with constraints have also been used to explore type systems for polymorphic references and assignment (Leroy and Weis, 1990; Wright 1992).

Extending and generalising the work of Kaes (1988), Wadler and Blott (1989) introduced the use of *predicated types* in their description of type classes. Using type class constraints in type expressions and providing rules which could be used to move constraints on a typing into the type of an object, Wadler and Blott were able to give a satisfactory treatment of polymorphic local definitions within their framework. Further developments of this work were described in (Blott, 1991) and have been used as a basis for the static semantics of Haskell given in (Peyton Jones and Wadler, 1992).

A closely related system was described by Smith (1991) whose main contribution was to show how the Wadler and Blott framework might be extended to include subtyping with implicit coercions. Another significant difference in Smith's work was to permit only satisfiable sets of constraints in the type of an object. Using a rather stronger notion of well-typed terms, Volpano and Smith (1991) showed that typability in the Wadler and Blott system is undecidable (without restrictions such as those used in Haskell on the form of overloading that is permitted). We discuss this more fully in Section 6.2.

An alternative formulation of type inference for type classes in Haskell was described by Nipkow and Snelting (1991) using a combination of Damas-Milner typing and order sorted unification which provides sufficient conditions to guarantee the existence of principal types. Unfortunately, it is not clear how their framework might be extended to our more general system.

In a recent paper, Kaes (1992) outlines a general purpose approach to systems of constrained type inference which is very similar to the framework described here, based on essentially the same set of typing rules as used for our presentation of the syntax-directed system in Section 3.3. However, much of Kaes' work is concerned with establishing the decidability of particular systems of predicates.

Chapter 4

Evidence

While the results of the preceding chapter provide a satisfactory treatment of type inference with qualified types, we have not yet made any attempt to discuss the semantics or evaluation of overloaded terms. For example, given a generic equality operator $(==)$ of type $\forall a. Eq\ a \Rightarrow a \to a \to Bool$ and integer valued expressions E and F, we can determine that the expression $E == F$ has type *Bool* in any environment which satisfies *Eq Int*. However, this information is not sufficient to determine the value of $E == F$; this is only possible if we are also provided with the value of the equality operator which makes *Int* an instance of *Eq*.

Our aim in the next two chapters is to present a general approach to the semantics and implementation of objects with qualified types based on the concept of *evidence*. The essential idea is that an object of type $\pi \Rightarrow \sigma$ can only be used if we are also supplied with suitable evidence that the predicate π does indeed hold. In this chapter we concentrate on the role of evidence for the systems of predicates described in Chapter 2 and then, in the following chapter, extend the results of Chapter 3 to give a semantics for OML.

As an introduction, Section 4.1 describes some simple techniques used in the implementation of particular forms of overloading and shows why these methods are unsuitable for the more general systems considered in this thesis. Our solution, presented in Section 4.2, is to extend the language of terms with constructs that permit the use and manipulation of evidence values, exploiting the symmetry between typed calculi and simple logical systems to guide us to a satisfactory formulation. The benefit of this approach is that it provides, at the very least, a good indication that our definitions are natural (in an informal sense) and hence that they will not cause unnecessary complications in subsequent work. Similar ideas are used to motivate the extension of the predicate entailment relation to describe the construction of evidence as described in Section 4.3.

The definitions for the treatment of evidence can also be motivated by more practical concerns. Section 4.4 outlines the range of possible choices of evidence in particular applications and, in the following sections, we show how established techniques used in the implementation of type classes (Section 4.5) and subtyping (Section 4.6) can be treated as particular instances of our approach. For the special case of the system of extensible records, we have been unable to find any previously documented implementation that makes use of analogous concepts, an observation which may at first sight appear to contradict our claims about the generality of the concept of evidence. However, as described in Section 4.7, choosing suitable evidence values for the system of predicates outlined in Section 2.4 leads us to discover a promising new representation for extensible records.

4.1 Simple implementations of overloading

In simple cases, the type of a particular term may be sufficiently well determined to enable an occurrence of an overloaded function to be replaced by the appropriate implementation. We might, for example, treat the expression $2 == 3$ as if it had been written as *primEqInt* 2 3 where *primEqInt* is the primitive equality test on integers with type $Int \rightarrow Int \rightarrow Bool$.

The situation is more complicated when overloading is combined with polymorphism, since it may not always be possible to determine completely which version of an overloaded operator is required in a particular context. For example, recall the definition of the `member` function in Section 2.2:

```
member x []      =  False
member x (y:ys)  =  x==y || member x ys
```

In a large program, this function might be used with many different types of list, each requiring a different implementation of (==) and so requiring a different version of `member` for each case. Implementations based on this approach will be considered in more detail in Section 6.1.5.

Another possibility is to adopt a run-time representation that uses tags to indicate the type of each object. Primitive overloaded functions can be implemented by scrutinising the tags of its arguments and applying the appropriate definition for values of that type. In this case, the role of the type system is simply to ensure that the evaluation of "a well-typed expression does not go wrong" in the sense that no primitive overloaded operator is ever applied to a value for which it is not defined. The implementation of 'polymorphic equality' in Standard ML of New Jersey (Appel, 1992) is based on this technique and a similar proposal (which also supports the use of other common overloaded operators) has been suggested for use in future versions of Haskell (Wadler, 1991).

An interesting variation on this technique would be to store the implementation of frequently used overloaded operators as part of the concrete representation of each run-time object. This would work particularly well in systems such as those described by (Johnsson, 1987; Peyton Jones, 1992) where each object includes a pointer to a vector of code addresses that could be used to store entry points to the implementation of specific overloaded operators. This would help to reduce some of the 'interpretive overhead' associated with the use of tagged data structures and would open up the possibilities for further optimisations. For example, the equality test stored with an empty list need not be the full definition of equality on lists, but simply a test to determine whether a second list is empty or not.

The main problems with these techniques are as follows:

- Only certain kinds of overloading can be dealt with in this way. In particular, it is not suitable for functions (or as a special case, constant values) for which the required overloading cannot be determined from the type of its arguments. For example, a function $f :: \forall a. Int \subseteq a \Rightarrow Int \rightarrow a$ cannot be implemented in this way since it is not possible to evaluate expressions of the form $f\ n$ (for integer values n) without more information about the context in which this expression appears to indicate what the result type should be.

- The need to include type information in the representation of an object may compromise run-time performance.

- One of the arguments to an overloaded function must be (at least partially) evaluated in order to determine which implementation of the overloaded function should be used. This may not be acceptable in the context of a non-strict language where the implementation for a particular instance of an overloaded function may not itself be strict in the argument that is evaluated.

For our purposes, the first of these three problems is by far the most significant since it implies that we cannot expect to find a general implementation of qualified types based on the methods described in this section. On the other hand, having identified this problem, it seems reasonable to expect that the implementation of a function with a qualified type will (in general) require additional parameters to provide information about the context in which its result will be used.

4.2 Overloading made explicit

There is a well known relationship, often described as the *Curry-Howard isomorphism* (Howard, 1980), between the terms of simply typed λ-calculus and the derivations of propositions in a formulation of propositional calculus. In particular, the use of hypotheses in a derivation corresponds to occurrences of variables in *lambda*-terms, while the type of each term can be identified with the proposition established by the corresponding derivation. We can highlight this relationship by writing the inference rules for the two systems side by side as follows:

$$A, x{:}\sigma \vdash x : \sigma \qquad\qquad A, S \vdash S$$

$$\frac{A \vdash E : \sigma \rightarrow \tau \quad A \vdash F : \sigma}{A \vdash EF : \tau} \qquad\qquad \frac{A \vdash S \Rightarrow T \quad A \vdash S}{A \vdash T}$$

$$\frac{A, x{:}\sigma \vdash E : \tau}{A \vdash \lambda x{:}\sigma.E : \sigma \rightarrow \tau} \qquad\qquad \frac{A, S \vdash T}{A \vdash S \Rightarrow T}$$

In particular, the rule for typing applications corresponds to the logical rule of *modus ponens*, while the rule for typing abstractions yields a form of the *deduction theorem*. Another significant feature of the correspondence is that the familiar concepts of β- and η-reduction can also be interpreted as proof-theoretic reductions between derivations.

In the terminology of (Girard, Lafont and Taylor, 1989), the Curry-Howard isomorphism highlights implicit symmetries between the language of terms and the underlying logic, and they argue that the design of each of these facets should be influenced by consideration of the other. As a further illustration, the polymorphic λ-calculus, originally formulated by Girard (1971) and independently by Reynolds (1974), includes constructs for type application and abstraction, corresponding respectively to the rules for eliminating and introducing (second order) universal quantification in a formulation of predicate calculus:

$$\frac{A \vdash E : \forall t.\sigma}{A \vdash E\tau : [\tau/t]\sigma} \qquad\qquad \frac{A \vdash \forall t.S}{A \vdash [T/t]S}$$

$$\frac{A \vdash E : \sigma \quad t \notin TV(A)}{A \vdash \lambda t.E : \forall t.\sigma} \qquad\qquad \frac{A \vdash S \quad t \text{ not free in } A}{A \vdash \forall t.S}$$

The principal feature that distinguishes a system of qualified types from other typing disciplines is the typing rules ($\Rightarrow E$) and ($\Rightarrow I$).

$$\frac{P\,|\,A \vdash E : \pi \Rightarrow \sigma \quad P \Vdash \pi}{P\,|\,A \vdash E : \sigma}\,(\Rightarrow E) \qquad \frac{P, \pi\,|\,A \vdash E : \sigma}{P\,|\,A \vdash E : \pi \Rightarrow \sigma}\,(\Rightarrow I)$$

Considering the correspondence between terms and logics illustrated by the examples above leads us to a natural extension of the term language that makes the role of evidence explicit. The main features of this system are as follows:

- **Evidence expressions**: A language of *evidence expressions* e denoting evidence values, including a (countably infinite) set of *evidence variables* v, disjoint from the sets of term and type variables. The set of evidence variables appearing (free) in an object X (in particular, in an evidence expression) will be denoted $EV(X)$.

- **Evidence construction**: A *predicate assignment* is a collection of elements of the form $(v : \pi)$ in which no evidence variable appears more than once. The $\Vdash$ relation is extended to a three place relation $P \Vdash e : \pi$ and we treat this with more operational significance, as an assertion that it is possible to 'construct' evidence e for the predicate π in any environment binding the variables in the predicate assignment P to appropriate evidence values. Notice that predicates now play a similar role for evidence expressions as types for simple λ-calculus terms.

  The *domain* of a predicate assignment P is the set of all evidence variables appearing in P and will be denoted by *dom* P.

- **Evidence abstraction**: The use of ($\Rightarrow I$) corresponds to an evidence abstraction of the form $\lambda v\!:\!\pi.E$.

  $$\frac{P, v\!:\!\pi, P'\,|\,A \vdash E : \sigma}{P, P'\,|\,A \vdash \lambda v\!:\!\pi.E : \pi \Rightarrow \sigma}$$

  Informally, an implicitly overloaded term E' of type $\pi \Rightarrow \sigma$ is represented by a term of the form $\lambda v\!:\!\pi.E$ with explicit treatment of overloading where v is an evidence variable and E is a term of type σ corresponding to E' using v in each place where evidence for π is needed.

- **Evidence application**: In a similar way, the use of ($\Rightarrow E$) corresponds to an evidence application of the form Ee:

  $$\frac{P\,|\,A \vdash E : \pi \Rightarrow \sigma \quad P \Vdash e\!:\!\pi}{P\,|\,A \vdash Ee : \sigma}$$

  Informally, an object of type $\pi \Rightarrow \sigma$ can be used as an object of type σ by applying it to suitable evidence for π.

- **Evidence reduction**: To describe the way that evidence values are manipulated during the execution of a program, the standard rules of computation must be augmented by a variant of β-reduction for evidence abstraction and application:

  $$(\lambda v.E)e \rhd_{\beta e} [e/v]E.$$

With the explicit use of evidence expressions, the order of the predicates in the type of an object (and hence the order of the evidence parameters taken by an overloaded value) can no longer be ignored; if E has type $\pi_1 \Rightarrow \pi_2 \Rightarrow \sigma$ and e_1, e_2 are evidence expressions for π_1 and π_2 respectively, then $Ee_1 e_2$ will be a term of type σ, but the term $Ee_2 e_1$ will not (in general) be well-typed. Fortunately, we can easily accommodate the necessary changes by dropping the assumption that the $(\_,\_)$ operator on predicates and predicate assignments is commutative and idempotent, treating it simply as an associative binary operator with a left and right identity $\emptyset$. In simpler terms, we work with lists of (labelled) predicates rather than predicate sets as in Chapter 3.

The only place that we have actually treated $(\_,\_)$ as anything other than a purely formal symbol was in the formulation of $(\Rightarrow I)$ in Figure 3.1 where we wrote P, π to denote a predicate set containing the predicate π. With the weaker interpretation, this would require π to be the last element in a list of predicates. This is easily remedied by writing the corresponding predicate assignment in the form $P, v\!:\!\pi, P'$ as in the second version of $(\Rightarrow I)$ above.

In practice, it is convenient to blur the distinction between sequences and individual objects. In particular, the following abbreviations will be very useful in subsequent work:

Object	Expression	Abbreviation
Predicate assignment	$v_1\!:\!\pi_1, \ldots, v_n\!:\!\pi_n$	$v\!:\!P$
Evidence assignment	$e_1\!:\!\pi_1, \ldots, e_n\!:\!\pi_n$	$e\!:\!P$
Qualified type	$\pi_1 \Rightarrow \ldots \Rightarrow \pi_n \Rightarrow \rho$	$P \Rightarrow \rho$
Evidence application	$(\ldots(Ee_1)\ldots)e_n$	Ee
Evidence abstraction	$\lambda v_1.\ldots\lambda v_n.E$	$\lambda v.E$

where $P = \pi_1, \ldots, \pi_n$ is a list of predicates, $v = v_1, \ldots, v_n$ is a list of evidence variables and $e = e_1, \ldots, e_n$ is a list of evidence expressions. When writing a predicate assignment in the form $v : P$ we assume implicitly that v does not include any duplicates. In particular, for a predicate assignment of the form $v : P, w : Q$, we assume that the sets of variable in v and w are disjoint. When there is no particular need to explicitly mention the domain of a predicate assignment we will often write just P in place of $v\!:\!P$, and we will also allow P to be treated as a list of predicates without explicitly removing the evidence variables.

4.3 Predicate entailment with evidence

The properties of predicate entailment described in Chapter 2 must also be extended to deal with predicate assignments and evidence expressions. A suitable set of rules is given in Figure 4.1, most of which are straightforward generalisations of the original rules for predicate entailment given in Figure 2.1.

Note that there are two rules which do not have counterparts in the original system with implicit overloading:

- Rule (*evars*) specifies that the only evidence variables that can appear in the evidence expression e given by an entailment $P \Vdash e\!:\!\pi$ are those which appear in the domain P. This is analogous to the result that all of the free variables appearing in a term that is well-typed under a given type assignment A must appear in the domain of A.

Standard properties:

(*id*) $$v\!:\!P \Vdash v\!:\!P$$

(*term*) $$v\!:\!P \Vdash \emptyset$$

(*fst*) $$v\!:\!P, w\!:\!Q \Vdash v\!:\!P$$

(*snd*) $$v\!:\!P, w\!:\!Q \Vdash w\!:\!Q$$

(*univ*) $$\frac{v\!:\!P \Vdash e\!:\!Q \quad v\!:\!P \Vdash e'\!:\!R}{v\!:\!P \Vdash e\!:\!Q, e'\!:\!R}$$

(*trans*) $$\frac{v\!:\!P \Vdash e\!:\!Q \quad v'\!:\!Q \Vdash e'\!:\!R}{v\!:\!P \Vdash [e/v']e'\!:\!R}$$

(*close*) $$\frac{v\!:\!P \Vdash e\!:\!Q}{v\!:\!SP \Vdash e\!:\!SQ}$$

Evidence variables:

(*evars*) $$\frac{v\!:\!P \Vdash e\!:\!Q}{EV(e) \subseteq v}$$

Derived rules:

(*rename*) $$\frac{v\!:\!P \Vdash e\!:\!Q}{w\!:\!P \Vdash [w/v]e\!:\!Q}$$

(*dist*) $$\frac{v\!:\!P \Vdash e\!:\!Q \quad v'\!:\!P' \Vdash e'\!:\!Q'}{v\!:\!P, v'\!:\!P' \Vdash e\!:\!Q, e'\!:\!Q'}$$

(*cut*) $$\frac{v\!:\!P \Vdash e\!:\!Q \quad v\!:\!P, w\!:\!Q \Vdash e'\!:\!R}{v\!:\!P \Vdash [e/w]e'\!:\!R}$$

Figure 4.1: Rules for predicate entailment with evidence.

- Rule (*rename*) can be used to rename the evidence variables bound in a particular predicate assignment and can be thought of as a form of α-conversion. This rule will often be used implicitly to justify the process of combining two entailments such as $v : P \Vdash e : Q$ and $v' : P' \Vdash e' : Q'$ in the rule (*dist*); if any of the variables in v' clash with those in v, then we can pick new evidence variables w' and obtain $v\!:\!P, w'\!:\!P' \Vdash e\!:\!Q, [w'/v']e'\!:\!Q'$.

In particular applications, we will usually assume that all of the rules in Figure 4.1 are (implicitly) included as part of the definition of $\Vdash$.

4.4 Evidence, predicates and implementations

Having motivated the definition and use of evidence in a fairly abstract way it is important to examine its role in particular applications of qualified types. On an informal level, an overloaded value of type $\forall\alpha_i.P \Rightarrow \tau$ can be interpreted as a function $\mathcal{I}$ mapping each collection of predicates of the form $[\tau_i/\alpha_i]P$ to an implementation with type $[\tau_i/\alpha_i]\tau$. Quite how much of $\mathcal{I}$ is dealt with at compile-time (type-checking) and how much is implemented at run-time varies according to the choice of evidence values that provides an intermediate step between predicates and implementations.

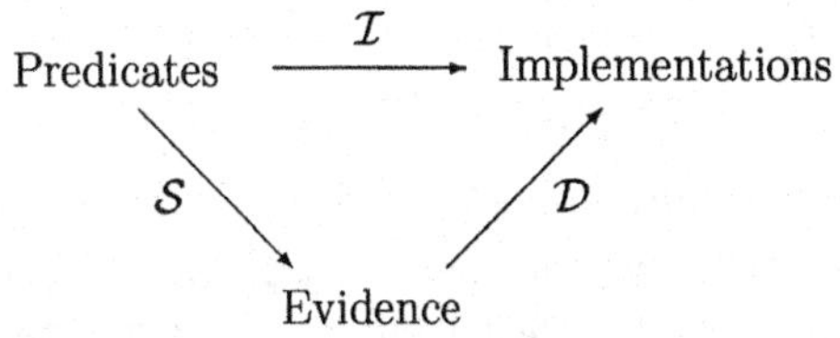

($\mathcal{S}$ and $\mathcal{D}$ are the *static* and *dynamic* components of $\mathcal{I}$ respectively.) In the simplest (and most abstract) case we can use the predicates themselves as evidence values taking the static component $\mathcal{S}$ to be the identity and setting $\mathcal{D} = \mathcal{I}$. For example, we might implement the function $f :: \forall a. Int \subseteq a \Rightarrow Int \to a$ mentioned in Section 4.1 by supplying the predicate $Int \subseteq a$ (with a bound to the appropriate type) as an additional parameter from which the required overloading can be determined.

Moving towards the other extreme, we might use terms as evidence values, taking $\mathcal{S}$ as the function that maps each predicate of the form $Eq\ \tau$ to a term representing the equality function on objects of type τ. In this case, the dynamic component $\mathcal{D}$ is (essentially) the identity.

These two extremes highlight a distinction made by Thatte (1992) between *prescriptive* and *descriptive* type systems i.e. those in which meaning and well-typing can be treated independently and those in which they are inseparable. As Thatte points out, any system in which the overloading of values cannot be completely determined during type checking will include elements of the prescriptive approach (in other words, having a non-trivial dynamic component) and hence most will fall somewhere between these two alternatives. For example, Thatte gives a (largely prescriptive) treatment of type class overloading based on the use of types as evidence values. The static component is the function that maps each class constraint of the form $C\ \tau$ to the type τ. The dynamic component is described using a polymorphic fixed-point operator and a new **typecase** construct to allow the definition of functions from types to values by 'pattern matching' on the form of a type expressions.

In the following sections we describe some specific (descriptive) choices of evidence values for each of the systems of predicates described in Chapter 2.

4.5 Type classes and dictionaries

In this section, we provide a brief indication of the use of evidence in the implementation of systems of type classes as described in Section 2.2, a topic we discuss in much greater detail in Chapters 7 and 8.

Following (Wadler and Blott, 1989) we refer to the evidence for a predicate of the form $C\ \tau$ as a *dictionary*. In the special case of the class `Eq` there is only one member function (the equality operator `(==)`) and an obvious choice of dictionary for a predicate `Eq a` is an equality test function with type `a -> a -> Bool` constructed using the definitions given in the corresponding instance declarations. For example, we might use `primEqInt` as evidence for `Eq Int` and `eqList primEqInt` as evidence for `Eq [Int]` where `eqList` is the function:

```
eqList                     :: (a -> a -> Bool) -> [a] -> [a] -> Bool
eqList eq []     []     = True
eqList eq []     (y:ys) = False
eqList eq (x:xs) []     = False
eqList eq (x:xs) (y:ys) = eq x y  &&  eqList eq xs ys
```

derived directly from the instance declaration for equality on lists.

Type classes with more than one member function can be dealt with using a dictionary that includes implementations for each member. The member functions themselves can be implemented as selector functions that extract the appropriate value from a dictionary. Superclasses can also be dealt with in this framework; for example, we might store a dictionary for an instance `Eq a` as a component of the dictionary for the instance `Ord a`. These extensions are discussed more fully in later chapters.

The rules for predicate entailment for type classes given in Section 2.2.4 can be extended to describe the construction of dictionaries. As a first step we use type class environments containing elements of the form:

$\mathit{Class}\ P \Rightarrow \pi$	representing a class declaration. Given a dictionary $d : \pi$, the superclass dictionary for a predicate π' appearing in P is denoted $d.\pi'$.
$D\colon \mathit{Inst}\ P \Rightarrow \pi$	representing an instance declaration. D is a dictionary constructor function that maps a collection of dictionaries $e\colon P$ to a dictionary De for π.

Dictionary expressions are written using the grammar:

$$\begin{array}{rcll} d & ::= & v & \textit{dictionary variable} \\ & | & d.\pi & \textit{superclass selection} \\ & | & De & \textit{dictionary construction} \end{array}$$

and the rules for dictionary construction with respect to an arbitrary type class environment Γ are given in Figure 4.2 .

$$(\mathit{super})\quad \frac{P \Vdash d\colon\pi}{P \Vdash (d.\pi')\colon\pi'} \quad (\mathit{Class}\ Q, \pi', Q' \Rightarrow \pi) \in \Gamma$$

$$(\mathit{inst})\quad \frac{P \Vdash e\colon P'}{P \Vdash De\colon\pi} \quad (D\colon \mathit{Inst}\ P' \Rightarrow \pi) \in \Gamma$$

Figure 4.2: Rules for type class entailment.

For example, the type class environment corresponding to the instance declarations in Section 2.2 is:

$$\begin{array}{l} \{\mathit{Class}\ \emptyset \Rightarrow \mathit{Eq}\ a, \\ \ \mathit{Class}\ (\mathit{Eq}\ a) \Rightarrow \mathit{Ord}\ a, \\ \ \texttt{primEqInt}\colon \mathit{Inst}\ \emptyset \Rightarrow \mathit{Eq}\ \mathit{Int}, \\ \ \texttt{eqChar}\colon \mathit{Inst}\ \emptyset \Rightarrow \mathit{Eq}\ \mathit{Char}, \\ \ \texttt{eqList}\colon \mathit{Inst}\ (\mathit{Eq}\ a) \Rightarrow \mathit{Eq}\ [a]\,\} \end{array}$$

where `eqList` is the function defined above and `eqChar` is the function:

```
eqChar          ::  Char -> Char -> Bool
eqChar c c'     =   primEqInt (ord c) (ord c')
```

derived from the instance declaration for equality on characters. In this simple case, the equality operator can be implemented as an identity function:

```
(==)     ::  (a -> a -> Bool) -> (a -> a -> Bool)
(==) eq  =   eq
```

As a more interesting example, the `member` function can be implemented using:

```
member                :: (a -> a -> Bool) -> a -> [a] -> Bool
member eq x []        = False
member eq x (y:ys)    = eq x y || member eq x ys
```

4.6 Subtyping and coercion

This section outlines a treatment for systems of subtyping based on the approach described in Section 2.3 using *coercion functions* mapping values of type σ to values of type σ' as evidence for predicates of the form $\sigma \subseteq \sigma'$. Instead of working directly with the coercions themselves we use a language of *coercion expressions* with syntax:

$$\begin{array}{rcll} e & ::= & v & \textit{coercion variable} \\ & | & id & \textit{trivial coercion} \\ & | & e \rightarrow e & \textit{function coercion} \\ & | & e \circ e & \textit{composition of coercions} \end{array}$$

The rules used to define the entailment relation in Figure 2.3 are extended to those in Figure 4.3 which also describe the calculation of the coercion corresponding to a given predicate.

$$\begin{array}{ll} (\textit{refl}) & P \Vdash id : \sigma \subseteq \sigma \\[1em] (\textit{trans-}\subseteq) & \dfrac{P \Vdash e : a \subseteq b \quad P \Vdash f : b \subseteq c}{P \Vdash (f \circ e) : a \subseteq c} \\[1em] (\textit{arrow}) & \dfrac{P \Vdash e : a \subseteq c \quad P \Vdash f : d \subseteq b}{P \Vdash (e \rightarrow f) : (c \rightarrow d) \subseteq (a \rightarrow b)} \end{array}$$

Figure 4.3: Rules for structural subtyping with coercion.

Writing C for the set of all coercions we define the semantics of a coercion expression (with respect to an environment η mapping coercion variables to elements of C) using:

$$\begin{array}{lcl} [\![v]\!] & = & \eta[\![v]\!] \\ [\![id]\!] & = & \lambda x.x \\ [\![f \rightarrow g]\!] & = & \lambda h.\lambda x.[\![g]\!](h([\![f]\!]\ x)) \\ [\![f \circ g]\!] & = & \lambda x.[\![g]\!]([\![f]\!]\ x) \end{array}$$

Using the obvious definitions, it is straightforward to establish the soundness of the rules in Figure 4.3 with respect to this interpretation.

4.7 Implementation of extensible records

Type systems with extensible records have been studied by a number of researchers but there have been surprisingly few attempts to describe how these systems might be dealt with in concrete implementations.

If the type of a given record is fully determined at compile-time, it may be possible to arrange for the values in each field to be held in contiguous storage locations, with the field corresponding to a given label at a fixed offset from the start of the record. For the general case, it is common to represent records as lists of label and value pairs; extracting a value from a record involves scanning the list to locate a pair with a given label. In principle, this might fail if no appropriately labelled is found, but in practice, the type system can be used to ensure that this does not happen.

Recently, Rémy (1992) has proposed a representation that stores the values held in a record as an array together with a pointer to a *header* (shared by other records with the same field structure) that is used to determine offsets into the array for each label. Extending a record with a new field is potentially expensive since it requires the calculation of a new header.

Independently of the work described here, Ohori (1992) gives a compilation method for a calculus of records which has much in common with the approach described below. Other than this, we are not aware of any previous work that makes use of concepts analogous to evidence in the implementation of extensible records. One simple (prescriptive) approach would be to consider a system in which the evidence for a predicate of the form $(r \textsf{ lacks } l)$ is the function:

$$(\_ \mid l = \_) \;::\; \forall t.\, r \rightarrow t \rightarrow \langle r \mid l : t\rangle$$

In a similar way, evidence for a predicate of the form $(r \textsf{ has } l : t)$ might be given by the pair of functions:

$$\begin{array}{lcl}(\_ \setminus l) & :: & r \rightarrow r \setminus l \\ (\_ .\, l) & :: & r \rightarrow t\end{array}$$

While reasonable from a theoretical point of view, these choices are not particularly useful for practical work since they do not say anything about how these operations are actually implemented.

In the rest of this section we outline a new implementation of extensible records that provides constant time selection and relatively inexpensive implementations of extension and restriction. In particular, there is no need to include any information about labels (either directly or as part of some header) in the representation of a record. We retain the efficiency of the implementation of records in the simple case where all the fields are known, with the additional benefit of supporting proper extensible records.

This representation was discovered by considering how the rules for predicate entailment given in Figure 2.4 might be extended to describe the construction of evidence. Whilst it would be wrong to draw any firm conclusions from this single example, we hope that similar considerations of evidence values might also be helpful in the discovery of concrete implementations for other applications of qualified types.

We assume that all records can be represented by arrays of equally sized cells. The fields in a record will be stored in such an array in increasing order of their labels. This relies on the choice of an arbitrary total order $<$ on the set of labels—we illustrate this here with a lexicographic ordering. As a simple example, the record $\langle w = 2,\ y = 3,\ x = \mathit{True}\rangle$ might be represented by:

2	*True*	3

There is no need to include representations for the labels since the positions of each field are completely determined by the set of labels $\{w,\ x,\ y\}$ and this information can be obtained from the type of the record, $\langle w : \mathit{Int},\ y : \mathit{Int},\ x : \mathit{Bool}\rangle$. More precisely, if L gives the set of labels in a record, then the position at which the value associated with label l can be found is given by $\mathit{pos}\ l\ L$, the number of elements in the set $\{\, l' \mid l' \in L,\ l' < l\,\}$.

The following diagram illustrates the process of extending a record with a new field:

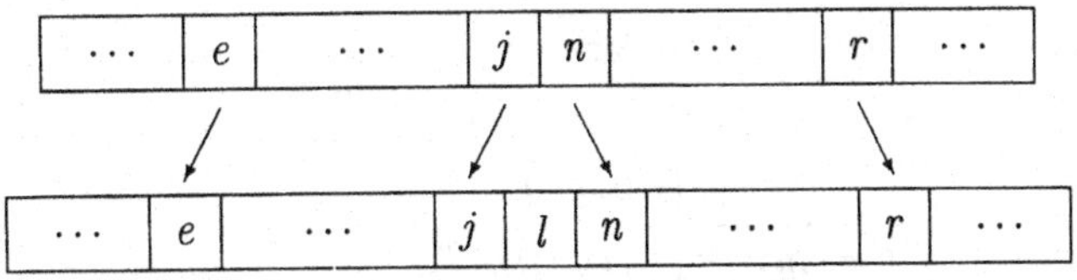

Note that all of the fields with labels that are less than that of the field being inserted remain in the same position in the array while the other entries are shifted up one position. If the set of labels in the original record is L, then a field labelled l should be inserted in position $\mathit{pos}\ l\ L$ as defined above. (For simplicity, we assume that the number of fields in a given record is stored as part of the concrete representation for record values. This ensures that the implementation can determine how much storage space should be allocated to hold the extended record.) The reverse process can be used to remove a field from a given record.

Suitable forms of evidence for the three kinds of predicate introduced in Section 2.4 are as follows:

- The evidence for a predicate of the form **record** r is the set of labels appearing in r which, by the comments above, completely determines the structure of records of type r.
- The evidence for a predicate of the form r **has** $l : t$ is an integer that specifies the position of the field labelled l in a record of type r.
- The evidence for a predicate of the form r **lacks** l is an integer that gives the position at which a field with label l could be inserted into a record of type r.

The definition of predicate entailment in Figure 2.4 is extended to describe the calculation of evidence values in Figure 4.4. Note that all of the comparisons between labels can be evaluated during the type checking process (so there is no need for a runtime representation of labels or of $<$).

The only kind of predicates used in the (qualified) types of programs involving records are those of the form r **has** $l\!:\!t$ and r **lacks** l and hence the form of evidence expressions needed for the execution of a program can be described by the syntax:

$$\begin{array}{rcll} e & ::= & 0 & \textit{zero offset} \\ & | & n & \textit{offset variable} \\ & | & e + 1 & \textit{successor} \\ & | & e - 1 & \textit{predecessor} \end{array}$$

Record formation:

$$P \Vdash \{\}:\textsf{record}\ \langle\rangle$$

$$\frac{P \Vdash L:\textsf{record}\ r \quad l \notin L}{P \Vdash L \cup \{l\}:\textsf{record}\ \langle r \mid l:t\rangle}$$

$$\frac{P \Vdash L:\textsf{record}\ r \quad l \in L}{P \Vdash L \setminus \{l\}:\textsf{record}\ r \setminus l}$$

Absent fields:

$$P \Vdash 0:\langle\rangle\ \textsf{lacks}\ l$$

$$\frac{P \Vdash L:\textsf{record}\ r \setminus l}{P \Vdash n:(r \setminus l\ \textsf{lacks}\ l)} \qquad n = pos\ l\ L$$

$$\frac{P \Vdash n:(r\ \textsf{lacks}\ l)}{P \Vdash m:(r \setminus l'\ \textsf{lacks}\ l)} \qquad m = \begin{cases} n, & l < l' \\ n-1, & l' < l \end{cases}$$

$$\frac{P \Vdash n:(r\ \textsf{lacks}\ l)}{P \Vdash m:(\langle r \mid l':t'\rangle\ \textsf{lacks}\ l)} \qquad m = \begin{cases} n, & l < l' \\ n+1, & l' < l \end{cases}$$

Present fields:

$$\frac{P \Vdash L:\textsf{record}\ \langle r \mid l:t\rangle}{P \Vdash n:(\langle r \mid l:t\rangle\ \textsf{has}\ l:t)} \qquad n = pos\ l\ L$$

$$\frac{P \Vdash n:(r\ \textsf{has}\ l:t)}{P \Vdash m:(r \setminus l'\ \textsf{has}\ l:t)} \qquad m = \begin{cases} n, & l < l' \\ n-1, & l' < l \end{cases}$$

$$\frac{P \Vdash n:(r\ \textsf{has}\ l:t)}{P \Vdash m:(\langle r \mid l':t'\rangle\ \textsf{has}\ l:t)} \qquad m = \begin{cases} n, & l < l' \\ n+1, & l' < l \end{cases}$$

Figure 4.4: Predicate entailment for extensible records with evidence.

In the special case of a record whose structure is completely determined at compile-time, simple constant folding techniques can be used to calculate integer offsets for each field without any run-time cost.

Chapter 5

Semantics and coherence

The principal aim of this chapter is to show how the concept of evidence can be used to give a semantics for OML programs with implicit overloading.

Outline of chapter

We begin by describing a version of the polymorphic λ-calculus called OP that includes the constructs for evidence application and abstraction described in the previous chapter (Section 5.1). One of the main uses of OP is as the target of a translation from OML with the semantics of each OML term being defined by those of its translation. In Section 5.2 we show how the OML typing derivations for a term E can be interpreted as OP derivations for terms with explicit overloading, each of which is a potential translation for E. It is immediate from this construction that every well-typed OML term has a translation and that all translations obtained in this way are well-typed in OP.

Given that each OML typing typically has many distinct derivations it follows that there will also be many distinct translations for a given term and it is not clear which should be chosen to represent the original term. The OP term corresponding to the derivation produced by the type inference algorithm in Section 3.4 gives one possible choice but it seems rather unnatural to base a definition of semantics on any particular type inference algorithm. A better approach is to show that any two translations of a term are semantically equivalent so that an implementation is free to use whichever translation is more convenient in a particular situation while retaining the same, well-defined semantics. In the words of (Breazu-Tannen et al., 1989), we need to show that 'the meaning of a term does not depend on the way that it was type checked', a property that they call *coherence*.

As we demonstrate in Section 5.3, there are examples for which a term may have semantically distinct translations and hence we cannot hope to establish a general coherence theorem. Instead, we settle for the less ambitious goal of discovering conditions that are sufficient to ensure that the semantics of a term are well-defined. Tests for these conditions would then be included as part of the type checking phase in a concrete implementation so that we reject not only those programs that do not type-check, but also those for which coherence cannot be guaranteed.

As part of this process, we need to specify exactly what it means for two terms to be equivalent. Rather than working with any particular semantic model, Section 5.4 gives a syntactic definition of (typed) equality between terms. This means that our results are valid in a model for which the axioms and rules used in the definition of equality are themselves valid. Clearly, it is preferable to make this definition as weak as possible, permitting a larger class of models, while at the same time retaining enough structure to give a useful and sensible characterisation of the equality between terms. One limitation of our framework is that we include an axiom for β-conversion, $(\lambda x.E)F = [F/x]E$, which is not sound in models of the λ-calculus with call-by-value semantics and hence our results are restricted to languages with lazy or call-by-name semantics. We discuss this point more fully in Section 5.9.

We have already seen how the type inference algorithm can be used to describe the relationship between the set of all OML typings for a term and a particular principal type scheme. It therefore seems sensible to extend the results of Chapter 3 in an attempt to describe the relationship between arbitrary translations and the translation determined by this algorithm. As a first step, Section 5.5 describes a semantic interpretation for the ordering relation ($\leq$) used extensively in our treatment of type inference. The basic idea is that an ordering of the form $\sigma \geq \sigma'$ can be described by a *conversion*; a closed OP term C of type $\sigma \to \sigma'$. The only effect of a conversion is to change the way in which evidence parameters are dealt with so that, if E is a term of type σ, then CE gives essentially the same term, repackaged with the less general type σ'.

Using the properties of conversions we extend the results for the syntax-directed system and the type inference algorithm in our earlier work to include the calculation of translations. These are described in Sections 5.6 and 5.7 respectively and we show that any translation of a term can be written in the form $C(\lambda w.E')v$ where C is a conversion of a particular type, E' is the translation produced by the type inference algorithm and v, w are fixed collections of evidence variables. Hence the task of establishing the equivalence of two arbitrary translations reduces to showing the equivalence of two terms of the form $C_1(\lambda w.E')v$ and $C_2(\lambda w.E')v$ where C_1 and C_2 are conversions of a particular type. One obvious approach is to find conditions that guarantee that these conversions are equivalent.

Section 5.8 investigates this possibility to obtain sufficient conditions for the equivalence of a pair of conversions and hence to guarantee coherence. In particular, we show that the type system is coherent for any term with an *unambiguous*principal type scheme (a simple syntactic condition), generalising an earlier result in (Blott, 1991) for the special case of a system of type classes. In addition, we show how our results can be adapted to applications where the restriction to terms with unambiguous type schemes is too severe. For example, we are able to give a satisfactory treatment of coherence for the system of extensible records described in Sections 2.4 and 4.7 despite the fact that the primitive field restriction operator has an ambiguous type.

Detailed proofs for the results of this chapter are included in Appendix A.

5.1 A version of polymorphic λ-calculus with qualified types

This section describes a version of the polymorphic λ-calculus extended with constructs for evidence application and abstraction. For ease of reference, we call the type system presented here OP, intended as a mnemonic for 'Overloaded Polymorphic λ-calculus'. The set of types

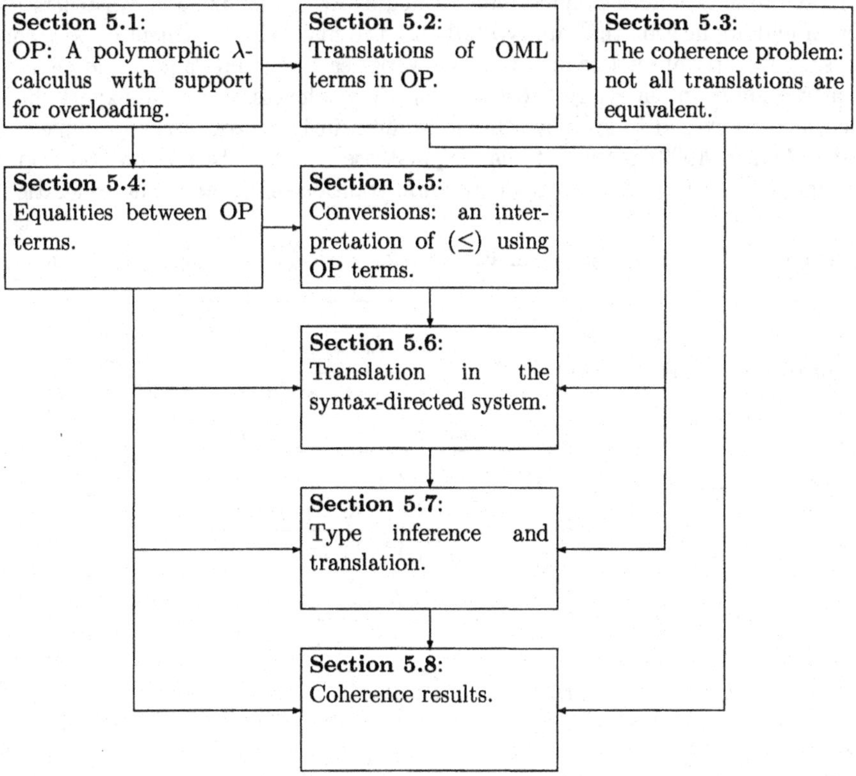

Figure 5.1: Outline of chapter

in OP is defined by the grammar:

$$\begin{array}{rcll} \sigma & ::= & t & \textit{type variables} \\ & | & \sigma \to \sigma & \textit{function types} \\ & | & \forall t.\sigma & \textit{polymorphic types} \\ & | & \pi \Rightarrow \sigma & \textit{qualified types} \end{array}$$

This is considerably more flexible than the structured language of types used in Chapter 3 since there is no distinction between simple types and type schemes. In particular, OP allows functions with polymorphic and/or overloaded values as their arguments. Note that constrained type schemes of the form $(P \,|\, \sigma)$ introduced in Section 3.2.1 can be written as the type $P \Rightarrow \sigma$ in this more general system.

The terms of OP are given by expressions of the form:

$$\begin{array}{rcll} E & ::= & x & \textit{term variables} \\ & | & EF & \textit{application} \\ & | & \lambda x.E & \textit{abstraction} \\ & | & Ee & \textit{evidence application} \\ & | & \lambda v.E & \textit{evidence abstraction} \\ & | & \textbf{let}\ x = E\ \textbf{in}\ F & \textit{local definition} \end{array}$$

Unlike most presentations of polymorphic λ-calculus we do not include constructs for type abstraction and application that are typically used to make the treatment of polymorphism explicit; such features are not required for the work described here, and would be an unnecessary distraction from our study of overloading. Nevertheless, we would expect the results described here to extend to such systems if required in later work. For example, (Peyton Jones and Wadler, 1990) point out that explicit use of type abstraction and application may provide useful information to guide program transformation and code generation in an optimising compiler.

The typing rules for OP are given in Figure 5.2. Strictly speaking, there is no need to

Standard rules:	(*var*)	$\dfrac{(x{:}\sigma) \in A}{P \mid A \vdash x : \sigma}$
	$(\to E)$	$\dfrac{P \mid A \vdash E : \sigma' \to \sigma \quad P \mid A \vdash F : \sigma'}{P \mid A \vdash EF : \sigma}$
	$(\to I)$	$\dfrac{P \mid A, x{:}\sigma' \vdash E : \sigma}{P \mid A \vdash \lambda x.E : \sigma' \to \sigma}$
Qualified types:	$(\Rightarrow E)$	$\dfrac{P \mid A \vdash E : \pi \Rightarrow \sigma \quad P \Vdash e{:}\pi}{P \mid A \vdash Ee : \sigma}$
	$(\Rightarrow I)$	$\dfrac{P, v{:}\pi, P' \mid A \vdash E : \sigma}{P, P' \mid A \vdash \lambda v.E : \pi \Rightarrow \sigma}$
Polymorphism:	$(\forall E)$	$\dfrac{P \mid A \vdash E : \forall t.\sigma}{P \mid A \vdash E : [\tau/t]\sigma}$
	$(\forall I)$	$\dfrac{P \mid A \vdash E : \sigma \quad t \notin TV(A) \cup TV(P)}{P \mid A \vdash E : \forall t.\sigma}$
Local definition:	(*let*)	$\dfrac{P \mid A \vdash E : \sigma \quad Q \mid A_x, x{:}\sigma \vdash F : \sigma'}{P, Q \mid A \vdash (\textbf{let}\ x = E\ \textbf{in}\ F) : \sigma'}$

Figure 5.2: Typing rules for OP.

include the **let** construct here since the typing rules of OP are sufficiently powerful to allow functions with polymorphic overloaded arguments and hence we can encode **let** $x = E$ **in** F as $(\lambda x.F)E$. The most important benefit of including the **let** construct is that it makes it much easier to treat the implicitly typed language of Chapter 3 as a (proper) sublanguage of OP. Another advantage is that it may sometimes be possible to generate better code for **let** expressions than for the equivalent term using a λ-abstraction (Peyton Jones, 1987).

5.2 Translation from OML to OP

From the definitions in the Sections 3.1 and 5.1 it is clear that every OML type scheme can be treated as an OP type. Furthermore, the typing rules of OML are a just a restricted version of the rules for OP, except that derivations in the latter involve predicate assignments rather than predicate sets and require explicit evidence abstraction and application in the rules ($\Rightarrow I$) and ($\Rightarrow E$) respectively. To formalise these ideas, we define a function *Preds* that maps each predicate assignment to the corresponding predicate set:

$$\begin{array}{lcl} \mathit{Preds}\ (P, P') & = & \mathit{Preds}\ P \cup \mathit{Preds}\ P' \\ \mathit{Preds}\ (v\!:\!\pi) & = & \{\pi\} \\ \mathit{Preds}\ \emptyset & = & \emptyset \end{array}$$

and a function *Erase* that maps OP terms with explicit overloading to terms in OML by deleting all occurrences of evidence variables and expressions:

$$\begin{array}{lcl} \mathit{Erase}\ (x) & = & x \\ \mathit{Erase}\ (EF) & = & (\mathit{Erase}\ E)\ (\mathit{Erase}\ F) \\ \mathit{Erase}\ (\lambda x.E) & = & \lambda x.(\mathit{Erase}\ E) \\ \mathit{Erase}\ (\mathbf{let}\ x = E\ \mathbf{in}\ F) & = & \mathbf{let}\ x = (\mathit{Erase}\ E)\ \mathbf{in}\ (\mathit{Erase}\ F) \\ \mathit{Erase}\ (Ee) & = & \mathit{Erase}\ E \\ \mathit{Erase}\ (\lambda v.E) & = & \mathit{Erase}\ E \end{array}$$

Similar tools are used in the investigation of the relationship between languages with implicit polymorphism (much like OP, but without overloading) and languages that use abstraction and application over types to make the use of polymorphism explicit (the standard example being Girard's 'System F'). See (Mitchell, 1990) for further details.

The correspondence between OML and OP suggested by the informal comments above can now be described by the following theorem:

Theorem 5.1 *If $P \mid A \vdash E : \sigma$ in OML, then there is an OP term E' and a predicate assignment P' such that $P = \mathit{Preds}\ P'$, $E = \mathit{Erase}\ E'$ and $P' \mid A \vdash E' : \sigma$ using a derivation of the same structure.*

The proof is straightforward, using induction on the structure of $P \mid A \vdash E : \sigma$. The term E' in the statement of the theorem will be referred to as a *translation* of E and we use the notation $P' \mid A \vdash E \leadsto E' : \sigma$ to refer to a translation of a term in a specific context. Note that, in the general case, an OML term will have many distinct translations in any given context, each corresponding to a different derivation of $P \mid A \vdash E : \sigma$ in OML.

The translations of OML terms can also be characterised more directly using the hybrid of the typing rules for OML and OP given in Figure 5.3. It is straightforward to show that $P' \mid A \vdash E \leadsto E' : \sigma$ according to the original definition of translations above if, and only if, the same judgement can be derived from these rules. In particular, we mention the following two theorems, the first of which establishes a soundness property indicating that any derivation using the rules includes both an OML derivation for the term involved and an OP derivation for its translation.

Theorem 5.2 *If $P \mid A \vdash E \leadsto E' : \sigma$ using the rules in Figure 5.3, then $E = \mathit{Erase}\ E'$ and there are derivations $P \mid A \vdash E' : \sigma$ in OP and $\mathit{Preds}\ P \mid A \vdash E : \sigma$ in OML each with the same structure as the first derivation.*

The second result shows that it is always possible to obtain a translation of a well-typed OML term using the rules given above (essentially by copying the structure of the original derivation):

$$(var)\quad \frac{(x:\sigma)\in A}{P\,|\,A\vdash x \leadsto x:\sigma}$$

$$(\to E)\quad \frac{P\,|\,A\vdash E\leadsto E':\tau'\to\tau \quad P\,|\,A\vdash F\leadsto F':\tau'}{P\,|\,A\vdash EF\leadsto E'F':\tau}$$

$$(\to I)\quad \frac{P\,|\,A_x, x{:}\tau'\vdash E\leadsto E':\tau}{P\,|\,A\vdash \lambda x.E\leadsto \lambda x.E':\tau'\to\tau}$$

$$(\Rightarrow E)\quad \frac{P\,|\,A\vdash E\leadsto E':\pi\Rightarrow\rho \quad P\Vdash e{:}\pi}{P\,|\,A\vdash E\leadsto E'e:\rho}$$

$$(\Rightarrow I)\quad \frac{P, v{:}\pi, P'\,|\,A\vdash E\leadsto E':\rho}{P, P'\,|\,A\vdash E\leadsto \lambda v.E':\pi\Rightarrow\rho}$$

$$(\forall E)\quad \frac{P\,|\,A\vdash E\leadsto E':\forall t.\sigma}{P\,|\,A\vdash E\leadsto E':[\tau/t]\sigma}$$

$$(\forall I)\quad \frac{P\,|\,A\vdash E\leadsto E':\sigma}{P\,|\,A\vdash E\leadsto E':\forall t.\sigma}\quad t\not\in TV(A)\wedge t\not\in TV(P)$$

$$(let)\quad \frac{P\,|\,A\vdash E\leadsto E':\sigma \quad Q\,|\,A_x, x{:}\sigma\vdash F\leadsto F':\tau}{P, Q\,|\,A\vdash (\textbf{let } x=E \textbf{ in } F)\leadsto(\textbf{let } x=E' \textbf{ in } F'):\tau}$$

Figure 5.3: Original type rules with translation

Theorem 5.3 *If $P\,|\,A\vdash E:\sigma$ in OML, then there is a derivation $P'\,|\,A\vdash E\leadsto E':\sigma$ for some predicate assignment P' with $P = Preds\ P'$ and some OP term E' such that $E = Erase\ E'$.*

The proofs for both of these results are straightforward and follow directly from the construction of the rules in Figure 5.3.

5.3 The coherence problem

The principal motivation for introducing OP was to enable the semantics of OML terms with implicit overloading to be described by the semantics of their translations in OP. In order to justify this approach we must show that:

- For each OML term E there is an OP term E' that is a translation of E. This follows directly from Theorem 5.3. Moreover, there is an effective way of calculating a translation for any well-typed term using the derivation given by Corollary 3.20 to guide the construction of the translation.

- Any translation of an OML term E is well-typed in OP. This has already been established in Theorem 5.2.

- The mapping from terms to translations must be well-defined. More accurately, we must show that any translations E_1 and E_2 of an OML term E given by derivations $P \mid A \vdash E \leadsto E_1 : \sigma$ and $P \mid A \vdash E \leadsto E_2 : \sigma$ are, in some precise sense, equivalent.

Whilst the first two properties have already been established, it is relatively simple to show that the third result does not hold in general. As an example, consider the term *out* (*in* x) under the evidence assignment $P = \{u : C\ \mathit{Int}, v : C\ \mathit{Bool}\}$ and the type assignment:

$$A = \{x : \mathit{Int},\quad \mathit{in} : \forall a.C\ a \Rightarrow \mathit{Int} \rightarrow a,\quad \mathit{out} : \forall a.C\ a \Rightarrow a \rightarrow \mathit{Int}\}$$

where C is a unary predicate symbol. Instantiating the quantified type variable in the type of *in* (and hence also in that of *out*) with the types *Int* and *Bool* leads to the following derivations with translations which are clearly not equivalent:

$$P \mid A \vdash \mathit{out}\ (\mathit{in}\ x) \leadsto \mathit{out}\ u\ (\mathit{in}\ u\ x) : \mathit{Int}$$
$$P \mid A \vdash \mathit{out}\ (\mathit{in}\ x) \leadsto \mathit{out}\ v\ (\mathit{in}\ v\ x) : \mathit{Int}$$

Given this example, we cannot hope to establish the general coherence result in the third item above; i.e. that all translations of an arbitrary OML term are semantically equivalent. In the rest of this chapter we work towards a more modest goal – to identify a collection of OML terms for which the coherence property can be established.

5.4 A definition of equality for OP terms

Before we can establish sufficient conditions to guarantee coherence, we need to specify formally what it means for two terms (specifically, two translations) to be equivalent. This section gives a syntactic characterisation of (typed) equality between OP terms using judgements of the form $P \mid A \vdash E = F : \sigma$ (with the implicit side-condition that both $P \mid A \vdash E : \sigma$ and $P \mid A \vdash F : \sigma$). Our task in the remaining sections of this chapter can now be described formally as:

> Given derivations $P \mid A \vdash E \leadsto E_1 : \sigma$ and $P \mid A \vdash E \leadsto E_2 : \sigma$ determine sufficient conditions to guarantee that $P \mid A \vdash E_1 = E_2 : \sigma$.

One of the reasons for including type information as part of the definition of equality is to avoid making unnecessary constraints on the choice of semantic model. Given a judgement $P \mid A \vdash E = F : \sigma$ we require only that E and F have the same meaning (which must be an element of the type denoted by σ) in environments that satisfy P and A. This is in contrast with an untyped judgement of the form $E = F$ that might be expected to hold in any semantic model, without consideration of the types of the objects involved.

5.4.1 Uniqueness of evidence

Another reason for using predicate assignments in the definition is to enable us to capture the 'uniqueness of evidence'; to be precise, we require that any evidence values e and f constructed by entailments $P \Vdash e : Q$ and $P \Vdash f : Q$ are semantically equivalent, in which case we write $P \vdash e = f : Q$. Since we only intend such judgements to be meaningful when both entailments hold, the definition of equality on evidence expressions can be described directly using:

$$P \vdash e = f : Q \quad \Leftrightarrow \quad P \Vdash e : Q \ \wedge \ P \Vdash f : Q.$$

This condition is essential if any degree of coherence is to be obtained. Without it, for example, it would be possible to have semantically distinct implementations of an overloaded operator that cannot be distinguished either by name or by type.

Uniqueness of evidence does not follow directly from the definition of $\Vdash$ and it is important to verify that this property holds for the predicate systems used in particular applications of qualified types. This, in turn, influences the design of particular predicate systems. For example, in the system of type classes described in Section 4.5, uniqueness of evidence is dealt with by ensuring that there is at most one definition that makes a given type an instance of a particular class.

5.4.2 Reduction of OP terms

In common with many treatments of typed λ-calculi, we will define the equality relation between terms using a notion of *reduction* between terms. More precisely, we use a judgement of the form $P \,|\, A \vdash E \rhd F : \sigma$ to describe a (typed) reduction from E to F with the implicit side condition that $P \,|\, A \vdash E : \sigma$. There is no need to include $P \,|\, A \vdash F : \sigma$ as a second side condition since it can be shown that this condition is implied by the first. This is a consequence of the *subject reduction theorem* – 'reduction preserves typing' – which is proved using standard techniques as in (Hindley and Seldin, 1986).

We split the definition of reduction into three parts, the first of which appears in Figure 5.4. We include the familiar definitions of β-conversion for evidence and term abstractions and **let** expressions and a rule of η-conversion for evidence abstractions.

(β)	$P \,|\, A \vdash (\lambda x.E)F \rhd [F/x]E : \sigma$
(β_e)	$P \,|\, A \vdash (\lambda v.E)e \rhd [e/v]E : \sigma$
$(\beta\text{-}let)$	$P \,|\, A \vdash (\mathbf{let}\ x = E\ \mathbf{in}\ F) \rhd [E/x]F : \sigma$
(η_e)	$\dfrac{v \notin EV(E)}{P \,|\, A \vdash (\lambda v.Ev) \rhd E : \sigma}$

Figure 5.4: Rules of computation

One unfortunate consequence of our approach is that the axiom (β) is not sound in models of the λ-calculus with call-by-value semantics and hence our results can only be applied to languages with lazy or call-by-name semantics. This limitation stems more from the difficulty of axiomatising call-by-value equality than from anything implicit in our particular application; for example, Ohori (1989) mentions similar problems in his work to describe a simple semantics for ML Polymorphism. This issue will be discussed more fully in Section 5.9.

A second collection of rules in Figure 5.5 is used to describe the renaming of bound variables in λ-abstractions, evidence abstractions and **let** expressions. Any such renaming is permitted so long as we avoid clashes with free variables.

$$(\alpha)\quad \frac{x \notin FV(\lambda y.E)}{P \,|\, A \vdash (\lambda y.E) \rhd (\lambda x.[x/y]E) : \sigma}$$

$$(\alpha_e)\quad \frac{v \notin EV(\lambda w.E)}{P \,|\, A \vdash (\lambda w.E) \rhd (\lambda v.[v/w]E) : \sigma}$$

$$(\alpha\text{-}let)\quad \frac{x \notin FV(\lambda y.E)}{P \,|\, A \vdash (\mathbf{let}\ y = E\ \mathbf{in}\ F) \rhd (\mathbf{let}\ x = E\ \mathbf{in}\ [x/y]F) : \sigma}$$

Figure 5.5: Rules for renaming bound variables

The final group of rules in Figure 5.6 are closely modelled on the original typing rules for OP in Figure 5.2. Their main application is to allow the reduction of subterms within a given term.

$$\frac{(x{:}\sigma) \in A}{P \,|\, A \vdash x \rhd x : \sigma}$$

$$\frac{P \,|\, A \vdash E \rhd E' : \sigma' \to \sigma \quad P \,|\, A \vdash F \rhd F' : \sigma'}{P \,|\, A \vdash EF \rhd E'F' : \sigma}$$

$$\frac{P \,|\, A_x, x{:}\sigma' \vdash E \rhd E' : \sigma}{P \,|\, A \vdash \lambda x.E \rhd \lambda x.E' : \sigma' \to \sigma}$$

$$\frac{P \,|\, A \vdash E \rhd E' : \pi \Rightarrow \sigma \quad P \vdash e = e' {:} \pi}{P \,|\, A \vdash Ee = E'e' : \sigma}$$

$$\frac{P, v{:}\pi, P' \,|\, A \vdash E \rhd E' : \sigma}{P, P' \,|\, A \vdash \lambda v.E \rhd \lambda v.E' : \pi \Rightarrow \sigma}$$

$$\frac{P \,|\, A \vdash E \rhd E' : \forall t.\sigma}{P \,|\, A \vdash E \rhd E' : [\tau/t]\sigma}$$

$$\frac{P \,|\, A \vdash E \rhd E' : \sigma \quad t \notin TV(A) \cup TV(P)}{P \,|\, A \vdash E \rhd E' : \forall t.\sigma}$$

$$\frac{P \,|\, A \vdash E \rhd E' : \sigma \quad P \,|\, A_x, x{:}\sigma \vdash F \rhd F' : \tau}{P \,|\, A \vdash (\mathbf{let}\ x = E\ \mathbf{in}\ F) \rhd (\mathbf{let}\ x = E'\ \mathbf{in}\ F') : \tau}$$

Figure 5.6: Structural laws for reductions between terms.

5.4.3 Equalities between OP terms

As we have already mentioned, equalities between OP terms will be represented by judgements of the the form $P \mid A \vdash E = F : \sigma$ with the implicit side condition that both $P \mid A \vdash E : \sigma$ and $P \mid A \vdash F : \sigma$. Figure 5.7 gives the definition of the equality between terms as the transitive, symmetric closure of the reduction relation described in the previous section. The first two rules ensure that equality is an equivalence relation. There is no

$$\frac{P\,|\,A \vdash E = F : \sigma}{P\,|\,A \vdash F = E : \sigma}$$

$$\frac{P\,|\,A \vdash E = E' : \sigma \quad P\,|\,A \vdash E' = E'' : \sigma}{P\,|\,A \vdash E = E'' : \sigma}$$

$$\frac{P\,|\,A \vdash E \rhd F : \sigma}{P\,|\,A \vdash E = F : \sigma}$$

Figure 5.7: Definition of equality between terms

need to include reflexivity here since this is a direct consequence of the structural rules in Figure 5.6. The last rule shows how reductions give rise to equalities. Note that in this case there is no need to establish that both $P\,|\,A \vdash E : \sigma$ and $P\,|\,A \vdash F : \sigma$ since the latter follows from the former by the subject reduction theorem mentioned above.

In practice, many of the rules used in the definition of equality above will be used implicitly in the proof of equalities between terms. The following example uses all three of the rules in Figure 5.7 as well as subject reduction to justify the fact that the intermediate steps are well-typed and illustrates the layout that we use for such proofs:

$$\begin{array}{rcll} P\,|\,A \vdash \textbf{let } x = E \textbf{ in } [F/x]F' & = & [E/x]([F/x]F') & (\beta\text{-}let) \\ & = & [[E/x]F/x]F' & \text{(substitution)} \\ & = & \textbf{let } x = [E/x]F \textbf{ in } F' : \sigma & (\beta\text{-}let) \end{array}$$

Notice that the context in which this equality is established (given by P, A and σ) is not significant. Examples like this are quite common and we will often avoid mentioning the context altogether in such situations, writing $\vdash E = F$ to indicate that E and F are equivalent in the sense that $P\,|\,A \vdash E = F : \sigma$ for any choice of P, A and σ for which the implicit side conditions hold.

The following proposition records some useful properties of **let** expressions including the result above, each of which follows directly from (β-*let*).

Proposition 5.4 *For any OP terms E, E' and F and distinct term variables x and y such that $y \notin FV(E)$:*

1. $\vdash (\textbf{let } x = E \textbf{ in } [F/x]F') = (\textbf{let } x = [E/x]F \textbf{ in } F')$.
2. $\vdash \lambda y.(\textbf{let } x = E \textbf{ in } F) = (\textbf{let } x = E \textbf{ in } \lambda y.F)$.
3. $\vdash E(\textbf{let } y = E' \textbf{ in } F') = (\textbf{let } y = E' \textbf{ in } EF')$.
4. $\vdash (\textbf{let } y = E' \textbf{ in } F')E = (\textbf{let } y = E' \textbf{ in } F'E)$.

The last three parts of this proposition are fairly standard, but the first is less familiar and it is worth illustrating why it is important in our work. Consider a system of type classes with a type class *Eq* such that $\emptyset \Vdash e : Eq\ Int$ and an equality function $(==) :: \forall a. Eq\ a \Rightarrow a \rightarrow a \rightarrow Bool$ used in the OML term:

$$\mathbf{let}\ f = (\lambda x.\lambda y.x == y)\ \mathbf{in}\ f\ 2\ 3$$

Since the local definition for function f is only ever applied to integer values, it is sufficient to treat f as having type $Int \rightarrow Int \rightarrow Bool$, with a corresponding translation:

$$\mathbf{let}\ f = (\lambda x.\lambda y.(==)\ e\ x\ y)\ \mathbf{in}\ f\ 2\ 3$$

However, the type inference algorithm uses $f :: \forall a. Eq\ a \Rightarrow a \rightarrow a \rightarrow Bool$ and results in a translation of the form:

$$\mathbf{let}\ f = (\lambda v.\lambda x.\lambda y.(==)\ v\ x\ y)\ \mathbf{in}\ f\ e\ 2\ 3.$$

The following calculation shows that these translations are equal and hence that it is possible to eliminate the evidence abstraction used in the second case.

$$\begin{array}{lll}
\multicolumn{2}{l}{\vdash \mathbf{let}\ f = (\lambda v.\lambda x.\lambda y.(==)\ v\ x\ y)\ \mathbf{in}\ f\ e\ 2\ 3} & \\
= & \mathbf{let}\ f = (\lambda v.\lambda x.\lambda y.(==)\ v\ x\ y)\ \mathbf{in}\ [f\ e/f](f\ 2\ 3) & \text{(substitution)} \\
= & \mathbf{let}\ f = [\lambda v.\lambda x.\lambda y.(==)\ v\ x\ y/f](f\ e)\ \mathbf{in}\ f\ 2\ 3 & \text{(Prop. 5.4(1))} \\
= & \mathbf{let}\ f = (\lambda v.\lambda x.\lambda y.(==)\ v\ x\ y)\ e\ \mathbf{in}\ f\ 2\ 3 & \text{(substitution)} \\
= & \mathbf{let}\ f = (\lambda x.\lambda y.(==)\ e\ x\ y)\ \mathbf{in}\ f\ 2\ 3 & (\beta)
\end{array}$$

As in the last step here, many equalities between terms can be obtained by replacing one subterm with an equivalent term. These steps are justified by the structural rules in Figure 5.6 and will often be used implicitly in proofs.

5.5 Ordering and conversion functions

5.5.1 Motivation and conversions between type schemes

One of the most important tools in the treatment of type inference described in Chapter 3 is the ordering relation $\leq$ used to describe when one (constrained) type scheme is more general than another. For example, assuming that $\emptyset \Vdash Eq\ Int$, the ordering:

$$Int \rightarrow Int \rightarrow Bool \quad \leq \quad \forall a. Eq\ a \Rightarrow a \rightarrow a \rightarrow Bool$$

might be used to justify replacing an integer equality function, say *primEqInt*, of type $Int \rightarrow Int \rightarrow Bool$ with a generic equality function $(==)$ with the more general type $\forall a. Eq\ a \Rightarrow a \rightarrow a \rightarrow Bool$. While valid in OML, this breaks down in OP due to the presence of evidence abstraction and application: Simply replacing *primEqInt* with $(==)$ in *primEqInt* 2 3 does not even give a well-typed expression! The correct approach would be to replace *primEqInt* by $(==)\ e$ where $\emptyset \Vdash e : Eq\ Int$.

This section describes an interpretation of orderings between type schemes as terms of OP that can be used to deal with examples like this. For each $\sigma' \leq \sigma$ we identify a particular collection of terms that we call *conversions* from σ to σ'. Each such conversion is a closed OP term $C : \sigma \rightarrow \sigma'$ and hence any term of type σ can be treated as having type σ' by applying the conversion C to it. One possible conversion for the example above is:

$$(\lambda x.xe) : (\forall a.Eq\ a \Rightarrow a \rightarrow a \rightarrow Bool) \rightarrow (Int \rightarrow Int \rightarrow Bool)$$

Note that the type of this conversion (as in the general case) cannot be expressed as an OML type scheme since it uses the richer structure of OP types.

For the purposes of type inference it would be sufficient to take any term C of type $\sigma \rightarrow \sigma'$ as a conversion for $\sigma' \leq \sigma$ since CE has type σ' for any term E of type σ. This is clearly inadequate if we are also concerned with the semantics of the terms involved; we can only replace E with CE if we can guarantee that these terms are equivalent, except perhaps in their use of evidence abstraction and application. More formally, we need to ensure that $Erase\ (CE) = Erase\ E$ for all OP terms E (or at least, all those occurring as translations of OML terms). Since $Erase\ (CE) = (Erase\ C)\ (Erase\ E)$, the obvious way to ensure that this condition holds is to require that $Erase\ C$ is equivalent to the identity term $id = \lambda x.x$.

It is tempting to define the set of conversions from σ to σ' as the set of all closed OP terms $C : \sigma \rightarrow \sigma'$ for which $Erase\ C$ is equivalent to id. In practice it is more convenient to choose a more conservative definition that gives a little more insight into the structure of conversions. The following definition is very closely modelled on the syntactic characterisation of the $\leq$ ordering in Proposition 3.4.

Definition 5.5 (Conversions – preliminary version)
Suppose that $\sigma = (\forall\alpha_i.Q \Rightarrow \tau)$ and $\sigma' = (\forall\beta_j.Q' \Rightarrow \tau')$ and that none of the variables β_j appear free in σ. A closed OP term C of type $\sigma \rightarrow \sigma'$ such that $Erase\ C$ is equivalent to id is called a conversion *from σ to σ', written $C : \sigma \geq \sigma'$, if there are types τ_i, evidence variables v and evidence expressions e such that:*

$$v : Q' \Vdash e : [\tau_i/\alpha_i]Q, \quad \tau' = [\tau_i/\alpha_i]\tau \quad and \quad \vdash C = \lambda x.\lambda v.xe.$$

Note that v and e are lists of evidence variables and expressions respectively. As a result, expanding the abbreviations introduced in Section 4.2, the equivalence above takes the form $\vdash C = \lambda x.\lambda v_1.\ldots.\lambda v_n.xe_1\ldots e_m$. It is straightforward to verify that $\lambda x.\lambda v.xe$ is itself a conversion from σ to σ'; it is obvious that $Erase\ (\lambda x.\lambda v.xe) = \lambda x.x$ and the following derivation establishes the required typing:

$$\dfrac{\dfrac{\dfrac{\dfrac{\dfrac{\dfrac{\dfrac{v : Q' \mid x : \sigma \vdash x : \sigma}{v : Q' \mid x : \sigma \vdash x : (\forall\alpha_i.Q \Rightarrow \tau)}\ \sigma = (\forall\alpha_i.Q \Rightarrow \tau)}{v : Q' \mid x : \sigma \vdash x : [\tau_i/\alpha_i](Q \Rightarrow \tau)}\ (\forall E)}{v : Q' \mid x : \sigma \vdash xe : [\tau_i/\alpha_i]\tau}\ (\Rightarrow E)}{v : Q' \mid x : \sigma \vdash xe : \tau'}\ \tau' = [\tau_i/\alpha_i]\tau}{\emptyset \mid x : \sigma \vdash \lambda v.xe : Q' \Rightarrow \tau'}\ (\Rightarrow I)}{\emptyset \mid x : \sigma \vdash \lambda v.xe : \sigma'}\ (\forall I)}{\emptyset \mid \emptyset \vdash \lambda x.\lambda v.xe : \sigma \rightarrow \sigma'}\ (\rightarrow I)$$

It follows that any OP term with type $\sigma \rightarrow \sigma'$ that is equivalent to $\lambda x.\lambda v.xe$ will also be a conversion from σ to σ'. On the other hand, we cannot assume that all conversions from σ

to σ' will be equivalent to this particular term since there may be more than one possible choice for the types τ_i and hence for the evidence expressions e in the definition above.

The following proposition establishes some simple properties of conversions that will be useful in subsequent work.

Proposition 5.6 *Suppose that σ, σ' and σ'' are type schemes. Then:*

1. $id : \sigma \geq \sigma$ *where* $id = \lambda x.x$ *is the identity term.*
2. *If* $C : \sigma \geq \sigma'$ *and* $C' : \sigma' \geq \sigma''$, *then* $C' \circ C : \sigma \geq \sigma''$ *where* $C' \circ C = \lambda x.C'(Cx)$.
3. *If σ is a type scheme and τ is a type, then* $id : \forall t.\sigma \geq [\tau/t]\sigma$. *In particular,* $id : Gen(A, \rho) \geq \rho$.

As with many of the results in this chapter, Proposition 5.6 extends earlier results from Chapter 3. In this particular case, the first two parts of the proposition correspond to the result that the ordering on type schemes is reflexive and transitive. From a categorical perspective, these results can be used to show that there is a category whose objects are type schemes and whose arrows are (equivalence classes of) conversions. The only additional properties needed to justify this are that the composition of equivalence classes is well-defined and associative with (the equivalence class of) *id* as unit, each of which is easily verified.

The following two propositions are useful for obtaining conversions between type schemes obtained using generalisation as described in Section 3.2.4. The first proposition deals with the interaction between generalisation and entailment, extending the result of Proposition 3.7.

Proposition 5.7 *Suppose that P and P' are predicate sets such that* $v' : P' \Vdash e : P$. *Then:*

$$(\lambda x.\lambda v'.xe) : Gen(A, P \Rightarrow \tau) \geq Gen(A, P' \Rightarrow \tau)$$

for any type assignment A and type τ.

The second result is useful when applying substitutions to type schemes obtained by generalisation, extending the result of Proposition 3.8:

Proposition 5.8 *If A is a type assignment, ρ is a qualified type and S is a substitution, then:*

$$id : SGen(A, \rho) \geq Gen(SA, S\rho).$$

Furthermore, there is a substitution R such that:

$$RA = SA \quad \text{and} \quad SGen(A, \rho) = Gen(RA, R\rho).$$

5.5.2 Conversions between constrained type schemes

The definition of conversions between type schemes extends to conversions between constrained type schemes. The obvious way to define a conversion for an ordering of the form $(P' \mid \sigma') \leq (P \mid \sigma)$ is as a term of type $(P \mid \sigma) \rightarrow (P' \mid \sigma')$, writing $(P \mid \sigma)$ as an abbreviation for the OP type $P \Rightarrow \sigma$.

Definition 5.9 (Conversions – general version)
Suppose that $\sigma = (\forall\alpha_i.Q \Rightarrow \tau)$ *and* $\sigma' = (\forall\beta_j.Q' \Rightarrow \tau')$ *and that none of the variables* β_j *appear free in* σ, P *or* P'. *A closed OP term* C *of type* $(P\,|\,\sigma) \to (P'\,|\,\sigma')$ *such that Erase* C *is equivalent to id is called a* conversion *from* $(P\,|\,\sigma)$ *to* $(P'\,|\,\sigma')$, *written* $C\!:\!(P\,|\,\sigma) \geq (P'\,|\,\sigma')$, *if there are types* τ_i, *evidence variables* v *and* w *and evidence expressions* e *and* f *such that:*

$$v\!:\!P', w\!:\!Q' \Vdash e\!:\!P, f\!:\![\tau_i/\alpha_i]Q, \quad \tau' = [\tau_i/\alpha_i]\tau \quad \textit{and} \quad \vdash C = \lambda x.\lambda v.\lambda w.xef\,.$$

Note that the definition of conversions between simple (i.e. unconstrained) type schemes is a just special case of this, obtained by taking $P = P' = \emptyset$.

It is immediate from the definition of conversions that $(P\,|\,\sigma) \geq (P'\,|\,\sigma')$ if and only if there is a conversion $C\!:\!(P\,|\,\sigma) \geq (P'\,|\,\sigma')$ (this may require renaming the bound variables of σ' to apply the definition of conversions). It follows that we can extend all of the properties of $(\leq)$ described in Section 3.2.3 to include the use of conversions as illustrated by the following three propositions.

For example, we have already mentioned that a qualified type of the form $P \Rightarrow \rho$ is equivalent to the constrained type scheme $(P\,|\,\rho)$. This is reflected, in a slightly more general form, by the following proposition:

Proposition 5.10 *For any qualified type* ρ *and predicate assignments* $v\!:\!P$ *and* $w\!:\!Q$ *there are conversions:*

$$id\!:\!(P, Q\,|\,\rho) \geq (P\,|\,Q \Rightarrow \rho) \quad \textit{and} \quad id\!:\!(P\,|\,Q \Rightarrow \rho) \geq (P, Q\,|\,\rho).$$

In particular, taking $P = \emptyset$, *there are conversions:*

$$id\!:\!(P\,|\,\rho) \geq P \Rightarrow \rho \quad \textit{and} \quad id\!:\!(P \Rightarrow \rho) \geq (P\,|\,\rho).$$

Another useful result is that $(P'\,|\,\sigma') \leq (P\,|\,\sigma)$ whenever $\sigma' \leq \sigma$ and $P' \Vdash P$. Extending this to describe the conversions involved gives:

Proposition 5.11 *If* $C\!:\!(R\,|\,\sigma) \geq (R'\,|\,\sigma')$ *and* $v'\!:\!P' \Vdash e\!:\!P$, *then there is a conversion:*

$$\lambda x.\lambda v'.C(xe)\!:\!(P, R\,|\,\sigma) \geq (P', R'\,|\,\sigma').$$

In particular, taking $R = \emptyset = R'$, *if* $C\!:\!\sigma \geq \sigma'$ *and* $v'\!:\!P' \Vdash e\!:\!P$, *then:*

$$\lambda x.\lambda v'.C(xe)\!:\!(P\,|\,\sigma) \geq (P'\,|\,\sigma').$$

We have already indicated that the ordering on constrained type schemes is preserved by substitutions (Proposition 3.5). The corresponding result for conversions is:

Proposition 5.12 *Suppose that* P *and* P' *are predicate assignments,* σ *and* σ' *are type schemes and that* $C\!:\!(P\,|\,\sigma) \geq (P'\,|\,\sigma')$. *Then:*

$$C\!:\!S(P\,|\,\sigma) \geq S(P'\,|\,\sigma')$$

for any substitution S *of types for type variables.*

In Proposition 5.6 we showed that, for the special case of (unconstrained) type schemes, reflexivity of $(\leq)$ corresponds to the identity conversion while transitivity of $(\leq)$ corresponds to composition of conversions. The next two propositions provide similar constructions, the first of which shows how the definitions of Proposition 5.6 extend to a category with arbitrary constrained type schemes as its objects.

Proposition 5.13 *For any type scheme σ and predicates P there is a conversion:*

$$id:(P\,|\,\sigma) \geq (P\,|\,\sigma).$$

Furthermore, if $C:(P\,|\,\sigma) \geq (P'\,|\,\sigma')$ and $C':(P'\,|\,\sigma') \geq (P''\,|\,\sigma'')$, then:

$$(C' \circ C):(P\,|\,\sigma) \geq (P''\,|\,\sigma'').$$

The next result gives an alternative way to extend Proposition 5.6, this time to describe a category whose objects are type schemes and whose arrows are conversions between type schemes with respect to an arbitrary fixed predicate assignment:

Proposition 5.14 *For any type scheme σ and predicate assignment $v:P$ there is a conversion:*

$$(\lambda x.\lambda v.x):\sigma \geq (P\,|\,\sigma).$$

Furthermore, if $C:\sigma \geq (P\,|\,\sigma')$ and $C':\sigma' \geq (P\,|\,\sigma'')$, then:

$$(\lambda x.\lambda v.C'(Cxv)v):\sigma \geq (P\,|\,\sigma'').$$

5.5.3 Conversions between type assignments

The definition of conversions can be extended to an ordering between type assignments. In fact, for the purposes of this work, it is sufficient to consider only the case of orderings of the form $A \geq A'$ and $A \geq (P\,|\,A')$, the first of which is just a special case of the second with $P = \emptyset$.

One simple approach would be to define a conversion for an ordering $A \geq (P \mid A')$ as a function that gives a conversion from $A(x)$ to $(P \mid A'(x))$ for each $x \in dom\ A$. However, whereas we might use a conversion $C:\sigma \geq (P\,|\,\sigma')$ to treat a term of type σ as having type σ', we will typically use a conversion between type assignments to simultaneously replace each occurrence of a variables mentioned in the type assignment with an appropriate new term. From this perspective it seems more sensible to think of a conversion between type assignments as a term substitution.

Furthermore, the translations of a term are calculated with respect to a particular predicate assignment (the first component in a derivation $v : P \mid A \vdash E \leadsto E' : \sigma$) and may involve the evidence variables in the domain of that assignment. It is therefore necessary to specify these variables explicitly as part of the type of the conversion.

Definition 5.15 (Conversions between type assignments)
A substitution C is a conversion *from a type assignment A to a constrained type assignment $(v:P\,|\,A')$, written $C:A \geq (v:P\,|\,A')$, if:*

- *dom* $A =$ *dom* A'.
- *For each* $x \in$ *dom* A *there is a conversion* $(\lambda x.\lambda v.Cx) : A(x) \geq (P \mid A'(x))$. *On the other hand, if* $x \notin$ *dom* A, *then* $C(x) = x$.

Note that a conversion between type assignments is not itself a term. The expression $C(x)$ appearing in the above definition denotes an application of a (meta-linguistic) substitution to a particular variable.

Continuing with the example above and assuming that $\emptyset \Vdash e : Eq\ Int$, one possible conversion for the type assignment ordering

$$\{(==) : Int \to Int \to Bool\} \quad \leq \quad \{(==) : \forall a.Eq\ a \Rightarrow a \to a \to Bool\}.$$

would be the substitution that maps $(==)$ to $(==)\ e$ but leaves every other variable unchanged. To see how this might be used, consider an OP term in which the $(==)$ has been treated as having type $Int \to Int \to Bool$. If we replace this integer equality function by a generic equality function with the more general type, then we need to include the evidence e for $Eq\ Int$ with every use of $(==)$. This is precisely the effect obtained by applying the conversion substitution to the original term.

Suppose that $C : A \geq (v : P \mid A')$. Since every conversion is a closed OP term, it follows that the only variable that appears free in a term of the form $C(x)$ is the variable x itself. The following results are easily established using this observation:

Proposition 5.16 *Suppose that* $C : A \geq (v : P \mid A')$ *and write* C_x *for the substitution such that* $C_x(x) \equiv x$ *and* $C_x E \equiv CE$ *for any term* E *such that* $x \notin FV(E)$. *Then:*

1. $C(\lambda x.E) = \lambda x.C_x E$,
2. $C(\textbf{let}\ x = E\ \textbf{in}\ F) = (\textbf{let}\ x = CE\ \textbf{in}\ C_x F)$,
3. $C_x : (A_x, x : \sigma) \geq (v : P \mid A_x, x : \sigma)$ *for any type scheme* σ, *and*
4. $[E/x](C_x F) = (C[E/x])F$ *for any terms* E *and* F.

Another useful consequence of the definition of conversions between type assignments is summarised by the following proposition:

Proposition 5.17 *If* $C : A \geq A'$, *then* $C : A \geq (v : P \mid A')$ *for any predicate assignment* $v : P$.

To see this, suppose that $C : A \geq A'$ so that $(\lambda x.Cx) : A(x) \geq A'(x)$ for every $x \in$ *dom* A. By Proposition 5.14 there is a conversion $(\lambda x.\lambda v.x) : A'(x) \geq (P \mid A'(x))$ and hence $(\lambda x.\lambda v.Cx) : A(x) \geq (P \mid A'(x))$.

5.6 Syntax-directed translation

The next two sections follow the development of Chapter 3 to describe the relationship between an arbitrary translation of an OML term and the translation corresponding to the derivation constructed by the type inference algorithm.

$$(var)^s \quad \frac{(x:(\forall \alpha_i.Q \Rightarrow \nu)) \in A \quad P \Vdash e:[\tau_i/\alpha_i]Q}{P \,|\, A \overset{s}{\vdash} x \rightsquigarrow xe : [\tau_i/\alpha_i]\nu}$$

$$(\to E)^s \quad \frac{P \,|\, A \overset{s}{\vdash} E \rightsquigarrow E' : \tau' \to \tau \quad P \,|\, A \overset{s}{\vdash} F \rightsquigarrow F' : \tau'}{P \,|\, A \overset{s}{\vdash} EF \rightsquigarrow E'F' : \tau}$$

$$(\to I)^s \quad \frac{P \,|\, A_x, x:\tau' \overset{s}{\vdash} E \rightsquigarrow E' : \tau}{P \,|\, A \overset{s}{\vdash} \lambda x.E \rightsquigarrow \lambda x.E' : \tau' \to \tau}$$

$$(let)^s \quad \frac{v':P' \,|\, A \overset{s}{\vdash} E \rightsquigarrow E' : \tau' \quad P \,|\, A_x, x:\sigma' \overset{s}{\vdash} F \rightsquigarrow F' : \tau}{P \,|\, A \overset{s}{\vdash} (\mathbf{let}\ x = E\ \mathbf{in}\ F) \rightsquigarrow (\mathbf{let}\ x = \lambda v'.E'\ \mathbf{in}\ F') : \tau}$$
$$\text{where } \sigma' = Gen(A, P' \Rightarrow \tau')$$

Figure 5.8: Syntax-directed typing rules with translation

We begin by extending the results of Section 3.3 to describe the construction of translations for the syntax-directed system using the typing rules in Figure 5.8.

As before, the structure of a derivation $P \,|\, A \overset{s}{\vdash} E \rightsquigarrow E' : \tau$ is uniquely determined by the syntactic structure of the OML term E. Note however that the translation E' need not be uniquely determined since there may be distinct choices for the evidence values e introduced by $(var)^s$. This of course is the source of the incoherence in the translation semantics of OML.

It is straightforward to show that the rules in Figure 5.8 are sound with respect to those in Figure 5.3 by induction on the structure of syntax-directed derivations.

Theorem 5.18 *If* $P \,|\, A \overset{s}{\vdash} E \rightsquigarrow E' : \tau$, *then* $P \,|\, A \vdash E \rightsquigarrow E' : \tau$.

The reverse process, to establish a form of completeness property by showing that every translation and typing obtained using the general rules in Figure 5.3 can, in some sense, be described by a syntax-directed derivation is considerably more difficult. As a first step, we can extend the properties of the original syntax-directed system outlined in Section 3.3.2 to include the calculation of translations. More precisely, if $v:P \,|\, A \overset{s}{\vdash} E \rightsquigarrow E' : \tau$, then each of the following results can be established by induction on the structure of this derivation (see the appendix for further details):

- $EV(E') \subseteq v$. **(Proposition 5.19)**
- $SP \,|\, SA \overset{s}{\vdash} E \rightsquigarrow E' : S\tau$ for any substitution S. **(Proposition 5.20)**
- If $Q \Vdash e:P$, then $Q \,|\, A \overset{s}{\vdash} E \rightsquigarrow [e/v]E' : \tau$. **(Proposition 5.21)**
- If $C:A' \geq (v:P \,|\, A)$, then $v:P \,|\, A' \overset{s}{\vdash} E \rightsquigarrow E'' : \tau$ and $v:P \,|\, A' \vdash CE' = E'' : \tau$. **(Proposition 5.22)**

The first of these results is an immediate consequence of the rule (*evars*) described in Section 4.3 and the following three propositions are direct extensions of Propositions 3.10, 3.11

and 3.12 respectively. Also, as an immediate corollary of Propositions 5.17 and 5.22 we obtain (with the same hypothesis as above):

- If $C : A' \geq A$, then $v : P \,|\, A' \overset{s}{\vdash} E \rightsquigarrow E'' : \tau$ and $v : P \,|\, A' \vdash CE' = E'' : \tau$. **(Corollary 5.24)**

Using these results, we can establish the following theorem as an extension of Theorem 3.15, again by structural induction on the derivation in the hypothesis:

Theorem 5.25 *If $v : P \,|\, A \vdash E \rightsquigarrow E' : \sigma$, then there is a predicate assignment $v' : P'$, a type τ' and a term E'' such that $v' : P' \,|\, A \overset{s}{\vdash} E \rightsquigarrow E'' : \tau'$ and $v : P \,|\, A \vdash C(\lambda v'.E'')v = E' : \sigma$ where $C : Gen(A, P' \Rightarrow \tau') \geq (P \,|\, \sigma)$.*

Note that the OP term $\lambda v'.E''$ appearing in this result can be treated as having type $Gen(A, P' \Rightarrow \tau')$ (using the soundness result, Theorem 5.18, from above). Furthermore, since $C : Gen(A, P' \Rightarrow \tau') \geq (P \,|\, \sigma)$ and v gives evidence variables for P, it follows that $C(\lambda v'.E'')v$ can be treated as having type σ as required.

5.7 Type inference and translation

It is reasonably easy to extend the definition of the type inference algorithm given in Section 3.4 to include the calculation of a translation using the rules in Figure 5.9. As before, these rules can be interpreted as an attribute grammar. The type assignment A and OML term E in a judgement of the form $P \,|\, TA \overset{W}{\vdash} E \rightsquigarrow E' : \tau$ are inherited attributes, while the predicate assignment P, substitution T, OP translation E' and type τ are synthesised.

$$(var)^W \quad \frac{(x : \forall \alpha_i . P \Rightarrow \tau) \in A \quad \beta_i \text{ and } v \text{ new}}{v : [\beta_i/\alpha_i]P \,|\, A \overset{W}{\vdash} x \rightsquigarrow xv : [\beta_i/\alpha_i]\tau}$$

$$(\to E)^W \quad \frac{P \,|\, TA \overset{W}{\vdash} E \rightsquigarrow E' : \tau \quad Q \,|\, T'TA \overset{W}{\vdash} F \rightsquigarrow F' : \tau' \quad T'\tau \overset{U}{\sim} \tau' \to \alpha}{U(T'P, Q) \,|\, UT'TA \overset{W}{\vdash} EF \rightsquigarrow E'F' : U\alpha}$$

where α is a new variable

$$(\to I)^W \quad \frac{P \,|\, T(A_x, x : \alpha) \overset{W}{\vdash} E \rightsquigarrow E' : \tau \quad \alpha \text{ new}}{P \,|\, TA \overset{W}{\vdash} \lambda x.E \rightsquigarrow \lambda x.E' : T\alpha \to \tau}$$

$$(let)^W \quad \frac{v : P \,|\, TA \overset{W}{\vdash} E \rightsquigarrow E' : \tau \quad P' \,|\, T'(TA_x, x : \sigma) \overset{W}{\vdash} F \rightsquigarrow F' : \tau'}{P' \,|\, T'TA \overset{W}{\vdash} (\textbf{let } x = E \textbf{ in } F) \rightsquigarrow (\textbf{let } x = \lambda v.E' \textbf{ in } F) : \tau'}$$

where $\sigma = Gen(TA, P \Rightarrow \tau)$

Figure 5.9: Type inference algorithm with translation

The following theorem shows that any typing and translation that is obtained using the type inference algorithm can also be derived using the rules for the syntax-directed system described in the previous section.

Theorem 5.26 *If* $P \mid TA \vdash^{W} E \leadsto E' : \tau$, *then* $P \mid TA \vdash^{s} E \leadsto E' : \tau$.

Combining this result with Theorem 5.18 we obtain:

Corollary 5.27 *If* $P \mid TA \vdash^{W} E \leadsto E' : \tau$, *then* $P \mid TA \vdash E \leadsto E' : \tau$.

This result is important because it shows that the 'translation' E' of an OML term E produced by the algorithm above is a valid translation of E (in the sense of Section 5.2) and hence, in particular, that it is a well-typed OP term.

Given that the algorithm described above calculates a principal type scheme for each well-typed OML term (as in Section 3.4.3), we will refer to the translations produced by this algorithm as *principal translations*. The following theorem provides further motivation for this terminology, extending the result of Theorem 3.19 and showing that every translation obtained using the syntax-directed system can be expressed in terms of a principal translation.

Theorem 5.28 *Suppose that* $v : P \mid SA \vdash^{s} E \leadsto E' : \tau$. *Then* $w : Q \mid TA \vdash^{W} E \leadsto E'' : \nu$ *and there is a substitution* R *such that* $S \approx RT$, $\tau = R\nu$, $v : P \Vdash e : RQ$ *and* $v : P \mid SA \vdash E' = [e/w]E'' : \tau$.

Finally, we can use this result to describe the relationship between arbitrary translations of an OML term and a principal translation:

Theorem 5.29 *If* $v : P \mid SA \vdash E \leadsto E' : \sigma$, *then* $w : Q \mid TA \vdash^{W} E \leadsto E'' : \nu$ *for some* $w : Q$, T, E'' *and* ν *and there is a substitution* R *and a conversion* $C : RGen(TA, Q \Rightarrow \nu) \geq (P \mid \sigma)$ *such that* $S \approx RT$ *and*

$$v : P \mid SA \vdash C(\lambda w.E'')v = E' : \sigma.$$

It is instructive to include the proof of this result here as an illustration of how the results in this and preceding sections can be used.

First of all, by Theorem 5.25, if $v : P \mid SA \vdash E \leadsto E' : \sigma$, then $v' : P' \mid SA \vdash^{s} E \leadsto F' : \tau'$ and $v : P \mid SA \vdash C'(\lambda v'.F')v = E' : \sigma$ for some $C' : Gen(SA, P' \Rightarrow \tau') \geq (P \mid \sigma)$.

Next, by Theorem 5.28 $w : Q \mid TA \vdash^{W} E \leadsto E'' : \nu$ and there is a substitution R such that $S \approx RT$, $\tau' = R\nu$, $v' : P' \Vdash e : RQ$ and $v' : P' \mid SA \vdash [e/w]E'' = F' : \sigma$, from which it follows that $\emptyset \mid SA \vdash \lambda v'.([e/w]E'') = \lambda v'.F' : Gen(SA, P' \Rightarrow \tau')$.

Note that:

$$\begin{array}{lll} RGen(TA, Q \Rightarrow \nu) & & \\ \quad \geq \; Gen(RTA, RQ \Rightarrow R\nu) & & \text{(Prop. 5.8, conversion } id\text{)} \\ \quad = \; Gen(SA, RQ \Rightarrow \tau') & & (S \approx RT \text{ and } \tau' = R\nu) \\ \quad \geq \; Gen(SA, P' \Rightarrow \tau') & & \text{(Prop. 5.7, conversion } \lambda x.\lambda v'.xe\text{)} \\ \quad \geq \; (P \mid \sigma) & & \text{(using conversion } C'\text{)} \end{array}$$

Composing these conversions we obtain:

$$C : RGen(TA, Q \Rightarrow \nu) \geq (P \mid \sigma)$$

where $C = \lambda x.C'(\lambda v'.xe)$, and then:

$$\begin{array}{rcll} v\!:\!P\,|\,SA \vdash C(\lambda w.E'')v & = & (\lambda x.C'(\lambda v'.xe))(\lambda w.E'')v & \text{(definition of } C\text{)} \\ & = & C'(\lambda v'.[e/w]E'')v & \text{(using } (\beta) \text{ and } (\beta_e)\text{)} \\ & = & C'(\lambda v'.F')v & \\ & = & E' : \sigma & \end{array}$$

which completes the proof.

5.8 Coherence results

Theorem 5.29 is important because it shows that any translation of an OML term E in a particular context can be written in the form $C(\lambda w.E')v$ where E' is a principal translation and C is the corresponding conversion. Applied to two arbitrary derivations $v\!:\!P\,|\,A \vdash E \leadsto E_1' : \sigma$ and $v\!:\!P\,|\,A \vdash E \leadsto E_2' : \sigma$, it follows that:

$$v\!:\!P\,|\,A \vdash E_1' = C_1(\lambda w.E')v : \sigma \quad \text{and} \quad v\!:\!P\,|\,A \vdash E_2' = C_2(\lambda w.E')v : \sigma$$

where C_1 and C_2 are conversions from the principal type scheme to $(P \mid \sigma)$. One obvious way to ensure that these translations are equal is to show that $\vdash C_1 = C_2$.

5.8.1 Equality of conversions

Taking a more slightly more general view, suppose that C_1, C_2 are conversions from σ to $(P' \mid \sigma')$. Without loss of generality, we can assume that $\sigma = (\forall \alpha_i.Q \Rightarrow \nu)$ and $\sigma' = (\forall \alpha_j'.Q' \Rightarrow \nu')$ where the variables α_j' only appear in $(Q' \Rightarrow \nu')$. Using the definition of conversions, it follows that:

$$\nu' = [\tau_i/\alpha_i]\nu \quad \text{and} \quad v'\!:\!P', w'\!:\!Q' \Vdash e\!:\!P, f\!:\![\tau_i/\alpha_i]Q$$

for some types τ_i and that $\vdash C_1 = \lambda x.\lambda v'.\lambda w'.xef$. Similarly for C_2 there are types τ_i' such that:

$$\nu' = [\tau_i'/\alpha_i]\nu \quad \text{and} \quad v'\!:\!P', w'\!:\!Q' \Vdash e'\!:\!P, f'\!:\![\tau_i'/\alpha_i]Q$$

and $\vdash C_2 = \lambda x.\lambda v'.\lambda w'.xe'f'$. Clearly, it is sufficient to show $e = e'$ and $f = f'$ to prove that the these two conversions are equivalent. The first equality is an immediate consequence of the uniqueness of evidence; both e and e' are evidence for the predicates P under the evidence assignment $v'\!:\!P', w'\!:\!Q'$ and hence must be equivalent. The same argument cannot in general be applied to the second equality since the predicates $[\tau_i/\alpha_i]Q$ may not be the same as those in $[\tau_i'/\alpha_i]Q$ due to differences between the types τ_i and τ_i'. Nevertheless, since $[\tau_i/\alpha_i]\nu = \nu' = [\tau_i'/\alpha_i]\nu$, it follows that $\tau_i = \tau_i'$ for all $\alpha_i \in TV(\nu)$. Notice then that, if $\{\alpha_i\} \cap TV(Q) \subseteq TV(\nu)$, the two predicate sets $[\tau_i/\alpha_i]Q$ and $[\tau_i'/\alpha_i]Q$ must be equal and hence $f = f'$ as required. We will give a special name to type schemes with this property:

Definition 5.30 (Unambiguous type schemes) *A type scheme* $\sigma = \forall \alpha_i.Q \Rightarrow \nu$ *is unambiguous if* $\{\alpha_i\} \cap TV(Q) \subseteq TV(\nu)$.

This definition coincides with that of an unambiguous type scheme in the treatment of type classes in Haskell, motivating our use of the same term here. Using this terminology, the discussion above shows that all conversions from an unambiguous type scheme to an arbitrary constrained type scheme are equivalent:

Proposition 5.31 *If* $C_1, C_2 : (P \mid \sigma) \geq (P' \mid \sigma')$ *are conversions and* σ *is an unambiguous type scheme then* $\vdash C_1 = C_2$.

5.8.2 Equality of translations

As an immediate corollary, it follows that, if the principal type scheme for a term E is unambiguous, then any two translations of E must be equivalent:

Theorem 5.32 *If* $v : P \mid A \vdash E \leadsto E'_1 : \sigma$ *and* $v : P \mid A \vdash E \leadsto E'_2 : \sigma$ *and the principal type scheme of* E *in* A *is unambiguous, then* $v : P \mid A \vdash E'_1 = E'_2 : \sigma$.

This generalises an earlier result established by Blott (1991) for the special case of the type system in (Wadler and Blott, 1989).

Theorem 5.32 is well-suited to use in concrete implementations of qualified types. The first step in type-checking any given source program is to use the type inference algorithm to calculate a principal type (and a corresponding translation that can be used to implement that program). If the program does not have a principal type, then it cannot be well-typed (Corollary 3.23) and will be rejected. If the principal type is not unambiguous, then we cannot guarantee a well-defined semantics and the program must again be rejected. For example, the principal type scheme of the term *out* (*in* x) in the example in Section 5.3 is $\forall a. C\ a \Rightarrow Int$ which is ambiguous. It follows that this program should be rejected since it is not possible to determine which overloading is required.

Practical experience with a concrete implementation of type classes based on syntax of Haskell (Jones, 1991c) suggests that the restriction to terms with unambiguous types does not usually cause any significant problems. However, examples using multiple parameter type classes (as described in Section 2.2.4) often lead to ambiguity since the mechanism for defining the corresponding relations between types is rather weak. Some suggestions for improving this will be described in Section 6.2.

From a theoretical point of view, there is no need to require that all of the types in the type assignment A are unambiguous. For example, if $(x : \sigma) \in A$ and σ is ambiguous, then the principal type of a term involving x given by the algorithm in Figure 5.9 will also be ambiguous, whereas a term that does not involve x would not be affected by this ambiguity. Nevertheless, in a practical implementation it will usually be sensible to avoid including any variable with an ambiguous type in a type assignment since any object defined in terms of those variables is essentially useless. In particular, in the rule for typing **let** expressions:

$$\frac{P \mid TA \overset{W}{\vdash} E : \tau \quad P' \mid T'(TA_x, x : \sigma) \overset{W}{\vdash} F : \tau'}{P' \mid T'TA \overset{W}{\vdash} (\mathbf{let}\ x = E\ \mathbf{in}\ F) : \tau'}$$

it would be reasonable to reject a program (or at least generate a warning message) if the inferred type scheme $\sigma = Gen(TA, P \Rightarrow \tau)$ is not unambiguous.

Note that Theorem 5.32 gives a condition that is sufficient, but not necessary, to guarantee coherence. Thus a concrete implementation based on the approach outlined above can be expected to reject some terms that have a well-defined meaning despite the fact that they have an ambiguous principal type. A well known example of this is the Haskell term `[] == []` that has an ambiguous principal type `Eq [a] => Bool`, but evaluates to `True` for any choice of type `a`. On the other hand, this fact cannot be established using the definition of equality in Section 5.4 and we might conjecture that the restriction to terms with unambiguous principal types is both necessary and sufficient to guarantee coherence with respect to such a formulation of provable equality. We will not consider this possibility any further here.

The restriction to unambiguous type schemes simplifies several aspects of our treatment of qualified types. For example, it restores the property of Damas-Milner typing, mentioned in Section 3.2.3, that $TV(\sigma) \subseteq TV(\sigma')$ whenever $\sigma \geq \sigma'$. This makes it possible to give a more convenient syntactic characterisation of the $(\leq)$ ordering. A second example is that the task of determining whether a particular OML typing $P \,|\, A \vdash E : \sigma$ is derivable is decidable if the process of determining whether $Q \Vdash R$ for any given Q and R is decidable, assuming that the principal type of E in A is unambiguous (see the comments in Section 3.4.4).

5.8.3 A weaker notion of ambiguity

Unfortunately, the restriction to unambiguous type schemes is too severe for some applications of qualified types. For example, in the system of extensible records described in Section 2.4, we suggested that the primitive operation of record restriction might be represented by a family of functions:

$$(\_ \setminus l) :: \forall r.\forall t.(r \ \mathsf{has}\ l : t) \Rightarrow r \rightarrow r \setminus l.$$

But this type scheme is ambiguous, and hence any values defined using this operator might also have ambiguous principal types. Notice however that, assuming we follow the approach suggested in Section 4.7, the evidence for a predicate of the form $(r \ \mathsf{has}\ l : t)$ is independent of the type t. Hence, repeating the argument in Section 5.8.1, we can guarantee a well-defined semantics for any term whose principal type scheme $\sigma = (\forall \alpha_i . Q \Rightarrow \nu)$ is *unambiguous* in the sense that $\{\alpha_i\} \cap AV(Q) \subseteq TV(\nu)$ where $AV(P)$ is defined by:

$$\begin{array}{lcl} AV(\emptyset) & = & \emptyset \\ AV(P, P') & = & AV(P) \cup AV(P') \\ AV(r \ \mathsf{has}\ l : t) & = & TV(r) \\ AV(r \ \mathsf{lacks}\ l) & = & TV(r) \end{array}$$

With this weaker definition, the type of the record restriction operator given above is unambiguous.

The same approach can be adapted to any system of predicates by defining $AV(Q)$ as a subset of $TV(Q)$ such that, if $P \Vdash e : SQ$ and $P \Vdash e' : S'Q$ for some substitutions S and S' such that $S\alpha = S'\alpha$ for each $\alpha \in AV(Q)$, then $P \vdash e = e' : SQ$. The simplest possible choice would be to take $AV(Q) = TV(Q)$ although it would obviously be preferable to give a definition that makes $AV(Q)$ as small as possible to increase the class of programs that will be accepted by the type system.

5.9 Comparison with related work

A number of researchers have investigated the coherence properties of particular type systems using a process of normalisation of typing derivations. Examples of this include systems with explicit subtyping (Breazu-Tannen et al., 1989; Curien and Ghelli, 1990), a form of implicit subtyping called *scaling* (Thatte, 1990) and an earlier treatment of type classes (Blott, 1991). The basic idea in each case is to give a collection of reduction rules and prove that they are confluent, that they preserve meaning and that any reduction sequence terminates (and hence, that the rules are strongly normalising). The confluence property guarantees the existence of a unique normal form and the fact that meaning is preserved by reduction is then sufficient to guarantee coherence.

In the work described in this chapter, the rules for reductions between terms in Section 5.4.2 correspond to reductions between derivations and the formulation of the syntax-directed system can be thought of as a means of identifying the 'normal forms' of a derivation. From this perspective, Theorem 5.25 can be interpreted as a proof that the reduction process terminates and that it preserves meaning. However, having established that the coherence property does not hold in the general case (Section 5.3) we do not guarantee the existence of unique normal forms or confluence.

The most important and novel feature of our work is the use of conversions to give a semantic interpretation to the ordering between constrained type schemes. In effect, a conversion acts as a record of the way in which one derivation is reduced to another. Some of this information is lost because we do not distinguish between conversions that are provably equal but, as we have seen, we retain sufficient detail to establish useful conditions that guarantee coherence.

Our use of conversions is closely related to the discussion of the relationship between two versions of the pure polymorphic λ-calculus, one with explicit type abstraction and application, the other without, described by Mitchell (1988) using *retyping functions*. Mitchell used these *retyping functions* (corresponding to our conversions) to describe minimal typings for a restricted set of terms, but it is not clear how his results might be extended to deal with larger classes of terms. Many of the difficulties are caused by the flexibility of the language of types in the systems considered by Mitchell (essentially the same as those in OP but without qualified types of the form $\pi \Rightarrow \sigma$). We have avoided these problems here by working with a source language based on a more restricted collection of type schemes.

One of the biggest limitations of our work is caused by the decision to include β-reduction in the definition of equality (Section 5.4.2). As an immediate consequence, the results in this chapter cannot be applied to languages with call-by-value semantics. The same problem occurs in other work, including the coherence proof in (Blott, 1991). One possibility would be to rework these results using an axiomatisation of equality for call-by-value semantics such as that given by Riecke (1990), but it would clearly be preferable to find a single formulation that can be used for both cases. We might therefore consider ways of avoiding β-reduction altogether. For example, a conversion $\lambda x.\lambda v.xe$ could be treated, not as a term of OP itself, but as a function in the meta-language, mapping each term E to the OP term $\lambda v.Ee$. Unfortunately, while this would eliminate many applications of β-reduction, there are several others for which there is no obvious alternative.

Another promising approach to establish coherence properties would be to use ideas from category theory as in (Reynolds, 1991) for a language with intersection types and subtyping and in (Hilken and Rhydeheard, 1991) for a system of type classes. One of the main attractions of the categorical approach from the theoretical standpoint is the increased generality resulting from a higher level of abstraction. The main benefit from a practical point of view is likely to be the 'variable-free' approach which avoids some of the messy technical details involving free and bound variables. As mentioned in Section 5.5, our treatment of conversions has a strong categorical flavour and we would hope to be able to extend the techniques developed here to provide a more general treatment of coherence for qualified types. Section 9.1 sketches some simple first steps towards this goal.

Chapter 6

Theory into practice

This chapter describes a number of features that might be useful in practical work with qualified types. We adopt a less rigourous approach than in previous chapters and we do not attempt to deal with all of the technical issues that are involved.

Section 6.1 suggests a number of techniques that can be used to reduce the size of the predicate set in the types calculated by the type inference algorithm, resulting in smaller types that are often easier to understand. As a further benefit, the number of evidence parameters in the translation of an overloaded term may also be reduced, leading to a potentially more efficient implementation.

Section 6.2 shows how the use of information about satisfiability of predicate sets may be used to infer more accurate typings for some terms and reject others for which suitable evidence values cannot be produced.

Finally, Section 6.3 discusses the possibility of adding the rule of subsumption to the type system of OML to allow the use of implicit coercions from one type to another within a given term.

It would also be useful to consider the task of extending the language of OML terms with constructs that correspond more closely to concrete programming languages such as recursion, groups of local binding and the use of explicit type signatures. One example where these features have been dealt with is in the proposed static semantics for Haskell given in (Peyton Jones and Wadler, 1992) but, for reasons of space, we do not consider this here.

6.1 Evidence parameters considered harmful

Using the algorithm described in Section 5.7 enables us to calculate, not just the principal type scheme of an OML term, but also a principal translation that can be used to implement that term. Assuming that the coherence conditions described in the previous chapter are satisfied, the principal translation is semantically equivalent to any other translation but it is not necessarily the best choice for an efficient implementation. This section describes some of the problems associated with the use of evidence parameters and suggests ways of obtaining alternative translations that can be used, either to reduce the number of parameters that are required, or to eliminate the use of evidence parameters altogether.

6.1.1 Simplification

With the implementation described in the previous chapter, an OML term E of type $(\forall\alpha_i.Q \Rightarrow \nu)$ is implemented by a translation of the form $\lambda w.E'$ where w is a collection of evidence variables for Q and E' is an OP term corresponding to E that uses these variables to obtain appropriate evidence values. More succinctly, the translation of a term whose type is qualified by a set of predicates Q requires one evidence abstraction for each element of Q. One obvious way to reduce the number of evidence parameters in this situation is to find a smaller set of predicates Q' that is equivalent to Q in the sense that each set entails the other. If the original translation is $\lambda w.E'$ and $w' : Q' \Vdash f : Q$, then we can treat the term as having type $(\forall\alpha_i.Q' \Rightarrow \nu)$ with translation $\lambda w'.(\lambda w.E')f$ which, using (β_e), is equivalent to $\lambda w'.[f/w]E'$. In this situation we have a compromise between reducing the number of evidence parameters required, and the cost of constructing the evidence f for Q from evidence for Q'.

We will refer to the process of finding a suitable choice of predicates Q' from a given collection of predicates Q as *simplification*. One way to extend our current type inference algorithm to support this feature would be to allow the rule:

$$\frac{w : Q \,|\, TA \overset{W}{\vdash} E \leadsto E'' : \nu \quad w : Q \Vdash f' : Q' \quad w' : Q' \Vdash f : Q}{w' : Q' \,|\, TA \overset{W}{\vdash} E \leadsto [f/w]E'' : \nu} \qquad (simp)$$

to be used at any stage in the type inference process to simplify the inferred predicate assignment.

Soundness of $(simp)$ follows immediately from Theorem 5.18 using the entailment $w' : Q' \Vdash f : Q$. The other entailment, $w : Q \Vdash f' : Q'$, is needed to ensure that the type inference algorithm still calculates principal types, even though the evidence f' that it constructs is not actually used in the resulting translation. In order to establish this property it is sufficient to show that the conclusions of Theorem 5.28 are preserved by $(simp)$. More precisely, it is sufficient to show that, if $P \Vdash e : RQ$, $P \,|\, SA \vdash E' = [e/w]E'' : \tau$ and $w : Q$ and $w' : Q'$ are related as above, then $P \Vdash [e/w]f' : RQ'$ and $P \,|\, SA \vdash E' = [[e/w]f'/w']([f/w]E'') : \tau$. Verification of this fact is straightforward and we do not include full details here. The proof relies on the equality $w : Q \vdash w = [f'/w']f : Q$ which follows from uniqueness of evidence by composing the two entailments above to obtain the second evidence expression.

The fact that the algorithm obtained by adding $(simp)$ to the rules in Figure 5.9 is non-deterministic does not cause any problems in practice. First of all, any two applications of $(simp)$ following one after the other can be reduced to a single application using the transitivity of $\Vdash$. Furthermore, since the only place that the predicate assignments are actually used in the type inference algorithm is in the rule for typing **let** expressions, the only place where there is any benefit from using $(simp)$ is immediately before using the typing for a term E in the typing of an expression of the form **let** $x = E$ **in** F. Finally, the choice of Q' in the formulation of $(simp)$ above is arbitrary. More realistically, a suitable simplification for a predicate assignment might be obtained using a function *simplify* such that *simplify*$(w : Q)$ returns a pair $(w' : Q', f)$ containing a simplified predicate assignment $w' : Q'$ and evidence f satisfying the conditions above. Given these observations, simplification might be dealt with using a deterministic type inference algorithm that does not include $(simp)$ and in which

$(let)^{\mathrm{W}}$ is replaced by:

$$\frac{w\!:Q \mid TA \stackrel{\mathrm{W}}{\vdash} E \rightsquigarrow E' : \tau \quad P' \mid T'(TA_x, x\!:\!\sigma) \stackrel{\mathrm{W}}{\vdash} F \rightsquigarrow F' : \tau'}{P' \mid T'TA \stackrel{\mathrm{W}}{\vdash} (\mathbf{let}\ x = E\ \mathbf{in}\ F) \rightsquigarrow (\mathbf{let}\ x = \lambda w'.[f/w]E'\ \mathbf{in}\ F) : \tau'}$$

where $\sigma = Gen(TA, Q' \Rightarrow \tau)$ and $(w'\!:Q', f) = simplify(w\!:Q)$.

Apart from reducing the number of evidence parameters required, simplification can sometimes help to avoid the kind of ambiguity problems described in Section 5.8.2. For a simple example, suppose that Any is a unary predicate symbol such that $\emptyset \Vdash e\!:Any\ \tau$ for any type τ. Then a term with an ambiguous principal type scheme $\forall a.Any\ a \Rightarrow \nu$ where $a \notin TV(\nu)$ can be treated as having the unambiguous type scheme $\forall a.\nu$. Notice that this example can also be dealt with using the approach outlined in Section 5.8.3 by defining $AV(Any\ \tau) = \emptyset$.

We have not yet discussed how a simplification of a particular predicate assignment might be calculated. Of course, this will typically vary from one system of predicates to another and the task of finding an optimal assignment Q' with which to replace a given assignment Q may be intractable. One fairly general approach is to determine a minimal subset $Q' \subseteq Q$ such that $Q' \Vdash Q$. To see that this is likely to be a good choice, note that:

- $Q \Vdash Q'$ by monotonicity of $\Vdash$ and hence Q' is equivalent to Q as required.
- Since $Q' \subseteq Q$, the number of evidence abstractions required using Q' is less than or equal to the number required when using Q.
- The construction of evidence for a predicate in Q using evidence for Q' is trivial for each predicate that is already in Q'.

6.1.2 Unnecessary polymorphism

The principal motivation for including the **let** construct in OML was to enable the definition and use of polymorphic and overloaded values. In practice, the same construct is also used for a number of other purposes:

- To avoid repeated evaluation of a value that is used at a number of points in an expression.
- To create *cyclic data structures* (when combined with recursion in a non-strict language).
- To enable the use of identifiers as abbreviations for the subexpressions of a large expression.

Unfortunately, the use of evidence parameters for the value defined in a **let** expression may mean that the evaluation of an overloaded term will not behave as intended in these situations. For example, if $f : \forall a.C\ a \Rightarrow Int \to a$, then we have a principal translation of the form:

$$\mathbf{let}\ x = f\ 0\ \mathbf{in}\ (x, x) \quad \rightsquigarrow \quad \mathbf{let}\ x = (\lambda v.f\ v\ 0)\ \mathbf{in}\ (x\ e, x\ e)$$

that treats x as a value of type $\forall a.C\ a \Rightarrow a$ so that the evaluation of $x\ e$ in the translation is no longer shared. The problem here is that the type system allows a stronger degree of polymorphism than the programmer might anticipate (or require). The principal type of this expression is $\forall a.\forall b.(C\ a,\ C\ b) \Rightarrow (a,\ b)$ and not $\forall a.C\ a \Rightarrow (a,\ a)$ as might be expected.

If it is known that the value produced by this expression will be only used in situations where both components of the pair are expected to have the same type, then we might use the following translation to guarantee shared evaluation:

$$\textbf{let}\ x = f\ 0\ \textbf{in}\ (x,\ x) \quad \leadsto \quad \textbf{let}\ x = f\ e\ 0\ \textbf{in}\ (x,\ x)$$

Note that this is only provably equal to the principal translation if we use the less general typing above.

In a more general situation, this optimisation can only be applied to an expression of the form **let** $x = E$ **in** F if we can guarantee that the same evidence values will be used for each occurrence of x in F. For example, if there is only one occurrence of x in F, then this condition certainly holds. While there is no problem with shared evaluation in this case, it is still useful to avoid redundant evidence parameters. A slightly more sophisticated version of this optimisation is described in Section 6.1.4 which describes a technique that can be used to detect a subset of evidence parameters, that can be guaranteed to have constant values.

6.1.3 The monomorphism restriction

In practical programming languages such as Haskell or ML, top-level declarations are treated as **let** expressions in which the scope of the defined variable is not fully determined at compile-time. As a result, we cannot hope to apply the kind of optimisations described in the previous section.

The solution to this problem used in the current version of Haskell is to provide a second form of local definition, **let poly** $x = E$ **in** F in which the variable x may be assigned a polymorphic, but unqualified type in the expression F:

$$\frac{P\,|\,A \vdash E \leadsto E' : \sigma \quad Q\,|\,A_x, x{:}\sigma \vdash F \leadsto F' : \tau \quad \sigma = \forall T.\tau'}{P, Q\,|\,A \vdash (\textbf{let poly}\ x = E\ \textbf{in}\ F) \leadsto (\textbf{let}\ x = E'\ \textbf{in}\ F') : \tau}$$

Note that we use the keyword **poly** to distinguish between the two forms of local definition. The current version of Haskell uses a more sophisticated rule although the basic principle is the same: a local definition of the form **let** $x = E$ **in** F is treated as a **let poly** binding if E is not a lambda abstraction and no explicit type signature has been declared for the variable x. Otherwise, the definition is treated as a standard **let** construct.

The fact that none of the predicates P used in the typing for E can be included in the type scheme σ means that the degree of polymorphism (roughly corresponding to the number of type variables in T) may be limited since $(\forall I)$ cannot be used to quantify over any type variable in P. This aspect of the Haskell type system is usually referred to as the *monomorphism restriction* since, in the extreme case, σ may be restricted to be a monomorphic type. The main advantage is that the translation does not introduce additional evidence parameters.

Type inference for expressions involving the **let poly** construct is reasonably straightforward. The only complication is that, having calculated a derivation $P\,|\,A \overset{W}{\vdash} E \leadsto E' : \tau'$ for E we must use the simplification process described in Section 6.1.1 to minimise $TV(P)$. This is necessary to ensure that we assign as general a type as possible to the variable declared in the local definition; it is not just the predicates themselves that serve as constraints on the typing, but also the type variables that they involve. This requires an extra condition on the predicate entailment relation, namely that for any predicate set P, there is an equivalent set P_0 such that $TV(P_0) \subseteq TV(Q)$ for any Q equivalent to P.

6.1.4 Constant and locally-constant overloading

This section describes a simple method for detecting when the values passed for a particular evidence parameter are the same for each use of a variable bound to an overloaded value. We begin by recalling the (*let*) rule that is used for typing local definitions in the type system of Chapter 3:

$$\frac{P \,|\, A \vdash E : \sigma \quad Q \,|\, A_x, x : \sigma \vdash E' : \tau}{P, Q \,|\, A \vdash (\mathbf{let}\ x = E\ \mathbf{in}\ E') : \tau}$$

This rule allows some of the predicates constraining the typing of E (i.e. those in P) to be retained as a constraint on the environment in the conclusion of the rule rather than being included in the type scheme σ. However, in the corresponding rule $(let)^s$ for the syntax-directed system, all of the predicates constraining the typing of E are included into the type $Gen(A, P \Rightarrow \tau)$ that is inferred for E:

$$\frac{P \,|\, A \overset{s}{\vdash} E : \tau \quad P' \,|\, A_x, x : Gen(A, P \Rightarrow \tau) \overset{s}{\vdash} E' : \tau'}{P' \,|\, A \overset{s}{\vdash} (\mathbf{let}\ x = E\ \mathbf{in}\ E') : \tau'}$$

Note that this requires the use of evidence parameters for all predicates in P, even if the evidence supplied for some of these parameters is the same for each use of x in E'. In particular, this includes *constant* evidence (corresponding to constant predicates; i.e. predicates with no free type variables) and *locally constant* evidence (corresponding to predicates, each of whose free variables appears free in A).

From the relationship between the type inference algorithm W and the syntax-directed system, it follows that W has the same behaviour; indeed, this is essential to ensure that W calculates principal types: If $x \notin FV(E')$, then none of the environment constraints described by P need be reflected by the constraints on the complete expression in P'.

However, if $x \in FV(E')$, it is possible to find a set $F \subseteq P$ such that $P' \Vdash F$ and hence the type scheme assigned to x can be replaced by $Gen(A, (P \setminus F) \Rightarrow \tau)$, potentially decreasing the number of evidence parameters required by x. To see this, suppose that $Gen(A, P \Rightarrow \tau) = \forall \alpha_i . P \Rightarrow \tau$. A straightforward induction, based on the hypothesis that $x \in FV(E')$, shows that $P' \Vdash [\tau_i/\alpha_i]P$ for some types τ_i. If we now define:

$$\begin{array}{lcll} FP(A,P) & = & \{ (v : \pi) \in P \mid TV(\pi) \subseteq TV(A) \} & \textit{free predicates} \\ BP(A,P) & = & P \setminus FP(A,P) & \textit{bound predicates} \end{array}$$

then $F = FP(A, P)$ is the largest subset of P that is guaranteed to be unchanged by the substitution $[\tau_i/\alpha_i]$, with the remaining elements of P in $B = BP(A, P)$. These observations suggest that $(let)^s$ might be replaced by:

$$\frac{P \,|\, A \overset{s}{\vdash} E : \tau \quad P' \,|\, A \overset{s}{\vdash} E' : \tau'}{P' \,|\, A \overset{s}{\vdash} (\mathbf{let}\ x = E\ \mathbf{in}\ E') : \tau'} \ (let)_f{}^s$$

if $x \notin FV(E')$ (the typing judgement involving E serves only to preserve the property that all subterms of a well-typed term are also well-typed) and:

$$\frac{P\,|\,A \overset{s}{\vdash} E : \tau \quad P'\,|\,A_x, x : Gen(A, B \Rightarrow \tau) \overset{s}{\vdash} E' : \tau' \quad P' \Vdash F}{P'\,|\,A \overset{s}{\vdash} (\mathbf{let}\ x = E\ \mathbf{in}\ E') : \tau'}\ (let)_b{}^s$$

where $F = FP(A, P)$ and $B = BP(A, P)$ in the case where $x \in FV(E')$.

Top level declarations can be dealt with using just $(let)_b{}^s$, since the scope of such a declaration can be taken to include all terms that might reasonably be evaluated within its scope, which of course includes terms involving the variable x.

6.1.5 A template-based implementation

Since the use of evidence parameters seems to cause so many problems, we might consider whether it is possible to find an alternative approach to translation that avoids the use of evidence parameters altogether. For example, one simple alternative to the implementation of type classes described in Section 4.5 that avoids the use of evidence parameters is to treat the bodies of `class` and `instance` declarations as templates (i.e. macros) for the generation of function definitions. With this approach, the expression `[1,3]==[2,4]` might be implemented as `eqListInt [1,3] [2,4]` using the following definitions generated from the instance declarations for equality on integers and on lists:

```
eqInt                    :: Int -> Int -> Bool
eqInt                     = primEqInt

eqListInt                :: [Int] -> [Int] -> Bool
eqListInt []      []      = True
eqListInt []      (y:ys)  = False
eqListInt (x:xs)  []      = False
eqListInt (x:xs)  (y:ys)  = eqInt x y && eqListInt xs ys
```

Distinct versions of each overloaded function such as `member` and `subset` may also be needed, but only for those instances of `Eq` for which they are specifically required in a given source program; for example, it might be necessary to generate code for finding members of lists of type `[[Int]]` but not for lists of type `[Int]`.

This template-based approach can be adapted to any application of qualified types. One simple way to describe the construction of suitable 'translations' for a given term is with a type inference algorithm using judgements of the form $P\,|\,A \overset{W}{\vdash} E \leadsto E' : \sigma$ **with** B where B is a collection of bindings of the form $x' = xe$. The value bound to x' will be a specialised version of the overloaded operator x with evidence parameters e. For example, the rule for inferring the type of a variable is as:

$$\frac{(x : (\forall \alpha_i . P \Rightarrow \tau)) \in A \quad \beta_i,\ v \text{ and } x' \text{ new}}{[\beta_i/\alpha_i]P\,|\,A \overset{W}{\vdash} x \leadsto x' : [\beta_i/\alpha_i]\tau\ \mathbf{with}\ \{x' = xv\}}$$

A simple optimisation to this rule would be to translate any variable x for which the corresponding predicate set P is empty as itself, rather than introducing a new variable x'.

It is straightforward to recast the rules ($\rightarrow I$), ($\rightarrow E$) and (*simp*) in this framework, and we will not include the details here. The rule for local definitions is more interesting and produces a translation of the form (**let** D **in** F) where D is a set of bindings $x = E$ of expressions to variables:

$$\frac{\begin{array}{c} v : P \,|\, TA \overset{\mathrm{W}}{\vdash} E \leadsto E' : \tau \ \textbf{with}\ B \\ \sigma = Gen(TA, P \Rightarrow \tau) \\ Q \,|\, T'(TA_x, x:\sigma) \overset{\mathrm{W}}{\vdash} F \leadsto F' : \nu \ \textbf{with}\ B' \end{array}}{Q \,|\, T'TA \overset{\mathrm{W}}{\vdash} \begin{array}{c} \textbf{let}\ x = E\ \textbf{in}\ F \\ \leadsto \\ \textbf{let}\ \{\, x' = [e/v]E' \mid (x' = xe) \in B' \,\}\ \textbf{in}\ F' \end{array} : \nu\ \textbf{with}\ B \cup B'_x}$$

(B'_x is used as an abbreviation for the set $\{\, (y' = ye) \in B' \mid y \not\equiv x \,\}$.) The number of bindings in the translation of a local definition (and indeed, the size of the binding sets B) can often be reduced by simplifying binding sets. For example, a binding of the form $x_2' = xf$ can be eliminated if we already have a binding $x_1' = xe$ where e and f are equivalent.

These rules do not produce genuine translations of OML terms (in the sense of Section 5.2). However, it is relatively easy to show how they correspond to the principal translations used in Chapter 5 by treating binding sets as substitutions.

There are three significant problems with the template-based implementation:

- It may lead to a code explosion; a small increase in the size of the input program may result in a much larger increase in the compiled version.
- Some important optimisations, particularly that of eliminating redundant bindings as described above, may be expensive to implement.
- Binding sets B must be included in the compiled representation of top-level definitions, and passed to a sophisticated linker with the ability to replicate and instantiate sections of parameterised code before obtaining object code in a suitable form for a conventional linker. In some cases, it may also be necessary to include additional information in the interfaces for program modules.

Despite this, it still seems likely that a satisfactory, general purpose implementation based on this approach may be possible. For example, as we describe in Chapter 8, the implementation of type classes in Gofer is closely related to the template-based approach (working at the level of classes rather than individual functions) but almost completely avoids the three problems mentioned above.

6.2 Satisfiability

One of the most important features of the systems of qualified types described in this thesis is the ability to move 'global' constraints on a typing derivation into the type of an object using ($\Rightarrow I$):

$$\frac{P, \pi \,|\, A \vdash E : \rho}{P \,|\, A \vdash E : \pi \Rightarrow \rho}$$

This is essential in many situations where overloading is combined with polymorphism: Without the ability to move predicates from the first component of a typing $P \,|\, A \vdash E : \rho$ into the type of an object we would not be able to apply $(\forall I)$ for any type variables appearing in $TV(P)$, severely limiting the use of polymorphism.

On the other hand, with the formulation of the typing rules used in the previous chapters there is no attempt to guarantee that the predicates introduced into the type of an object using $(\Rightarrow I)$ are satisfiable. As we have already mentioned, an object of type $\pi \Rightarrow \rho$ can only be used if we can provide evidence for the predicate π. If no such evidence can be obtained, then any object with this type is useless.

This problem was noted by Volpano and Smith (1991) for the special case of the system of type classes described in (Wadler and Blott, 1989). With this in mind, they gave a stronger definition of well-typing that includes testing for satisfiability of an inferred type scheme and showed that this makes the process of determining whether a particular term is well-typed undecidable in an restricted version of the Wadler-Blott system. The framework used in this thesis allows us to separate typability from predicate entailment and to identify the problem as undecidability of the latter. Nevertheless, the difficulty remains.

On the one hand we could simply ignore the problem since it will never be possible to resolve the overloading for an object with an unsatisfiable type scheme and hence any attempt to use it will fail. On the other hand, it would certainly be useful if the type system could be used to identify such objects at the point where they are defined and produce suitable error diagnostics to assist the programmer. One possibility would be to modify the rule for typing **let** expressions with:

$$\frac{P \,|\, A \vdash E : \sigma \quad Q \,|\, A_x, x{:}\sigma \vdash F : \tau \quad P_0 \ \mathsf{sat}\ \sigma}{P, Q \,|\, A \vdash (\mathbf{let}\ x = E\ \mathbf{in}\ F) : \tau}$$

to ensure satisfiability with respect to a fixed set of predicates P_0, where:

$$P_0 \ \mathsf{sat}\ (\forall \alpha_i . P \Rightarrow \tau) \quad \Leftrightarrow \quad \exists \nu_i . P_0 \Vdash [\nu_i/\alpha_i]P.$$

The following properties of this relationship between predicate sets and type schemes are easily established and show that this notion of *satisfiability* is well-behaved with respect to our use of polymorphism, entailment and ordering:

- If $P \ \mathsf{sat}\ \sigma$, then $SP \ \mathsf{sat}\ S\sigma$ for any substitution S.
- If $P \ \mathsf{sat}\ \sigma$ and $Q \Vdash P$, then $Q \ \mathsf{sat}\ \sigma$.
- If $P \ \mathsf{sat}\ \sigma'$ and $\sigma \geq (P \,|\, \sigma')$, then $P \ \mathsf{sat}\ \sigma$.

We conjecture that, if we restrict our attention to derivations $P \,|\, A \vdash E : \sigma$ for which $P_0 \Vdash P$, then the development of a principal type algorithm and coherence conditions described in the previous chapters will extend naturally to deal with this extension. Note however that we will require decidability of $P_0 \ \mathsf{sat}\ \sigma$ for arbitrary P_0 and σ to ensure decidability of type checking.

Another, more positive, application of satisfiability that does not appear to have been considered elsewhere is to allow the use of more accurate types for particular objects. As an example, consider the function $\lambda r.(r.l,\ r.l)$ using the record selection operator described in Section 2.4 which has principal type scheme:

$$\forall r.\forall a.\forall b.(r \text{ has } l\!: a,\ r \text{ has } l\!: b) \Rightarrow r \rightarrow (a, b).$$

On the other hand, for any given record type r, the types assigned to the variables a and b must be identical since they both correspond to the same field in r. It would therefore seem quite reasonable to treat f as having a *principal satisfiable type scheme*:

$$\forall r.\forall a.(r \text{ has } l\!: a) \Rightarrow r \rightarrow (a, a).$$

To see how this might be dealt with more formally, recall the treatment of the ordering between type schemes in Section 3.2.1. Writing the set of generic instances of a type scheme as:

$$[\![\forall \alpha_i.P \Rightarrow \tau]\!] \quad = \quad \{\, Q \Rightarrow [\nu_i/\alpha_i]\tau \mid \nu_i \in \mathit{Type},\ Q \Vdash [\nu_i/\alpha_i]P \,\},$$

the ordering on type schemes is described by:

$$\sigma \leq \sigma' \quad \Leftrightarrow \quad [\![\sigma]\!] \subseteq [\![\sigma']\!].$$

In a similar way can define the *generic satisfiable instances* of a type scheme with respect to a predicate set P_0 as:

$$[\![\forall \alpha_i.P \Rightarrow \tau]\!]^{sat}_{P_0} \quad = \quad \{\, [\nu_i/\alpha_i]\tau \mid \nu_i \in \mathit{Type},\ P_0 \Vdash [\nu_i/\alpha_i]P \,\}$$

and define a satisfiability ordering, again with respect to P_0, by:

$$\sigma \leq^{sat}_{P_0} \sigma' \quad \Leftrightarrow \quad [\![\sigma]\!]^{sat}_{P_0} \subseteq [\![\sigma']\!]^{sat}_{P_0}$$

We can formalise the notion of principal satisfiable type in the same way as in Section 3.4.3 using the $(\leq^{sat}_{P_0})$ ordering in place of $(\leq)$. For the example above, both of the type schemes given are principal satisfiable type schemes for the term $\lambda r.(r.l,\ r.l)$. The first of these is the type scheme that would be obtained using our type inference algorithm, but it would clearly be preferable if the algorithm could be modified to give the second alternative. Further investigation is needed to discover effective procedures or heuristics for calculating more informative types that can be used to support this extension.

The use of principal satisfiable type schemes would also be useful to eliminate some of the problems with terms that would otherwise have ambiguous principal types. One application where this would be particularly useful is for work with multiple parameter type classes where ambiguities often seem to occur. For example, in (Jones, 1990), we presented a type class for describing duality between lattices with a definition of the form:

```
class Dual b a => Dual a b where comp :: a -> b
```

where `comp` represents a complement function. One of the simplest instances for this class is:

```
instance Dual Bool Bool where
    comp True  = False
    comp False = True
```

Unfortunately, even simple terms involving `comp` have ambiguous principal type schemes. For example:

```
comp . comp :: (Dual a b, Dual b c) => a -> c
```

Despite this, if the above declaration is the only instance of `Dual` that matches the predicate `Dual Bool a`, then there is only one possible interpretation for the expression `let f = comp . comp in f False` and the ambiguity can be avoided.

As we have shown in this section, predicate satisfiability has several attractive applications, but we should also mention some of the difficulties of using information of this kind in concrete implementations. For example, as highlighted in (Jones, 1990), a system of type classes can be used to write programs that are highly modular and easily extended. In particular, the complete set of instance declarations making up the definition of a particular overloaded operator may be distributed across a number of distinct program modules that may not be visible to the compilation system when processing particular modules. As a result, it will often not be possible to use information about satisfiability. For example, it would probably not be sensible to treat the `member` function defined in a module containing only the definitions:

```
class Eq a where (==) :: a -> a -> Bool
member x []     = False
member x (y:ys) = x==y || member x ys
```

as being ill-typed, simply because the module does not define any instances of `Eq`.

6.3 Incorporating the rule of subsumption

Although we have indicated how systems of predicates can be used to describe subtyping(Section 2.3), the type systems presented in Chapters 3 and 5 can only be used to reason about languages with explicit coercions. More precisely, for derivation $P \,|\, A \vdash E \leadsto E' : \sigma$, the translation E' will only involve a coercion if one of the free variables appearing in E is assigned a qualified type in A that involves a predicate of the form $\tau' \subseteq \tau$.

More flexible systems of subtyping allow coercions to be used at arbitrary points in a translation using the rule of *subsumption*:

$$\frac{P \,|\, A \vdash E : \tau' \quad P \Vdash \tau' \subseteq \tau}{P \,|\, A \vdash E : \tau}$$

The corresponding rule for translations which makes the process of inserting coercions explicit is:

$$\frac{P \,|\, A \vdash E \leadsto E' : \tau' \quad P \Vdash c : \tau' \subseteq \tau}{P \,|\, A \vdash E \leadsto c[E'] : \tau}$$

where $c[E']$ denotes the application of the coercion c to the term E'.

Follow each application of one of the other typing rules with an implicit coercion, it is straightforward to see that, for any term E whose free variables appear in the domain of a type assignment A and for any type τ, there is a predicate set P such that $P \mid A \vdash E : \tau$. However, the predicate sets involved in these typings may not be satisfiable or may be unnecessarily complex. Thus the most difficult problem for type inference using the rule of subsumption is the need to reject terms with unsatisfiable type schemes (as described in the last section) and to minimise the use of coercions. These issues are discussed more fully in (Fuh and Mishra, 1989, 1990; Mitchell, 1991; Smith 1991).

The coherence of languages with explicit typing and subsumption has been established by Breazu-Tannen et al. (1989) and by Curien and Ghelli (1990). On the other hand, the task of ensuring coherence for an implicitly typed language with subsumption is likely to be considerably more difficult. In the first instance, it seems unlikely that a system that allows user-defined coercions will be able to guarantee the 'uniqueness of evidence' condition that is central to the work in Chapter 5. It is also possible that the ambiguity condition formulated in Section 5.8.2 may be too restrictive in some cases. For example, Fuh and Mishra (1989) indicate that the recursively defined term:

$$\textit{napply} = \lambda f.\lambda x.\lambda n.\textbf{if}\ n == 0\ \textbf{then}\ x\ \textbf{else}\ f\ (\textit{napply}\ f\ x\ (n-1))$$

has the (rather complex) principal type scheme:

$$\forall\{\alpha, \beta, \nu_x, \nu, \upsilon\}.(\nu_x \subseteq \upsilon, \beta \subseteq \upsilon, \upsilon \subseteq \nu, \upsilon \subseteq \alpha) \Rightarrow (\alpha \to \beta) \to (\nu_x \to \textit{Int} \to \nu).$$

This type is ambiguous since υ appears only in the predicate set of the type scheme and furthermore, as Fuh and Mishra point out, any attempt to eliminate this type variable would be unsound because it would not be possible to capture the relationship between the types assigned to α, β, ν_x and ν.

Chapter 7

Type classes in Haskell

This chapter expands on the implementation of type classes in Haskell using dictionary values as proposed by Wadler and Blott (1989) and sketched in Section 4.5. For brevity, we refer to this approach to the use of type classes as HTC. The main emphasis in this chapter is on concrete implementation and we adopt a less rigourous approach to formal properties of HTC than in previous chapters. In particular, we describe a number of optimisations that are necessary to obtain an efficient implementation of HTC – i.e. to minimise the cost of overloading. We do not consider the more general problems associated with the efficient implementation of non-strict functional languages like Haskell which are beyond the scope of this thesis.

Section 7.1 describes an important aspect of the system of type classes in Haskell which means that only a particularly simple form of predicate expression can be used in the type signature of an overloaded function. The set of predicates in a Haskell type signature is usually referred to as the *context* and hence we will use the term *context reduction* to describe the process of reducing the context to an acceptable form. Context reduction usually results in a small context, acts as a partial check of satisfiability and helps to guarantee decidability of predicate entailment. Unfortunately, it can also interfere with the use of data abstraction and limits the possibilities for extending the Haskell system of type classes.

The main ideas used in the implementation of HTC are described in Section 7.2 including the treatment of default definitions which were omitted from our previous descriptions. Section 7.3 highlights the importance of finding translations that minimise the amount of dictionary construction used during the execution of a program. Section 7.4 concentrates on an important special case – sharing dictionary values in recursive programs to avoid repeating the construction of the same dictionaries on each recursive call of a particular function. Other opportunities for sharing are described in Section 7.5, with particular attention to sharing in hierarchies of dictionaries. Finally, Section 7.6 outlines a rather different approach, suggesting an implementation of dictionary constructors as memo functions.

Some of the examples used in this chapter (each of which is written using the concrete syntax of Haskell) are degenerate and are unlikely to be of use in practical applications. Nevertheless, we believe that they are representative of the kind of problems that can occur in such programs. We are particularly concerned with the use of type classes for large programming projects where a system of modules supporting some form of separate compilation is essential. This imposes an additional restriction on the compilation system: It is clearly unacceptable to adopt a system in which the ability to obtain an efficient implementation of a function relies on access to the source code for a value defined in another module.

7.1 Context reduction

An important aspect of the Haskell system is that only predicates of the form `C a` (where `C` is a type class name and `a` is a type variable) may appear in the contexts of overloaded functions. Any other context obtained during the type inference process must be reduced to this form using rules derived from the `class` and `instance` declarations appearing in the program concerned. As an example, given the function definition:

```
f x ys  =  [x] == ys
```

we may infer that `f` has type `a -> [a] -> Bool` with the context `Eq [a]` (i.e. for any type `a` such that `[a]` is an instance of `Eq`). Using the corresponding instance declaration this constraint is reduced to `Eq a` and the actual typing that will be used for `f` is:

```
f :: Eq a => a -> [a] -> Bool
```

This process can be thought of as a partial attempt to check for satisfiability of the predicate `Eq [a]`; had there been no instance for equality on lists, an error condition would be signaled by the type checker. On the other hand, no attempt is made to determine whether there is any type `a` for which the final context `Eq a` holds.

One advantage of context reduction is that it usually results in fairly simple contexts in inferred type signatures and deals naturally with the process of eliminating predicates for specific instances of classes that can be statically determined during type-checking. The restriction to predicates of the form `C a` is also useful as a simple means of ensuring the decidability of type checking (or more accurately, of predicate entailment), where each of the predicates in the context part of an instance declaration must be of this form for some type variable `a` appearing in the type expression to the right of the `=>` symbol. A simple argument on the structure of the type expressions involved can be used to prove that any attempt to construct a dictionary for a given predicate will terminate. Several researchers, for example (Volpano and Smith, 1991), have considered what extensions can be made to the form of Haskell instance declarations without loosing this property.

Another motivation for the use of context reduction in Haskell was to attempt to minimise the number of dictionary parameters used in the translations of overloaded functions. Unfortunately, there are also a number of examples where the number of dictionary parameters may actually be increased. For example, a function with inferred context `Eq (a,b)` could be implemented using a single dictionary parameter for this instance, but the corresponding HTC context is `(Eq a, Eq b)` which leads to a translation with two dictionary arguments.

In many cases, the contexts obtained by the reduction process are quite natural, but there are also some examples where the contexts are less easy to justify. For example, consider the following program which might be used to define subset inequality and set equality on an abstract data type of sets:

```
data Set a = Set [a]
```

```
instance Eq a => Ord (Set a) where
    Set xs <= Set ys  =  all (\x -> member x ys) xs

instance Ord (Set a) => Eq (Set a) where
    x == y  =  x <= y  &&  y <= x
```

The use of the predicate `Ord (Set a)` in the second instance declaration reflects the fact that the ordering function `(<=)` is used to compare set values in the definition of `(==)` on sets. This context is not legal in Haskell and the declaration must be rewritten as:

```
instance Eq a => Eq (Set a) where
    x == y  =  x <= y  &&  y <= x
```

Given only this declaration, it is not particularly clear why the context `Eq a` should be necessary.

Another problem with context reduction is that it interferes with the use of data abstraction. Consider an HTC program that makes considerable use of the equality operation on sets defined above and hence containing many functions whose type signatures include predicates of the form `Eq a` as a result of comparisons between sets. Suppose that we decide to change the representation of sets to use ordered lists with the subset ordering defined by:

```
instance Ord a => Ord (Set a) where
    Set xs <= Set ys  =  compare xs ys
     where compare []     ys              = True
           compare (x:xs) []              = False
           compare (x:xs) (y:ys) | x==y = compare xs ys
                                 | x<y  = False
                                 | y<x  = compare (x:xs) ys
```

To make this work we must now rewrite each predicate of the form `Eq a` in the original program arising out of a comparison between sets as `Ord a`. This breaks a fundamental principle of abstraction; it should be possible to change the implementation of an abstract datatype without any changes to the programs that make use of that code.

By contrast, had we avoided the use of context reduction, the only place that any changes would be necessary would be in the implementation of the abstract datatype, replacing the original instance declaration with that given above. This is the only place where a predicate of the form `Eq a` must be replaced by `Ord a`; at every other point in the program the use of an equality operation on sets is reflected by the predicate `Eq (Set a)` that does not need to be changed.

To preserve true abstraction we should not allow a program module containing the definition of an abstract datatype to export the context part of any instance declarations for objects of that type. For the example above, the interface for a module defining the set datatype might contain the definitions:

```
data Set a              -- abstract datatype of sets
instance Eq (Set a)     -- equality
instance Ord (Set a)    -- ordering
```

and each use of one of the set operations reflected by the use of predicates of the form Eq (Set a) or Ord (Set a). Note that it would then be possible for a program using this interface to access the set datatype to be accepted by the compilation system, but generate a link-time error if a dictionary for a particular instance Eq (Set t) cannot be constructed. This is analogous to attempting to create an executable version of a program without linking in an appropriate library.

Using context reduction in the type inference process will sometimes result in inferred typings that are not principal. For example, the principal type of the expression (\xs -> xs==[]) is Eq [a] => [a] -> Bool, but the Haskell typing is Eq a => [a] -> Bool. This is of little practical concern with the current definition of Haskell; even though the predicates Eq a and Eq [a] are not equivalent (the second may be inferred from the first, but the converse does not hold), the restrictions on the form of Haskell instance declarations ensure that whenever one holds, then so does the other. On the other hand, if the syntax of instance declarations were to be relaxed, as suggested by a number of researchers and implemented in Gofer, then the loss of principal types would become more significant. For example, in a program containing the instance declarations of the form:

```
instance Eq Int where ...
instance Eq [Int] where ...
instance Eq [Bool] where ...
```

the expression (\xs -> xs==[]) would not be acceptable unless we allowed a predicate of the form Eq [a] as part of its type.

Another way in which context reduction can limit the form of instance declarations that can be used is illustrated by an extension implemented as part of Haskell B. (Augustsson, 1991) that allows overlapping instance declarations such as:

```
instance Class Char where ...
instance Class a => Class [a] where ...
instance Class [Char] where ...
```

This feature might, for example, be used to define a function show that produces a printable representation of certain objects, printing strings (represented by lists of characters) in the form "xyz" but using the standard notation such as [x,y,z] for other kinds of list. Unfortunately, the use of context reduction means that we cannot guarantee uniqueness of evidence needed as part of the framework used to establish coherence in Chapter 5. For example, the expression:

```
let f xs = show (xs ++ xs) in f "x"
```

could result in a translation that evaluates to "xx" or in an alternative that produces "['x','x']", depending on the way that this expression is type checked. The problem is caused by the fact that context reduction allows a predicate of the form Eq [a] to be reduced to Eq a before the type a is known.

7.2 Implementation of type classes in HTC

This section outlines a simple implementation of type classes in HTC based on the original approach described by Wadler and Blott (1989) and subsequently in more detail by Hammond and Blott (1989).

As a preliminary we mention one feature of the Haskell system of type classes that was not mentioned in earlier chapter, namely the ability to support the use of *default definitions*. For example, the definition of the class Eq given in the standard prelude for Haskell (Hudak et al., 1992) is a little more complex than the definition used in Section 2.2:

```
class Eq a where
    (==), (/=) :: a -> a -> Bool              -- member functions
    x /= y      = not (x==y)                  -- default definitions
```

Note that Eq has two member functions but includes a default definition for the (/=) operator in terms of (==), so that only the latter need be specified to define an instance of Eq. Alternative definitions for (/=) can be provided in specific instances by giving an appropriate definition in the corresponding instance declaration. The most common reasons for overriding a default definition are to give a more efficient implementation or to specify a different semantics for the value in question.

In a similar way, the full definition of the class Ord includes default definitions for all of its member functions except (<=) so that, only this single function needs to be defined to construct an instance of the class:

```
class Eq a => Ord a where
    (<), (<=), (>), (>=) :: a -> a -> Bool -- member functions
    max, min             :: a -> a -> a

    x <  y               = x <= y && x /= y    -- default definitions
    x >= y               = y <= x
    x >  y               = y < x
    max x y | x >= y = x
            | y >= x = y
    min x y | x <= y = x
            | y <= x = y
```

Note how the assumption that Eq is a superclass of Ord is used in the default definition for (<) which uses both (<=) from Ord and (/=) from Eq.

7.2.1 Implementation of HTC dictionaries

The general form of evidence for a type class constraint in HTC is a dictionary containing implementations for each of the member functions for that instance. For example, the following type definition gives a suitable representation for dictionaries for the class Eq:

```
data EqD a = EqDict (a -> a -> Bool)    -- (==)
                    (a -> a -> Bool)    -- (/=)
```

An overloaded value of type `Eq a => sometype` can now be implemented as a function of type `EqD a -> sometype` where the additional parameter supplies the appropriate dictionary value. Member functions are treated in the same way, implemented as dictionary selector functions:

```
eq, neq            :: EqD a -> (a -> a -> Bool)
eq  (EqDict e n) = e   -- extract definition of (==)
neq (EqDict e n) = n   -- extract definition of (/=)
```

These operations are used to access the values of member functions in the implementation of other kinds of overloaded functions. For example, the definitions of `member` and `subset` in Section 2.2.1 might be implemented using the translations:

```
member             :: EqD a -> (a -> [a] -> Bool)
member d x []       = False
member d x (y:ys) = eq d x y || member x ys

subset             :: EqD a -> ([a] -> [a] -> Bool)
subset d xs ys      = all (\x -> member d x ys) xs
```

As a further example, the default definition of `(/=)` can be implemented using:

```
defNeq        :: EqD a -> (a -> a -> Bool)
defNeq d x y = not (eq d x y)
```

Each instance declaration in a given program is used to generate a corresponding *dictionary constructor*. A simple example is given by the dictionary constructor for the instance `Eq Int`:

```
eqDInt :: EqD Int
eqDInt  = EqDict primEqInt (defNeq eqDInt)
```

This results in a cyclic data structure, using the dictionary `eqDInt` that is being defined to obtain the correct parameterisation for `defNeq`.

The same approach can be used in more general examples and, in the case of a parameterised dictionary constructor, a local definition must be used to obtain the required cyclic data structure and avoid a potential space leak[1]:

```
eqDList   :: EqD a -> EqD [a]
eqDList d  = let d1 = EqDict (eqList d) (defNeq d1) in d1
```

Following (Wadler and Blott, 1989), a suitable definition for the `eqList` function used above can be derived from the instance declaration for `Eq [a]` giving:

```
eqList                      :: EqD a -> [a] -> [a] -> Bool
eqList d []     []     = True
eqList d []     (y:ys) = False
eqList d (x:xs) []     = False
eqList d (x:xs) (y:ys) = eq d x y && eq (eqDList d) xs ys
```

[1]The `let` construct in Haskell introduces a potentially recursive group of local bindings and corresponds to the `letrec` or `whererec` constructs in other languages. It should not be confused with the **let** construct used in the formal treatment of OML.

The implementation of superclasses in HTC is straightforward if we allow the dictionary for a particular instance of a class to include dictionaries for each of its superclasses, in addition to the implementations for each of its member functions. For example, the following data type definition and the associated family of selector functions provide a representation for dictionaries of the the class Ord:

```
data OrdD a = OrdDict (a -> a -> Bool)     -- (<)
                      (a -> a -> Bool)     -- (<=)
                      (a -> a -> Bool)     -- (>)
                      (a -> a -> Bool)     -- (>=)
                      (a -> a -> a)        -- max
                      (a -> a -> a)        -- min
                      (EqDict a)           -- superclass Eq

lessThan   (OrdDict lt le gt ge mx mn sceq) = lt
lessOrEq   (OrdDict lt le gt ge mx mn sceq) = le
...
scEqOfOrd  (OrdDict lt le gt ge mx mn sceq) = sceq
```

Note in particular the function `scEqOfOrd :: OrdD a -> EqD a` which extracts the superclass dictionary for `Eq a` from the dictionary for `Ord a`. As an illustration of the use of `scEqOfOrd`, the default definition of `(<)` in the definition of `Ord` can be implemented as:

```
defLessThan d x y = lessOrEq d x y && neq (scEqOfOrd d) x y
```

Dictionary constructor functions are defined in the same way as before, taking care to give appropriate values for superclass dictionaries. For example, the instance declaration:

```
instance Ord a => Ord [a] where
    []     <= xs     = True
    (x:xs) <= []     = False
    (x:xs) <= (y:ys) = x<y || (x==y && xs<=ys)
```

can be used to generate a dictionary constructor of the form:

```
ordDList   :: OrdD a -> OrdD [a]
ordDList d  = let d1 = OrdDict (defLessThan d1)
                               (ltOrEqList d)
                               ...
                               (defMin d1)
                               (eqDList (scEqOfOrd d)) in d1
```

7.3 The problem of repeated construction

The performance of any implementation of HTC using dictionaries is very much dependent on the costs associated with dictionary construction and selection of member functions. A typical implementation will store the components of a dictionary in a contiguous array, for which the process of selecting a member function has an obvious and efficient implementation. Construction of a dictionary amounts to allocation and initialisation of the values to be held in it. This too can be implemented reasonably efficiently in constant time, particularly if heap space is allocated directly from a contiguous block of free memory. Even so, dictionary construction is still likely to be (at least) an order of magnitude more expensive than member function selection, and it is difficult to see how this might be reduced.

While it is obviously sensible to try to minimise the cost of each of these individual operations, it is also sensible to try and minimise the number of times that they are actually needed. The same idea motivates standard optimisation techniques such as common subexpression elimination in imperative languages and full laziness in non-strict functional languages.

There are a number of additional reasons why dictionary construction should be kept to a minimum:

- Allocation of dictionaries in the heap reduces the amount of heap available for other parts of the program.
- The number of garbage collections required increases with heap use and hence with greater rates of dictionary construction.
- Multiple copies of a single dictionary are redundant and waste heap space.
- The evaluation of a value held in a dictionary cannot be shared with physically distinct copies of the same dictionary.

The following sections describe a number of situations in which dictionary construction can be reduced by careful sharing of dictionary values.

7.4 Repeated construction caused by recursion

Functional programs typically make extensive use of recursion so it is particularly important to ensure that such programs can be implemented efficiently. In a dictionary-based implementation of HTC, special precautions must be taken to avoid repeating the construction of dictionaries for each recursive function call.

Section 7.4.1 shows both how this problem can occur and how it it can be avoided by using a slightly more sophisticated translation. The same techniques are extended to groups of mutually recursive overloaded functions in Section 7.4.2. We also highlight two issues that do not seem to have been noticed elsewhere; the need for a restricted form of full-laziness as described in Section 7.4.3, and the problems caused by (indirectly) recursive dictionary constructors illustrated in Section 7.4.4.

7.4.1 Recursion in the definition of overloaded functions

Recall the recursive definition of the equality on lists given in Section 7.2 in which the translation of the equation `(x:xs)==(y:ys) = x==y && xs==ys` is given by:

```
eqList d (x:xs) (y:ys) = eq d x y && eq (eqDList d) xs ys
```

Since the dictionary expression `eqDList d` appears on the right hand side of this definition, the construction of this dictionary will be once repeated for each element of the argument list in an expression such as `[1,2,3]==[1,2,3]`.

In this example, we can use a form of partial evaluation or some other compiler driven transformation, based on the calculation:

```
eq (eqDList d) = eq (let d1 = EqDict (eqList d) (defNeq d1) in d1)
               = let d1 = EqDict (eqList d) (defNeq d1) in eq d1
               = eqList d.
```

Substituting this into the definition above gives:

```
eqList d (x:xs) (y:ys) = eq d x y && eqList d xs ys
```

which does not involve `eqDList` and so avoids the need for dictionary construction altogether. Whilst this approach is useful in particular cases, the calculations required will typically require the use of arbitrarily complex laws that the compilation system cannot reasonably be expected to apply. If for example, we had used the line:

```
(x:xs)==(y:ys)  =  x==y && not (xs/=ys)  -- rather perverse!
```

as part of the definition of equality on lists, then it would not be possible to avoid the repeated construction of a dictionary value without using a law of the form `not (not x) = x`.

A more practical solution, described in (Peyton Jones and Wadler, 1992) in a slightly different form, is to move the translation of the equality on lists into the definition of the dictionary constructor. In so doing, the problematic expression `eqDList d` can be replaced with a direct reference to the dictionary being constructed:

```
eqDList   :: EqD a -> EqD [a]
eqDList d = let d1                   = EqDict eqList (defNeq d1)
                eqList []      []    = True
                                     .
                                     .
                eqList (x:xs) (y:ys) = eq d x y && eq d1 xs ys
            in  d1
```

Having written the definition in this way, we can obtain an equivalent translation by lifting the definition of `eqList` to give a new top-level function. This kind of transformation will in any case be used in any implementation that incorporates some form of lambda lifter, but is also useful in the discussion of mutually recursive functions in the next section.

```
eqDList    :: EqD a -> EqD [a]
eqDList d  = let d1 = EqDict (eqList d d1) (defNeq d1) in  d1

eqList                      :: EqD a -> EqD [a] -> [a] -> [a] -> Bool
eqList d d1 []      []      = True
                            .
                            .
eqList d d1 (x:xs) (y:ys) = eq d x y && eq d1 xs ys
```

Notice that with this formulation, the equality test **eqList** is parameterised by dictionaries for the actual overloadings required, and not (as might be implied by context reduction) from some smaller group of dictionaries from which they may be constructed.

In general, the translation of a recursively defined overloaded function `f` that uses dictionary values `d1'`, ..., `dm'` constructed from dictionary parameters `d1`, ..., `dn` must be written in the form:

```
f d1 ... dn  =  let d1' = ...
                        .
                        .
                    dm' = ...
                in
                let f' x1 ... xk  = expr
                in  f'
```

where the use of dictionary constructor functions is restricted to the right hand side of the definitions of `d1'`, ..., `dm'`. Recursive calls to `f` in the original definition must be replaced by calls to `f'` in `expr`. This ensures that the values of any constructed dictionaries are shared by all recursive calls to `f'` and, at the same time, guarantees that none of these dictionary values will be constructed more than once for any single redex of the form `f d1 ... dn`.

As it stands, there is little to be gained by using this translation for recursive functions that do not involve dictionary construction. For example, rewriting the translation of **member** as:

```
member   :: EqD a -> (a -> [a] -> Bool)
member d = let member' x []     = False
               member' x (y:ys) = eq d x y || member' x ys
           in  member'
```

gains very little except perhaps in an implementation that does not rely on lambda lifting due to the reduced number of arguments to **member'**. In any other implementation, the use of lambda lifting results in a final program of the form:

```
member d              = member' d
member' d x []        = False
member' d x (y:ys) = eq d x y || member' d x ys
```

where the definition of **member'** is now precisely that given in the original translation in Section 7.2 and the equation for **member** results in an additional (small) run-time overhead unless special care is taken to eliminate that equation using η-reduction as described by (Peyton Jones, 1987).

7.4.2 Mutually recursive groups of functions

The same basic ideas can be extended to groups of mutually recursive definitions, although in this case, it is easier to give the translations in their lifted form rather than using local definitions. To illustrate this, consider the mutually recursive functions defined by:

```
f, g  ::  Eq a => a -> a -> Bool
f x y  =  x==y      ||  g x y
g x y  =  [x]==[y]  ||  f x y
```

Using the standard process we infer that `f` has type
`a -> a -> Bool` for any type a such that `Eq a`, whilst g has the same type but restricted to those types a such that `Eq [a]`. This leads to the following translations:

```
f, g     ::  EqD a -> a -> a -> Bool
f d x y  =  eq d x y                 || g d x y
g d x y  =  eq (eqDList d) [x] [y]  || f d x y
```

Note that the construction of the dictionary `eqDList d` will potentially be repeated each time that the function `g` is called. This can be avoided (at the expense of an additional dictionary parameter) using a more sophisticated translation such as:

```
f, g          ::  EqD a -> a -> a -> Bool
f d            =  f1 d (eqDList d)
g d            =  g1 d (eqDList d)

f1, g1        ::  EqD a -> EqD [a] -> a -> a -> Bool
f1 d d1 x y   =  eq d  x   y    ||  g1 d d1 x y
g1 d d1 x y   =  eq d1 [x] [y]  ||  f1 d d1 x y
```

In this example, we can think of `f` and `g` as corresponding to entry points to the system of equations defined by the original equations while `f1` and `g1` can be thought of as transitions within that system. The construction of `eqDList d` can only occur on entry to the system of equations, either through `f` or through `g`, and hence will no longer be repeated with each recursive call as in the original translation.

The translation given above is essentially equivalent to that suggested in (Peyton Jones and Wadler, 1992) which, for the current example, would be:

```
f d = let f1 x y  =  eq d  x   y    || g1 x y
          g1 x y  =  eq d1 [x] [y]  || f1 x y
          d1      =  eqDList d
      in  f1

g d = let f1 x y  =  eq d  x   y    || g1 x y
          g1 x y  =  eq d1 [x] [y]  || f1 x y
          d1      =  eqDList d
      in  g1
```

One obvious advantage of our formulation is that it automatically avoids the duplication of the code for the functions `f1` and `g1` in the example above.

7.4.3 The need for a form of full-laziness

The following example illustrates the need for (at least a restricted form of) full laziness to avoid repeated dictionary construction in certain situations. This provides motivation for including the more general transformations as a part of the compilation system in a dictionary based implementation of HTC.

Consider a function `doToOne` of type `Eq a => a -> Bool` whose implementation uses the dictionary parameter corresponding to the instance `Eq a` to construct one or more additional dictionaries. The exact definition of this function is not important; a simple example having the required properties is:

```
doToOne   :: Eq a => a -> Bool
doToOne x = [x] == [x]
```

The fact that the implementation of `doToOne` involves the construction of a dictionary will (in general) be hidden from the compilation system if the definition of `doToOne` appears in an external module.

Now suppose that we define a function `doToList` given by:

```
doToList          :: Eq a => [a] -> [Bool]
doToList []        = []
doToList (x:xs) = doToOne x : doToList xs
```

Notice that `doToList` is equivalent to the function `map doToOne` (and indeed, the definition of `doToList` might even be generated automatically by a sophisticated compiler that unrolls the definition of `map` in an attempt to optimise the expression `map doToOne`).

The translation of `doToList` is as follows:

```
doToList            :: EqD a -> [a] -> [Bool]
doToList d []        = []
doToList d (x:xs) = doToOne d x : doToList d xs
```

Any attempt to evaluate the complete list produced by an application of this function will repeat the construction of the redex `doToOne d` (and hence repeat the dictionary construction in `doToOne`) for each element of the argument list.

Happily, the same observation also makes the solution to this problem quite obvious. The essential step is to abstract not just the appropriate dictionaries required as in Section 7.4.1, but also the application of each overloaded operator to its dictionary arguments. For the current example, this gives the translation:

```
doToList   :: EqD a -> [a] -> [Bool]
doToList d = doToList'
             where doToList' []     = []
                   doToList' (x:xs) = doToOne' x : doToList' xs
                   doToOne'         = doToOne d
```

An additional benefit of this translation is that the garbage collector can reclaim the storage used for dictionary values as soon as the implementations of the appropriate member functions have been extracted from it.

The second translation of `doToList` is exactly what we might expect to obtain using a translation to fully-lazy form as described in (Holst, 1990; Peyton Jones and Lester, 1991).

The basic motivation for such transformations is that no expression need be evaluated more than once after its free variables have been bound to particular values. Given the translation of a particular function in the form:

```
f d1 ... dn = let f' x1 ... xm = expr in f'
```

any occurrences of an overloaded function applied to dictionary values constructed from `d1`, ..., `dn` will be a free expression in the definition of `f'` and hence will be abstracted (possibly as part of some enclosing maximally free expression) by the transformation to fully-lazy form.

Since every overloaded function can be expected to make use of at least one overloaded operator, even if dictionary construction is not involved, it it is sensible to extend the transformation given in Section 7.4.1 so that the translation of any overloaded function takes the form:

```
f d1 ... dn  =  let d1' = ...               -- dictionary values
                        .
                        .
                    dm' = ...
                in
                let o1  = ...               -- overloaded functions
                        .
                        .
                    op  = ...
                in
                let f' x1 ... xk = expr    -- function definition
                in  f'
```

where `o1`, ..., `op` are the overloaded operators abstracted from `expr`.

In justifying the optimisation for the example above, we have implicitly assumed that the translation of `doToOne` was written in such a way as to guarantee that `doToOne d` is a redex. A suitable translation with this property for the sample definition of `doToOne` given above:

```
doToOne   :: EqD a -> a -> Bool
doToOne d = let doToOne' x = eqd1 [x] [x]
                eqd1       = eq d1
                d1         = eqDList d
            in  doToOne'
```

As a further example, a revised translation for `member` that makes use of the optimisations described in this chapter is:

```
member   :: EqD a -> (a -> [a] -> Bool)
member d = let member' x []     = False
               member' x (y:ys) = eqd x y || member' x ys
               eqd              = eq d
           in  member'
```

The only overloaded function involved here is a member function `eq` that is implemented as a selector function and does not require any form of dictionary construction. Nevertheless, this definition is still an improvement over the previous versions since it ensures that the selection from the dictionary (i.e. evaluation of `eq d`) is evaluated at most once, after which the remaining portions of the dictionary `d` may be discarded as described above.

In the interests of clarity, we will generally avoid giving full translations in the following sections, safe in the knowledge that these can in any case be obtained from the translations given using a standard transformation to fully-lazy form.

As a final comment, it is interesting to return to the observation made at the beginning of this section that `doToList` is equivalent to `map doToOne`. Had we used this equivalence to define `doToList`, then the translation obtained would be:

```
doToList   :: EqD a -> [a] -> [Bool]
doToList d = map (doToOne d)
```

Note that the redex `doToOne d` will now only be constructed a single time. Thus the use of higher order functions may ultimately give better performance than the explicit recursive definitions obtained by unrolling in a system that does not implement at least the restricted form of full laziness described in this section.

7.4.4 Recursion in dictionary constructors

The same kinds of problem described above in the context of recursive user defined overloaded functions can also occur with compiler generated functions such as the dictionary constructors corresponding to each `instance` declaration in a given program. A similar range of techniques must therefore be used to avoid unnecessary repeated construction of dictionary values. The problems discussed in this section do not appear to be widely known and (for example) are not dealt with in translations given in (Peyton Jones and Wadler, 1992).

As an example, consider the type of arbitrary branching labelled trees defined by:

```
data Tree a = Node a [Tree a]
```

The standard definition of equality on trees of this kind is described by the following instance declaration:

```
instance Eq a => Eq (Tree a) where
    Node x xs == Node y ys   =  x==y  &&  xs==ys
```

Using the approach described in Section 7.4.1, we obtain the following definition for the corresponding dictionary constructor:

```
eqDTree   :: EqD a -> EqD (Tree a)
eqDTree d = let d1 = EqDict (eqTree d) (defNeq d1) in d1

eqTree    :: EqD a -> Tree a -> Tree a -> Bool
eqTree d  = let eqTree' (Node x xs) (Node (y ys)
```

```
                   = eq d x y  &&  eq d2 xs ys
               d2 = eqDList (eqDTree d)
           in eqTree'
```

Unfortunately, this definition will potentially repeat the construction of the dictionaries `eqDTree d` and `eqDList (eqDTree d)` for each individual node in the tree.

A more efficient implementation can be obtained by providing **`eqTree`** with access to the dictionary `eqDTree d` as well as the dictionary parameter `d` from which it is obtained:

```
eqDTree d = let d1 = EqDict eqTree (defNeq d1)
                d2 = eqDList d1
                eqTree (Node x xs) (Node y ys)
                   = eq d x y  &&  eq d2 xs ys
            in  d1
```

Lifting out the definition of `eqTree` gives:

```
eqDTree d = let d1 = EqDict (eqTree d d2) (defNeq d1)
                d2 = eqDList  d1
            in  d1

eqTree d d2 (Node x xs) (Node y ys)
   = eq d x y  &&  eq d2 xs ys
```

This shows that an efficient implementation of equality on trees should be parameterised by dictionaries that reflect the actual overloadings required (i.e. `Eq a` and `Eq [Tree a]`) rather than by dictionaries from which those overloadings may be obtained (i.e. `Eq a`).

7.5 Other opportunities for shared dictionaries

In the previous section, we focussed on the use of a syntactic condition – functional dependency and, in particular, recursion – to detect places in a given source program where repeated dictionary construction can be avoided. By contrast, this section describes a number of situations in which the information produced by the type checker can be used to discover further opportunities for shared dictionaries. Unfortunately, there are also a number of examples in which repeated construction seems to be unavoidable.

7.5.1 Simple examples

The translation of the definition of a particular function is in part determined by the algorithm used to reduce an inferred context to the form required in an implementation of HTC. It is often the case that there are several different ways of reducing a given context to an acceptable form, yielding translations that are operationally distinct, although (one would hope!) semantically equivalent. As a simple example, consider the function defined by:

```
f      ::  Eq a => a -> a -> Bool
f x y  =   [x]==[y] && [y]==[x]
```

From this definition, we may infer that `f` has type `a -> a -> Bool` with context `(Eq [a], Eq [a])` in which the repeated predicate corresponds to the repeated use of `(==)` in the definition. There are two ways of reducing this context to the single predicate `Eq a`:

- One possibility is to reduce each predicate separately to give `(Eq a, Eq a)` and then simplifying to `Eq a`. This corresponds to the translation:

```
f         ::  EqD a -> a -> a -> Bool
f d x y   =   eq (eqDList d) [x] [y]  && eq (eqDList d) [y] [x]
```

  that (potentially) repeats the construction of the dictionary `eqDList d`.

- A more efficient translation can be obtained by explicitly sharing a single dictionary for `Eq [a]` between its two uses. This corresponds to simplifying the original context first to `Eq [a]` and then reducing this to `Eq a`:

```
f         ::  EqD a -> a -> a -> Bool
f d x y   =   eq d1 [x] [y]  &&  eq d1 [y] [x]
              where d1 = eqDList d
```

Note that the second translation can be obtained from the first using an optimisation based on common subexpression elimination (Aho, Sethi and Ullman, 1986). Such techniques are not generally used in the implementation of non-strict functional languages since they can introduce unanticipated (and of course, unwanted) space leaks (Peyton Jones, 1987, Section 23.4.2).

A rather more tricky problem is illustrated by the following pair of definitions:

```
g       ::  (Eq a, Eq b) => a -> b -> Bool
g x y   =   [x]==[x]  &&  [y]==[y]

h       ::  Eq a => a -> Bool
h x     =   g x x
```

whose translations are as follows:

```
g'            :: EqD a -> EqD b -> a -> b -> Bool
g' da db x y = eq (eqDList da) [x] [x] && eq (eqDList db) [y] [y]

h'            :: EqD a -> a -> Bool
h' da x       = g' da da x x
```

The expressions `(eqDList da)` and `(eqDList db)` in the translation of `g` will both result in the construction of a dictionary, even if `da` and `db` are equal as in the translation of `h`.

It is relatively easy to construct examples in which the number of times that a dictionary will be constructed is exponential in the depth of the calling graph. To illustrate this point consider the family of functions with `g_0 = g`, `h_0 = h` and functions `g_n` and `h_n` for positive natural numbers `n` given by the pseudo-definition:

```
g_n          :: (Eq a, Eq b) => a -> b -> Bool
g_n x y       = h_(n-1) x && h_(n-1) y

h_n          :: Eq a => a -> Bool
h_n x         = g_n x x
```

Then the evaluation of `h_3 1` and `h_6 1` will repeat the construction of `eqDList eqDInt` 8 and 64 times each respectively.

For this particular example, it is possible to reduce the problems of repeated construction by giving explicit type signatures `g_n :: Eq a => a -> a -> Bool` (for each `n`) that (when combined with the optimisations described in Section 7.4) will avoid the construction of all but one dictionary. There are two problems with this solution; first of all, a restricted typing may place an unacceptable limit on an otherwise general purpose function. Secondly, it may be unreasonable to expect a programmer both to determine when such a problem occurs and then to choose the best places to insert suitable type signatures.

An alternative approach is to use a second set of functions in the translation of this family of definitions, that separates the construction of dictionaries from their use. To begin with, we introduce the following variants of the translations given above that use additional dictionary parameters to avoid the construction of dictionary values:

```
g_0', g_n'         :: EqD [a] -> EqD [a] -> a -> b -> Bool -- n>=1
g_0' dla dlb x y = eq dla [x] [x] && eq dlb [y] [y]
g_n' dla dlb x y = h_(n-1)' dla x  && h_(n-1)' dlb y

h_n'               :: EqD [a] -> a -> Bool                  -- n>=0
h_n' dla x          = g_n' dla dla x
```

Given these definitions, we can recode the translations of each of `g_n` and `h_n` as:

```
g_n                :: EqD a -> EqD b -> a -> b -> Bool      -- n>=0
g_n da db           = g_n' (eqDList da) (eqDList db)

h_n                :: EqD a -> a -> Bool                    -- n>=0
h_n da              = h_n' (eqDList da)
```

Using the analogy of Section 7.4.2, the functions in the second group of definitions may be thought of as a entry points to those in the first. In order to be able to detect opportunities for this kind of optimisation, the compilation system will require a sophisticated analysis, working at the level of complete source modules rather than single groups of mutually recursive definitions as in the previous sections. Even then, the translation given above can only be produced if the definitions for all of the functions involved appear in a single module.

7.5.2 Sharing in hierarchies

In the case of the example `f` in the previous section, the compilation system need only detect identical predicates in the inferred context to obtain the required translation In general, the construction of a dictionary will require the construction of a small hierarchy of dictionary values, both as superclass dictionaries and as parameters to dictionary constructors. It is therefore possible that the inferred context for a given predicate may contain two predicates for which the corresponding dictionary hierarchies are not disjoint. In such cases, it is clearly desirable to arrange for the overlapping portions to be shared between each dictionary construction.

As a simple example, consider the function:

```
f x ys zss  =  [x]<=ys  ||  [ys]==zss
```

that has type `a -> [a] -> [[a]] -> Bool` for any type `a` such that `Ord [a]` and `Eq [[a]]`. The corresponding HTC typing is:

```
f :: Ord a => a -> [a] -> [[a]] -> Bool
```

and we have a translation of the form:

```
f d  =  let f' x ys zss = lessOrEq d1 [x] ys || eq d2 [ys] zss
            d1          = ... dictionary for Ord [a] ...
            d2          = ... dictionary for Eq [[a]] ...
        in  f'
```

There are two ways to construct suitable dictionaries `d1` and `d2` from a dictionary `d` for `Ord a`. Considering each dictionary separately, we obtain:

```
d1 = ordDList d
d2 = eqDList (eqDList (scEqOfOrd d))
```

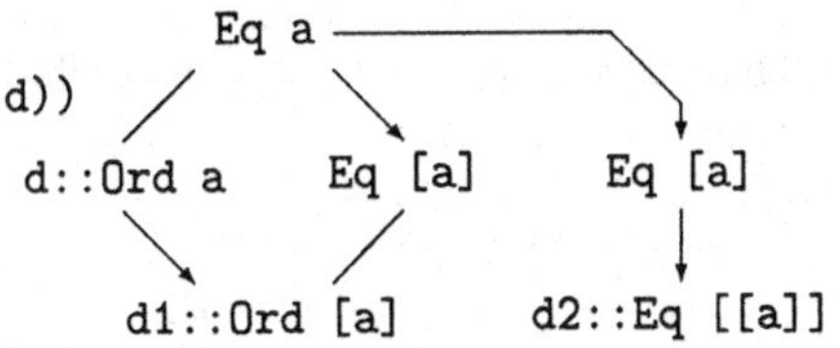

The diagram on the right illustrates the corresponding hierarchy (lines marked with arrow heads indicate the use of dictionary constructors, other lines correspond to superclass inclusions; an expression of the form `d::Ord a` indicates that `d` is a dictionary for the instance `Ord a`). Note that this requires two copies of the dictionary for `Eq [a]`.

As an alternative, we can construct the dictionary for `d2` using part of the hierarchy constructed for `d1`:

```
d1 = ordDList d
d2 = eqDList (scEqOfOrd d1)
```

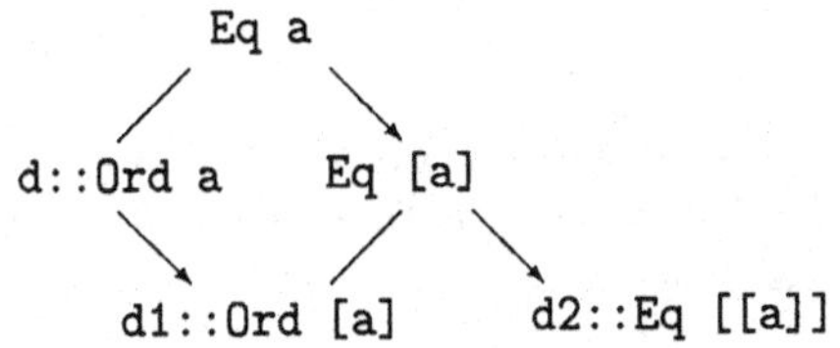

Unfortunately, it is not always possible to arrange for all of the overlapping parts of a dictionary hierarchy to be shared using only the standard form of dictionary constructor functions. To illustrate this, suppose that a program contains the declarations:

```
class Eq a => Demo a where ...
instance Demo a => Demo [a] where ...
```

and suppose that the inferred context for a function `f` is `(Ord [a], Demo [a])`. The corresponding HTC context is `(Ord a, Demo a)` and the translation of `f` will be of the form:

```
f          :: OrdD a -> DemoD a -> ...
f od dd    = let d1 = ordDList od       -- dictionary for Ord [a]
                 d2 = demoDList dd      -- dictionary for Demo [a]
             in
                 ... d1 ... d2 ...
```

where `demoDList` is the dictionary constructor corresponding to the instance declaration for `Demo` given above. Note that the construction of `d1` is completely independent from that of `d2`. Even if we assume that the dictionaries `od` and `dd` share the same superclass dictionary for the instance `Eq a`, the full hierarchy needed still duplicates the dictionary for `Eq [a]` as shown in the following diagram:

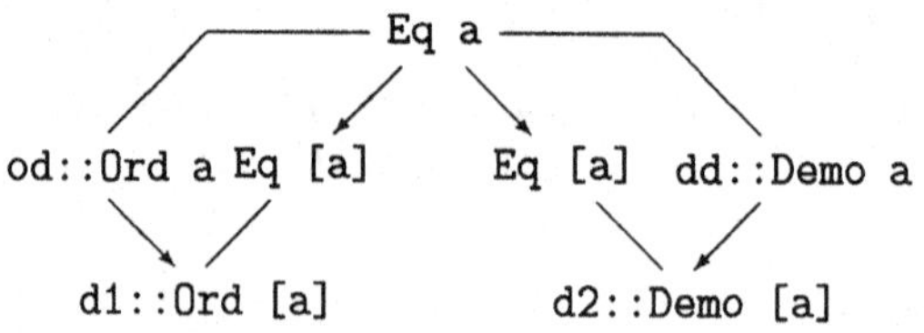

This problem can be solved by applying the same technique to dictionary constructor functions as was used with ordinary functions in Section 7.5.1. Specifically, we provide two 'entry points' for each dictionary constructor, one of which takes additional parameters as required to avoid construction of any auxiliary dictionaries. The appropriate definitions for instances of the form `Ord [a]` are as follows:

```
ordDList        :: OrdD a -> OrdD [a]
ordDList d       = ordDList' d (eqDList (scEqOfOrd d))

ordDList'       :: OrdD a -> EqD [a] -> OrdD [a]
ordDList' d d1 = d2 where d2 = OrdDict (defLessThan d2)
                                       (listLessOrEq d)
                                       ...
                                       ...
                                       d1
```

Note that the definition of `ordDList` is equivalent to the previous definition given in Section 7.2. The dictionary constructors for instances of the form `Demo [a]` are defined in a similar way, with types:

```
demoDList       :: DemoD a -> DemoD [a]
demoDList'      :: DemoD a -> EqD [a] -> DemoD [a]
```

Using these functions, there are a number of ways of defining a translation for `f` which ensures that a single dictionary for `Eq [a]` is shared between the dictionaries for `Ord[a]` and `Demo [a]`, one of which is:

```
f         :: OrdD a -> DemoD a -> ...
f od dd = let d1 = ordDList'  od ed        -- dict for Ord [a]
              d2 = demoDList' dd ed        -- dict for Demo [a]
              ed = eqDList (sqEqOfOrd od) -- dict for Eq [a]
          in
              ... d1 ... d2 ...
```

The collection of dictionaries used in this definition is illustrated by:

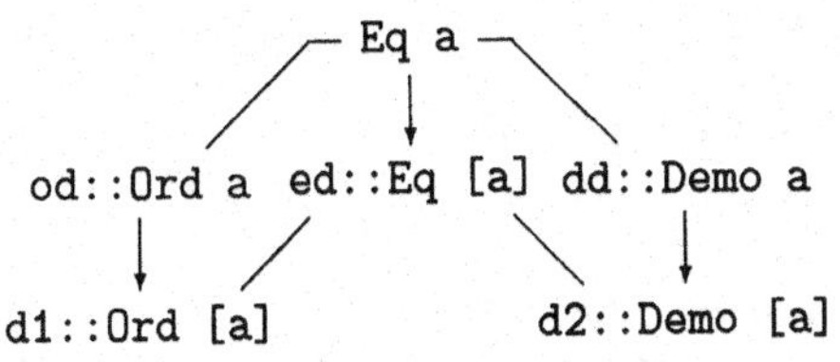

7.5.3 Repetition in superclass hierarchies

A particularly important special case of the kind of problems described in the previous section occurs in the construction of the superclass hierarchy for a given dictionary. To illustrate the basic problem, consider the following simple hierarchy of classes and superclasses, based on an example given in (Wadler and Blott, 1989) to illustrate the use of superclasses.

```
class Top a where
    t :: a -> a

class Top a => Left a where
    l :: a -> a

class Top a => Right a where
    r :: a -> a

class (Left a, Right a) => Bottom a where
    b :: a -> a
```

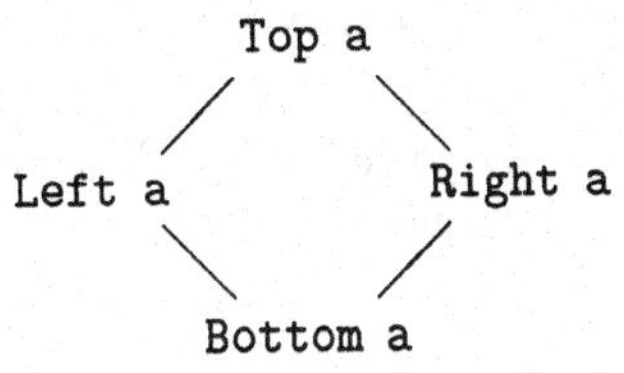

As before, we introduce an representation for the dictionaries of each of these classes, including a collection of superclass selectors.

```
data TopD a    = TopDict    (a -> a)
data LeftD a   = LeftDict   (a -> a) (TopD a)
data RightD a  = RightDict  (a -> a) (TopD a)
data BottomD a = BottomDict (a -> a) (LeftD a) (RightD a)

scTofL (LeftDict   l td)    = td     -- superclass selectors
scTofR (RightDict  r td)    = td
scLofB (BottomDict b ld rd) = ld
scRofB (BottomDict b ld rd) = rd
scTofB                      = scTofL . scLofB
```

For convenience, we have included the selector `scTofB` that returns a dictionary for `Top a` from a dictionary for `Bottom a`. Note that we could have equally well defined this by `scTofB = scTofR . scRofB`, corresponding to a second path between the two dictionaries in the diagram above.

Now suppose that we have a program containing instance declarations of the form `C a => C [a]` for each of the classes `Top`, `Left`, `Right` and `Bottom`. Assuming that the implementations for the member functions in each of these instances are described by functions

`tList`, `lList`, `rList` and `bList` respectively, the corresponding dictionary constructors are:

```
topDList       :: TopD a -> TopD [a]
topDList td     = TopDict (tList td)

leftDList      :: LeftD a -> LeftD [a]
leftDList ld    = LeftDict (lList ld) (topDList (scTofL ld))

rightDList     :: RightD a -> RightD [a]
rightDList rd   = RightDict (rList rd) (topDList (scTofR rd))

bottomDList    :: BottomD a -> BottomD [a]
bottomDList bd = BottomDict (bList bd) (leftDList  (scLofB bd))
                                       (rightDList (scRofB bd))
```

Any attempt to construct a dictionary for an instance of the form `Bottom [a]` using just these functions will require the construction of two distinct dictionaries for `Top [a]`, one as a superclass of the dictionary for `Left [a]` and the other as a superclass of the dictionary for `Right [a]`.

This problem can be solved using the same techniques as in the previous sections; providing a second set of dictionary constructors that use additional parameters to avoid dictionary construction:

```
topDList'               :: TopD a -> TopD [a]
topDList'    td          = TopDict (tList td)

leftDList'              :: LeftD a -> TopD [a] -> LeftD [a]
leftDList'   ld td       = LeftDict (lList ld) td

rightDList'             :: RightD a -> TopD [a] -> RightD [a]
rightDList'  rd td       = RightDict (rList rd) td

bottomDList'            :: BottomD a -> LeftD [a] -> RightD [a]
                               -> BottomD [a]
bottomDList' bd ld rd = BottomDict (bList bd) ld rd
```

Using these functions we can implement the original set of dictionary constructors in such a way that the same dictionary for `Top [a]` is shared between both the `Left` and `Right` superclasses of `Bottom [a]`:

```
topDList           = topDList'
leftDList     ld = leftDList' ld (topDList' (scTofL ld))
rightDList    rd = rightDList' rd (topDList' (scTofR rd))
bottomDList  bd = bottomDList' bd ld rd
                   where rd = rightDList' (scRofB bd) td
                         ld = leftDList'  (scLofB bd) td
                         td = topDList'   (scTofB bd)
```

If the example above seems rather artificial, it is perhaps worth pointing out that the standard prelude in Haskell defines a rather more complicated hierarchy of standard classes:

```
                 Eq                Text
               /    \            /
          Ord          Num
             \       /     \
              Real           Fractional
             /    \         /          \
     Integral        RealFrac           Floating
                            \          /
                              RealFloat
```

Now consider an instance of the form `RealFloat (Complex a)` where `Complex a` is the type of complex numbers where the real and imaginary parts are elements of some numeric type `a` (ranging over those types in the class `RealFloat`). Evaluating the complete dictionary structure for this example without taking the precautions described in this section will result in the construction of seventeen dictionaries (only nine are actually required) including four distinct copies of the dictionary for `Eq (Complex a)`.

7.6 Alternative implementations of dictionary construction

The examples in the previous sections suggest that complex optimisation techniques must be used to minimise the amount of construction (Section 7.4) and duplication (Section 7.5) of dictionaries in an efficient implementation of HTC. This leads us to consider alternative implementations of dictionary construction that limit the impact of these problems even if such optimisations are not used.

One possibility is to implement dictionary constructors as (lazy) memo functions. With this scheme, each dictionary constructor maintains a set of pointers to previously constructed (and possibly only partially evaluated) dictionaries for specific instances that are still present in the heap. The compiled code for a parameterised dictionary code firsts checks the pointer set to see if the dictionary to be constructed has already been allocated in the heap. A previously constructed dictionary is returned if possible, although a new dictionary will be built (and added to the appropriate pointer set) if necessary.

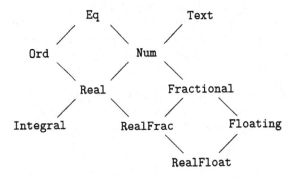

While this would certainly improve the space cost of dictionary construction, it is not at all clear what effect it would have on the time required to 'construct' a single dictionary. Except in the case of very small pointer sets, it is unlikely that searching the pointer set could be implemented more efficiently than a linear sequence of machine instructions to build a dictionary value in the heap.

A number of interesting variations on this scheme can be obtained by modifying the behaviour of the garbage collector:

- As it stands, we would expect the pointer to a given dictionary to be removed from the pointer set when the storage for that dictionary is reclaimed during garbage collection.
- Alternatively, we could arrange to retain all dictionaries during garbage collection, possibly taking the opportunity to move them out of the garbage collected heap altogether. Thus, once a particular dictionary has been constructed, it will remain in storage (even if it is never used again) until the program terminates, and will be shared by every subsequent attempt to construct the same dictionary.
- In an attempt to reduce the cost of examining the pointer set to determine whether a particular dictionary has already been constructed, we might also consider a hybrid of the implementation approaches that have been discussed in which:
  - Dictionaries are initially allocated on the heap without any attempt to detect repeats.
  - At most one copy of any given dictionary is retained during garbage collection.

  This scheme still suffers from many of the defects cited in Section 7.3, but does go some way towards eliminating the costs (in terms of both space and repeated evaluation) of maintaining distinct versions of a single dictionary.

Practical experience is needed to investigate the absolute costs of each of these alternatives, and to determine what (if any) performance gains can be achieved.

Chapter 8

Type classes in Gofer

This chapter describes GTC, an alternative approach to the use of type classes that avoids the problems associated with context reduction, while retaining much of the flexibility of HTC. In addition, GTC benefits from a remarkably clean and efficient implementation that does not require sophisticated compile-time analysis or transformation. As in the previous chapter we concentrate more on implementation details than on formal properties of GTC.

An early description of GTC was distributed to the Haskell mailing list in February 1991 and subsequently used as a basis for Gofer, a small experimental system based on Haskell and described in (Jones, 1991c). The two languages are indeed very close, and many programs that are written with one system in mind can be used with the other with little or no changes. On the other hand, the underlying type systems are slightly different: Using explicit type signature declarations it is possible to construct examples that are well typed in one but not in the other.

Section 8.1 describes the basic principles of GTC and its relationship to HTC. The only significant differences between the two systems are in the methods used to simplify the context part of an inferred type. While HTC relies on the use of context reduction, GTC adopts a weaker form of simplification that does not make use of the information provided in `instance` declarations.

Section 8.2 describes the implementation of dictionaries used in the current version of Gofer. As an alternative to the treatment of dictionaries as tuples of values in the previous chapter, we give a representation which guarantees that the translation of each member function definition requires at most one dictionary parameter. This scheme is not restricted to implementations of GTC and would be equally well-suited to an implementation of HTC.

Finally, Section 8.3 describes the concrete implementation of type class overloading used in the current version of Gofer, including the representation and abstract machine support for dictionary values.

8.1 The basic principles of GTC

Studying the examples in the previous chapter we can identify a simple idea that can be used to avoid the problems of context reduction in many of these cases: The translation of an overloaded function should be parameterised with the dictionaries that will actually be required, rather than some set of dictionaries from which they may be constructed. This is the principal motivation for the development of GTC.

The inferred context of an overloaded function can be simplified by removing duplicates and eliminating predicates that can be obtained from a superclass or for which the overloading required is completely determined (if, for example, the type at which an overloaded function is used is a monotype). The following definitions illustrate each of these techniques:

```
ex1   :: Eq a => a -> Bool   -- inferred context: (Eq a, Eq a)
ex1 x = x==x || x==x

ex2   :: Ord a => a -> Bool  -- inferred context: (Eq a, Ord a)
ex2 x = x==x || x<=x

ex3   :: Int -> Bool         -- inferred context: (Eq Int, Ord Int)
ex3 x = x==4 || x<=2
```

In addition, the process of context reduction in HTC allows the use of instance declarations to replace a given predicate with (zero or more) predicates on simpler types. This is illustrated by the following example:

```
ex4   :: Eq a => a -> Bool   -- inferred context: (Eq [a])
ex4 x = [x]==[x]             -- using HTC
```

Notice that this is exactly the point at which dictionary constructor functions (and hence dictionary construction) are introduced; using the techniques described in the previous section we obtain the translation:

```
ex4    :: EqD a -> a -> Bool
ex4 da = let dla         = eqDList d
             ex4' x = eq dla [x] [x]
         in  ex4'
```

The fact that this requires the construction of a dictionary is hidden. As a result, many implementations will implement the expression `(ex4 0 && ex4 1)` using the translation `(ex4 eqDInt 0 && ex4 eqDInt 1)` which repeats the construction of a dictionary for `Eq [Int]`.

To determine the type of a function using GTC we follow essentially the same process as above except that we do not allow the use of instance declarations to simplify a context where this would require the use of a dictionary constructor function. Thus the types assigned to each of the functions `ex1`, `ex2` and `ex3` using GTC are the same as those given above, but the typing for `ex4` becomes `Eq [a] => a -> Bool` with translation:

```
ex4     :: EqD [a] -> a -> Bool
ex4 d x = eq d [x] [x]
```

It is no longer necessary to arrange for `ex4 d` to be treated as a redex (and indeed, to do so might result in a less efficient implementation since no work can be shared in this way).

Notice that, in contrast with GTC, it is the responsibility of the caller (and not of the function being called) to construct whatever dictionary values are required.

The formal definition of predicate entailment (with respect to a type class environment Γ) in GTC is given by extending the standard rules for predicate entailment with the rule:

$$\frac{P \Vdash d\!:\!\pi' \quad (\mathit{Class}\ Q, \pi, Q' \Rightarrow \pi') \in \Gamma}{P \Vdash (d.\pi)\!:\!\pi}$$

This is the same as the rule (*super*) in Figure 4.2. Note however that we do not include any rule corresponding to (*inst*) and hence the definition of ⊩ does not make use of the information supplied by `instance` declarations. As a result, the dictionary values obtained using this weaker definition of predicate entailment do not involve dictionary construction.

Dictionary constructor functions will only be used to obtain dictionaries for specific (usually monotype) instances of a class. In addition, the construction of these dictionaries can be performed at compile-time or at run-time treating the dictionaries as top-level constants. The formal details of dictionary construction for GTC (including the construction of recursive dictionary structures in Section 8.2.2) will not be described here. The basic principles can be illustrated by considering the expression `[[1,2]]==[[2]]` which has inferred typing `Eq [[Int]] => Bool`, indicating that a dictionary for `Eq [[Int]]` is needed. The expression can then be evaulated using the translation `eq eqDListListInt [[1,2]] [[2]]` with dictionary constants defined by:

```
eqDInt          :: EqD Int          -- dictionary for Eq Int
eqDInt           = ...              -- details as before

eqDListInt      :: EqD [Int]        -- dictionary for Eq [Int]
eqDListInt       = eqDList eqDInt

eqDListListInt  :: EqD [[Int]]      -- dictionary for Eq [[Int]]
eqDListListInt   = eqDList eqDListInt
```

Note that this corresponds very closely to the template-based approach described in Section 6.1.5, except that it works at the level of classes, defining separate dictionaries for each instance rather than individual functions. On the other hand, the code defining the equality on lists is shared between all dictionaries for instances of `Eq` for types of the form `[a]`, avoiding the potential code explosion caused by the naive implementation of the template-based approach.

The fact that the `ex4` function requires the construction of a dictionary is reflected by the predicate `Eq [a]` in its type. In particular applications, to evaluate the expression `(ex4 0 && ex4 1)` for example, we can pass the appropriate dictionary value to `ex4` using the translation `(ex4 eqDListInt 0 && ex4 eqDListInt 1)` and sharing a single copy of the dictionary. On the other hand, if we use `ex4` in a definition such as:

```
ex5  :: Eq [a] => a -> Bool
ex5 x = ex4 x && ex4 x
```

where the required overloading for `ex4` is not fully determined, then the constraint `Eq [a]` in the type of `ex4` is passed onto the callers of `ex5` as reflected by the type signature.

In this way, GTC pushes the process of dictionary construction up through the call tree towards the root which is usually required to have a particular monomorphic type. As we move up the tree, the set of instances of overloaded operators that are actually required in the lower portions of the tree becomes increasingly well-defined so that, by the time we reach the root, the translated program involves only constant dictionaries and all overloading has been resolved.

As a further illustration of the way in which GTC avoids the problem of repeated construction, consider the functions `doToOne` and `doToList` described in Section 7.4.3. The GTC typings for these functions are:

```
doToOne  :: Eq [a] => a -> Bool
doToList :: Eq [a] => [a] -> Bool
```

and the corresponding translations are:

```
doToOne               :: EqD [a] -> a -> Bool
doToOne dla x          = eq dla [x] [x]

doToList              :: EqD [a] -> [a] -> Bool
doToList dla []        = []
doToList dla (x:xs) = doToOne dla x : doToList dla xs
```

Even if these two definitions, neither of which involves the construction of a dictionary, appear in separate modules and are called from a third, there will still be no danger of repeated construction. A transformation to fully-lazy form might still be useful, for example, to avoid the repeated evaluation of `eq dla`, but this is no longer essential for an efficient implementation.

8.2 The Gofer implementation of dictionaries

This section describes an alternative to the representation of dictionaries as fixed-sized tuples of values as used in the description of HTC in the previous chapter. This representation has been used as the basis for the concrete implementation of Gofer described in the next section. Formal properties of the underlying predicate system (such as verification of uniqueness of evidence) will not be addressed here.

8.2.1 A notation for records with subtyping

For convenience we will describe the representation of dictionaries in Gofer using a simple form for record values with implicit subtyping.

Record values will be denoted by expressions of the form:

```
{ l1 = v1, ..., ln = vn }
```

where `l1`, ..., `ln` are distinct labels and `v1`, ..., `vn` are expressions whose values are associated with the corresponding labels in the record. In a similar way, we will write the type of this record as:

```
{ l1 :: t1, ..., ln :: tn }
```

where `t1`, ..., `tn` are the types of the expressions `v1`, ..., `vn` respectively. As before, the order in which the components of a record or record type are listed has no bearing on the value of type denoted. Thus `{x=1, y=2}` and `{y=2, x=1}` represent the same record whose type may be written as either `{x::Int, y::Int}` or `{y::Int, x::Int}`.

For the purposes of this work, we assume that the sets of label and function names used in a particular program are disjoint and we write the operation of record selection (extracting the value associated with label `l` in a record `r`) as `(l r)` rather than `r.l` as used, for example, in Section 2.4.

Following Cardelli (1988), we say that a record type `r` is a *subtype* of another record type `s` if every labelled field in `s` also appears with the same type in `r`. In other words, a value of type `r` can be used in any situation where a value of type `s` is required. For example, `{x::Int, y::Int}` is a subtype of `{x::Int}` and elements of either type can be used as arguments of the function:

```
xPlusOne     :: {x::Int} -> Int
xPlusOne rec = x rec + 1
```

The record type formed by combining all of the fields in a record of type `r` with another of type `s` with disjoint sets of labels will be written `s|r`. Note that `r` is a subtype of `s` if and only if `r` is equivalent to `s|s'` for some `s'`.

8.2.2 Dictionaries as records

As in the representation for dictionaries in HTC, the dictionary value corresponding to a particular instance of a type class must contain implementations for each of the member functions at that instance. In the special case of the class `Eq`, we can describe this by saying that the type of a dictionary for an instance of the form `Eq t` must be a subtype of `EqD t` where:

```
type EqD a = { eq  :: a -> a -> Bool,
               neq :: a -> a -> Bool }
```

Not surprisingly, the default definition for the `(/=)` operator takes the same form as in the implementation of HTC:

```
defNeq         :: EqD a -> (a -> a -> Bool)
defNeq d x y   = not (eq d x y)
```

The dictionaries corresponding for particular instances of `Eq` add additional fields to the record structure of `EqD t`. In the special case of equality on integers, no additional structure is necessary and the following definition suffices:

```
eqDInt          :: EqD Int
eqDInt           = { eq = primEqInt, neq = defNeq eqDInt }
```

In general, the dictionary for a given instance of a class also includes dictionaries for each predicate in the context part of the instance declaration. In the case of equality on lists, any dictionary for an instance of the form `Eq [a]` will also contain a dictionary for `Eq a`:

```
type EqDList a = EqD [a] | { eqa :: EqD a }

eqDList    :: EqD a -> EqDList a
eqDList d   = let d1 = { eq  = eqList d1,
                         neq = defNeq d1,
                         eqa = d }
              in  d1

eqList                     :: EqDList a -> [a] -> [a] -> Bool
eqList d []      []         = True
eqList d []      (y:ys)     = False
eqList d (x:xs)  []         = False
eqList d (x:xs)  (y:ys)     = eq (eqa d) x y  &&  eq d xs ys
```

As a further example, consider the definition of equality on trees described in Section 7.4.4. The correct instance declaration for GTC is as follows:

```
instance (Eq a, Eq [Tree a]) => Eq (Tree a) where
    Node x xs == Node y ys  =  x==y  &&  xs==ys
```

The context part of this declaration is justified by the fact that, in order to compare two trees of type `Tree a`, we need to be able to compare values of type `a` and lists of type `[Tree a]`. The corresponding implementation is given by:

```
type EqDTree a = EqD (Tree a) | { eqa :: EqD a,
                                  eqf :: EqD [Tree a] }

eqDTree      :: EqD a -> EqD [Tree a] -> EqD (Tree a)
eqDTree d df = let d1 = { eq = eqTree d1, neq = defNeq d1,
                          eqa = d, eqf = df }
               in  d1

eqTree       :: EqDTree a -> Tree a -> Tree a -> Bool
eqTree d1 (Node x xs) (Node y ys)
             = eq (eqa d1) x y  &&  eq (eqf d1)
```

To illustrate the use of the dictionary constructors in these examples, the following definitions show how we can obtain dictionary values for a function using an equality test on trees of type `Tree [Int]`:

```
d1 = eqDList d2      :: EqDList (Tree [Int])
d2 = eqDTree d3 d1   :: EqDTree [Int]
d3 = eqDList d4      :: EqDList Int
d4 = eqDInt          :: EqD Int
```

These definitions can be expanded, either at compile-time or run-time, to obtain:

```
d1 = { eq = eqList d1, neq = defNeq d1, eqa = d2 }
d2 = { eq = eqTree d2, neq = defNeq d2, eqa = d3, eqf = d1 }
d3 = { eq = eqList d3, neq = defNeq d3, eqa = d4 }
d4 = { eq = primEqInt, neq = defNeq d4 }
```

Superclasses are implemented in much the same way as before. For example, the type of a dictionary for an instance `Ord t` will be a subtype of `OrdD t` where:

```
type OrdD a = { lt :: a -> a -> Bool,  le :: a -> a -> Bool,
                gt :: a -> a -> Bool,  ge :: a -> a -> Bool,
                mx :: a -> a -> a,     mn :: a -> a -> a,
                sceq :: EqD a }
```

It is interesting to note that the definitions of `eqList` and `eqTree` given above do not appear to follow our general rule that efficient implementations of overloaded functions should be parameterised by the complete set of dictionaries that they require. For example, the definition of `eqList` is parameterised by a dictionary for `Eq [a]`, but there is no longer any need to add another dictionary parameter for `Eq a` since this can be obtained from the `eqa` field of the first dictionary. In a similar way, every function used to implement a member function in a particular class can be given a translation that requires at most one dictionary parameter.

8.2.3 An optimisation to reduce the number of dictionary parameters

As we have described it above, the GTC system does not make use of the information supplied in `instance` declarations to simplify the the context part of an inferred type. In some cases, this may mean that the GTC translation of an expression requires more dictionary parameters than the corresponding HTC translation (the reverse is also true – see the discussion in Section 7.1). As an example, consider the function defined by `f x = x==x && [x]==[x]` that has GTC typing `(Eq a, Eq [a]) => a -> Bool` with a translation requiring two dictionary parameters, while the HTC typing is `Eq a => a -> Bool` and leads to a translation requiring only one parameter.

The current implementation of Gofer takes advantage of the representation for dictionaries described here to support an optimisation that can often reduce the size of contexts in inferred types and hence reduce the number of dictionary parameters needed. To see how this is possible, note that any dictionary `d` for an instance of the form `Eq [a]` contains a dictionary `eqa d` for `Eq a`. Thus the example above can be treated as having type `Eq [a] => a -> Bool` with translation:

```
f       :: EqDList a -> a -> Bool
f dla x = eq (eqa dla) x x && eq dla [x] [x]
```

More generally, the reduction process can be described by extending the definition of predicate entailment with the rule:

$$\frac{P \Vdash \pi \quad (\mathit{Inst}\ P' \Rightarrow \pi) \in \Gamma \quad \pi' \in P'}{P \Vdash \pi'}$$

In retrospect, it is not clear whether this idea should be used since it makes the rules for simplifying contexts somewhat less intuitive and can sometimes break the use of data abstraction in much the same way as context reduction in HTC (Section 7.1). It is likely that this optimisation will not be supported in future versions of Gofer except, perhaps, when the simplified context is specifically requested by an explicit type signature declaration provided by the programmer.

8.3 A concrete implementation

Despite the use of variable size records and subtyping, it is relatively straightforward to obtain an efficient mapping of the implementation described in the previous section onto a conventional machine. This section describes the approach taken in the current implementation of Gofer and highlights some further advantages of the representations chosen for the GTC approach to type classes.

8.3.1 Representation of dictionaries

For each class there is a corresponding record type `ClassD a` whose components are the member functions and super class dictionaries common to all instances of that class. Every dictionary for an instance of this class will have a type of the form `ClassD t|Specifics t` where the record type `Specifics t` contains values determined by the form of the instance declaration used to construct the given dictionary. As a result, every dictionary for an instance of the class can be represented by an array of values with an initial portion corresponding to the type `ClassD t` and a second corresponding to `Specifics t`. There is no need to store the labels for the fields in each record since each label can be associated with a fixed offset in a dictionary of the appropriate subtype of `ClassD t`. Thus the potentially expensive operation of searching for the value of a field in a labelled record can be implemented by a simple array access.

The diagram below illustrates one possible concrete representation for the dictionary values `d1`, `d2`, `d3` and `d4` used in the previous section to give an equality test on trees of type `Tree [Int]`. In each case, the implementations of `(==)` and `(/=)` are held in the first and second positions respectively so that, for any instance `Eq t`, the appropriate definition of either operator can always be extracted from the corresponding position in the dictionary, regardless of the type `t`.

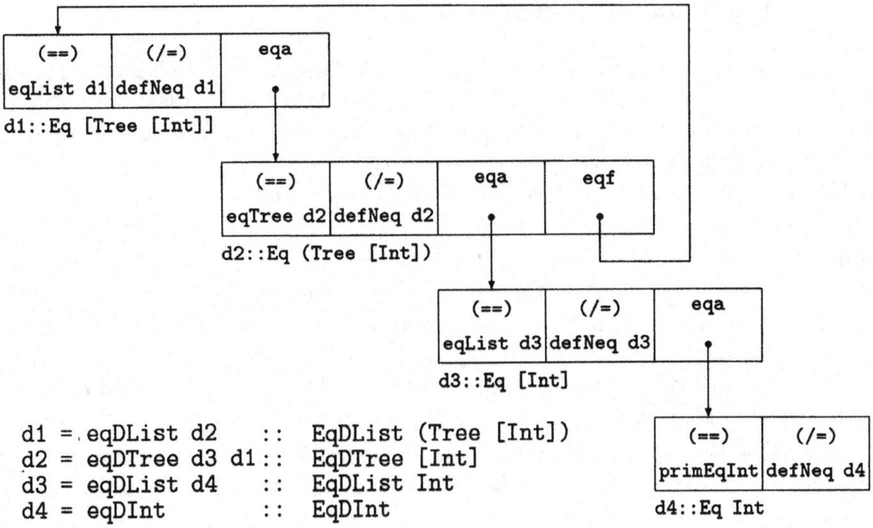


```
d1 = eqDList d2     ::  EqDList (Tree [Int])
d2 = eqDTree d3 d1  ::  EqDTree [Int]
d3 = eqDList d4     ::  EqDList Int
d4 = eqDInt         ::  EqDInt
```

The fact that GTC treats dictionary values as constants whose structure and mutual dependencies can be fully determined at compile-time (or perhaps, in a system with separate compilation, at link time) has a number of useful benefits:

- The complete set of dictionaries required in any given program can be calculated, and a suitable amount of storage can be allocated and initialised at link time. There is no need to store dictionary values within the main garbage collected heap.

- Dictionary constructor functions (such as `eqDList` and `eqDTree`) are replaced by a general dictionary construction mechanism within the compilation system that is used whenever the type inference system can determine that a specific instance of a given class is needed. By implementing this as a memo function along the lines suggested in Section 7.6, we can guarantee that there is at most one dictionary for any given instance of a class and hence avoiding the problems described in Section 7.5. Using this technique, collections of mutually recursive dictionary values such as the example illustrated above can be constructed without any risk of non-termination. The use of memo functions within the compilation system obviously has no impact on the performance of the compiled program.

  A further small, but useful, benefit of this approach is that there is no need to provide a runtime representation for dictionary constructor functions such as `eqDList` and `eqDTree`.

- There is no need for delayed evaluation (using closures for example) of dictionary expressions; each dictionary constant will already be in weak head normal form (in the sense that each of its components may be accessed without further evaluation). In particular, there is no need to check to see if a dictionary value has been evaluated before extracting a value from it, as would typically be expected in a system using lazy evaluation. Note that this only applies to the dictionaries themselves and not to the values that they contain which will still need to be evaluated at runtime in the usual manner.

8.3.2 Abstract machine support

The current implementation of Gofer is based on an abstract machine with a small instruction set, similar in many ways to the Chalmers G-Machine (Augustsson, 1984; Johnsson, 1984), but extended with a single instruction to support GTC overloading. The same basic approach should also be applicable to other families of abstract machine such as TIM (Fairbairn and Wray, 1987) and the Spineless Tagless G-machine (Peyton Jones, 1992).

The Gofer abstract machine evaluates an expression held as a (potentially cyclic) graph, 'unwinding' the spine of the outermost function application, and recording each function argument on a stack. The value at the head of the application points to a set of machine instructions that carry out an appropriate graph rewrite using the values held on the stack. (The stack is also used to record temporary values during each rewrite.) This evaluation process continues until the expression graph has been reduced to the required normal form. See (Peyton Jones, 1987) for further details and background.

To give a flavour of the Gofer abstract machine, the definition of function composition given by `compose f g x = f (g x)` might be compiled to the following sequence of machine instructions:

```
compose: LOAD   argument x ; arguments f, g, x on stack
         LOAD   argument g
         MKAP   1          ; apply g to x
         LOAD   argument f
         MKAP   1          ; apply f to (g x)
         UPDATE root       ; overwrite redex for lazy evaluation
         RETURN
```

The `LOAD` instruction used here pushes a specified value onto the top of the stack and the `MKAP n` instruction replaces the top `n+1` values on the stack by the result of appling the top value to the remaining `n` arguments. A number of additional instructions are used to implement pattern matching, local definitions and certain optimisations, whose description is beyond the scope of this thesis.

Dictionaries and overloading are supported by adding a single instruction, `DICT n`, that replaces the value on the top of the stack (which must be a pointer to a dictionary) with the value stored in the `n`th position of the dictionary. The same instruction can therefore be used to access both class members and superclass or instance specific dictionaries. The type checking process ensures that `DICT` instructions are only executed when the value on the top of the stack is indeed a pointer to a dictionary, in the same way that we normally expect it to ensure that `MKAP` instructions are only ever executed when the value on the top of the stack is a function. For example, the lambda expression `(\x -> x == x)` has type `Eq a => a -> Bool` with translation `(\d x -> eq d x x)`, and compiles to the following code:

```
LOAD   argument x ; second argument to (==)
LOAD   argument x ; first  argument to (==)
LOAD   argument d ; fetch dictionary for Eq a
DICT   1          ; member function in first slot
MKAP   2          ; apply member to args
```

```
UPDATE root
RETURN
```

As a second example, including the use of DICT instructions to access superclass dictionaries, consider the function:

```
f              ::  Eq [a] => a -> a -> [a] -> Bool
f x y xs        =  x==y || xs==[y]
```

which has translation:

```
f              ::  EqDList a -> a -> a -> [a] -> Bool
f dla x y xs    =  eq (eqa dla) x y || eq dla xs [y]
```

The following sequence of instructions gives one possible implementation for this function:

```
CONST  []          ; push constant [] onto stack
LOAD   argument y
CONST  (:)         ; push constant (:) onto stack
MKAP   2           ; NB. [y] abbreviates y : []
LOAD   argument xs
LOAD   argument d  ; fetch dictionary for Eq [a]
DICT   1           ; extract definition of (==)
MKAP   2           ; and apply to xs and [y]
LOAD   argument y
LOAD   argument x
LOAD   argument d  ; fetch dictionary for Eq [a]
DICT   3           ; get subdictionary for Eq a
DICT   1           ; extract definition of (==)
MKAP   2           ; and apply to x and y
CONST  ||
MKAP   2
UPDATE root
RETURN
```

Note that there is no need to provide a runtime representation for member functions and superclass or instance specific dictionary selectors; each of these is implemented using the DICT instruction that can typically be implemented very compactly and efficiently as a single instruction on many conventional machines.

A particularly useful optimisation when generating code that makes use of overloaded functions at specific instances of a class can be described by a simple peephole optimisation. If d is a pointer to a particular fixed dictionary, then the sequence of instructions:

```
CONST d            ; push dictionary onto stack
DICT  m            ; extract mth element
```

is used to access the mth element d[m] of the dictionary pointed to by d. Since type checking (and hence, construction of dictionary values) is completed before code generation, it is possible to determine the value of d[m] and, if it is a constant, replace the instructions above with the single instruction:

```
CONST d[m]          ; push mth element of dictionary d
```

Note that, in the special case where `d[m]` is itself a dictionary, this instruction might in turn be combined with a further `DICT` instruction using the same optimisation. For example, using this technique, the code for `(\n -> n==0)` might be:

```
INT    0           ; push integer constant onto stack
LOAD   argument n
CONST  primEqInt   ; integer equality test
MKAP   2
UPDATE root
RETURN
```

which completely avoids any of the costs of defining `(==)` as an overloaded function.

Optimisations of this kind were described in (Wadler and Blott, 1989; Hammond and Blott, 1989), but it is pleasing to see how easily they can be implemented on the abstract machine described in this section.

8.3.3 Some comments on performance

In an attempt to gain some insight into the costs of GTC overloading using dictionary parameters, the current version of Gofer includes implementations of generic equality and ordering functions of type `a -> a -> Bool` and of monomorphic integer arithmetic functions of type `Int -> Int -> Int` as built-in primitives. Using these functions, we have been able to compare the performance of overloaded programs with the corresponding alternatives using generic or monomorphic functions. In each case, these programs have been run using the same version of the Gofer system (by selecting between different versions of the standard prelude) so that factors such as the performance of the graph reduction engine, memory allocation and garbage collection are common to both.

Whilst more detailed investigation is needed before drawing firm conclusions, our experience so far suggests that the overloaded versions of the programs considered actually run faster and use less memory (by a factor of two in some cases)! The principal reasons for this appear to be:

- There is no need for any run-time type checking with the overloaded version of the program. On the other hand, an attempt to compare two integer values, for example, using the generic equality function must first evaluate both of its arguments and check that they are indeed integer values before the required comparison can be made.
- Evaluation and storage for the values of member functions is shared between all uses of any given dictionary.

This is a very promising result, suggesting that the use and implementation of overloaded functions need not have the significant effect on performance that was anticipated with early implementations of Haskell (Hammond and Blott, 1989). However, further investigation is needed before any firm conclusions can be drawn from these results.

It is also important to make sure that the number of dictionary parameters used in the translations of individual functions, and the number of dictionary constants used in the translations of complete programs are not too large. Our experience with Gofer suggests that neither of these potential problems occurs in practical applications.

Chapter 9

Summary and future work

In this thesis we have developed a general formulation of overloading based on the use of qualified types. Applications of qualified types can be described by choosing an appropriate system of predicates and we have illustrated this with particular examples including Haskell type classes, explicit subtyping and extensible records. We have shown how these ideas can be extended to construct a system that combines ML-style polymorphism and overloading in an implicitly typed programming language. Using the concept of evidence we have extended this work to describe the semantics of overloading in this language, establishing sufficient conditions to guarantee that the meaning of a given term is well-defined. Finally, we have described techniques that can be used to obtain efficient concrete implementations of systems based on this framework.

From a theoretical perspective, some of the main contributions of this thesis are:

- The formulation of a general purpose system that can be used to describe a number of different applications of overloading.
- The extension of standard results, for example the existence of principal types, to the type system of OML.
- A new approach to the proof of coherence, based on the use of conversions.

From a practical perspective, we mention:

- The implementation of overloading using the template-based approach, and the closely related implementation of type class overloading in Gofer.
- A new implementation for extensible records, based on the use of evidence.
- The use of information about satisfiability of predicate sets to obtain more informative inferred types.

Throughout this thesis we have concentrated on the use of polymorphism and qualified types in implicitly typed, purely functional languages using extensions of Milner's framework. Nevertheless, the basic features of qualified types can also be incorporated in other type systems – for example, in explicitly typed polymorphic λ-calculus as illustrated in (Jones, 1992a). The same techniques should, in principle, extend to other kinds of language although we have not attempted to investigate this here.

The following sections describe three additional areas for further study, outlining some preliminary ideas in each case.

9.1 Towards a categorical semantics

This section sketches a simple categorical semantics for a version of simply typed λ-calculus that supports qualified types but not polymorphism. It is hoped that the ideas described here will serve as a useful starting point for future work, to extend the semantics to include polymorphism and generalise the coherence results in Chapter 5 to a wider class of semantic models.

We write $S \times T$ for the product of two objects S and T and $\mathit{fst}: S \times T \to S$ and $\mathit{snd}: S \times T \to T$ for the first and second projects respectively. The universal property for products ensures that, for any $f : X \to S$ and $g : X \to T$, there is a unique arrow $\langle f, g\rangle : X \to S \times T$ such that $\mathit{fst} \cdot \langle f, g\rangle = f$ and $\mathit{snd} \cdot \langle f, g\rangle = g$. In particular, for any pair of arrows $f : X \to S$ and $g : Y \to T$, there is a unique arrow $(f \times g) = \langle f \cdot \mathit{fst}, g \cdot \mathit{snd}\rangle : X \times Y \to S \times T$ such that: $f \cdot \mathit{fst} = \mathit{fst} \cdot (f \times g)$ and $g \cdot \mathit{snd} = \mathit{snd} \cdot (f \times g)$.

Definition 9.1 *A categorical model of a predicate system consists of a category* Pred *with a terminal object* $\emptyset$ *and binary product* $(\_,\_)$ *whose objects and arrows represent predicates (or predicate assignments) and entailments respectively.*

Entailments of the form $v : P \Vdash e : Q$ are described by arrows $P \xrightarrow{e} Q$ and the basic rules of predicate entailment are summarised in the right hand column of Figure 9.1 with the corresponding rules from Figure 4.1 on the left. A full treatment would require a notion

(id)	$v : P \Vdash v : P$	$P \xrightarrow{id} P$
$(term)$	$v : P \Vdash \emptyset$	$P \xrightarrow{term} \emptyset$
(fst)	$v : P, w : Q \Vdash v : P$	$P, Q \xrightarrow{fst} P$
(snd)	$v : P, w : Q \Vdash w : Q$	$P, Q \xrightarrow{snd} Q$
$(univ)$	$\dfrac{v : P \Vdash e : Q \quad v : P \Vdash f : R}{v : P \Vdash e : Q, f : R}$	$\dfrac{P \xrightarrow{e} Q \quad P \xrightarrow{f} R}{P \xrightarrow{\langle e,f\rangle} Q, R}$
$(trans)$	$\dfrac{v : P \Vdash e : Q \quad w : Q \Vdash f : R}{v : P \Vdash [e/w]f : R}$	$\dfrac{P \xrightarrow{e} Q \quad Q \xrightarrow{f} R}{P \xrightarrow{e} Q \xrightarrow{f} R}$

Figure 9.1: Categorical interpretation of predicate entailment.

of substitution on objects of Pred but we do not consider this here and hence there is no rule corresponding to $(close)$. More significantly, since the categorical form of predicate entailments is variable-free there is no need to include rules corresponding to $(evars)$ and $(rename)$.

Definition 9.2 *A categorical model of simply typed λ-calculus with qualified types consists of:*

- *A predicate system* Pred *as in Definition 9.1.*
- *A cartesian closed category* C *such that any objects A and B have a product $A \times B$, an exponential $[A \to B]$ and an arrow $eval : [A \to B] \times A \to B$. The adjoint transpose of an arrow $f : C \times A \to B$ is written $\lambda f : C \to [A \to B]$ and is the unique arrow with the property that $f = eval \cdot (\lambda f \times id)$.*
- *A functor $\mathcal{E}$:* Pred $\to$ C *mapping predicates to evidence values that preserves terminals and finite products (in particular, we require $\mathcal{E}(P, Q) \cong \mathcal{E}P \times \mathcal{E}Q$). For any entailment $P \xrightarrow{e} Q$, the arrow $\mathcal{E}P \xrightarrow{\mathcal{E}e} \mathcal{E}Q$ should be uniquely determined by P and Q alone to guarantee 'uniqueness of evidence'.*

Each typing judgement $P \,|\, A \vdash E : \tau$ corresponds to an arrow $\mathcal{E}P \times A \xrightarrow{E} T$. The complete set of typing rules are given in Figure 9.2, again with the categorical semantics in the right hand column and the corresponding typing rule on the left.

The task of establishing coherence is equivalent to showing that any two arrows $\mathcal{E}P \times A \xrightarrow{E} T$ and $\mathcal{E}P \times A \xrightarrow{E'} T$ such that $Erase(E) = Erase(E')$ are equal. This corresponds very closely to a standard notion of coherence in category theory. For example, MacLane (1971) refers to a coherence theorem as an assertion that 'every diagram (of a certain class) commutes'.

9.2 Constructor classes

Throughout this thesis we have used predicates on types to assign types to overloaded values and we have seen many examples where this is useful. On the other hand, there are some examples where an apparently natural application of overloading that cannot be described in a convenient manner in this way. This section describes an extension that allows the use of predicates on a language of type constructors, including types as a special case, resulting in a much more flexible system.

As an example, consider the standard `map` function used to apply a function to each of the elements of a given list. Using the definition given in the Haskell standard prelude (Hudak et al., 1992), this function has type `(a -> b) -> ([a] -> [b])` and satisfies the familiar laws:

```
map f . map g  =  map (f . g)
map id         =  id
```

In categorical terms, this shows that there is a *functor* from types to types whose object part maps any given type `a` to the list type `[a]` and whose arrow part maps each function `f :: a -> b` to the function `map f :: [a] -> [b]`. Similar constructions are used with a wide range of other datatypes. For example:

```
data  Tree a  =  Leaf a  |  Tree a :^: Tree a
```

$$P \mid A, x{:}\tau \vdash x : \tau \qquad \mathcal{E}P \times (A \times T) \xrightarrow{snd \cdot snd} T$$

$$\frac{P \mid A \vdash x : \tau}{P \mid A, y{:}\tau' \vdash x : \tau} \qquad \frac{\mathcal{E}P \times A \xrightarrow{x} T}{\mathcal{E}P \times (A \times T) \xrightarrow{id \times fst} \mathcal{E}P \times A \xrightarrow{x} T}$$

$$\frac{P \mid A \vdash E : \tau' \to \tau \quad P \mid A \vdash F : \tau'}{P \mid A \vdash EF : \tau} \qquad \frac{\mathcal{E}P \times A \xrightarrow{E} [T' \to T] \quad \mathcal{E}P \times A \xrightarrow{F} T'}{\mathcal{E}P \times A \xrightarrow{\langle E,F \rangle} [T' \to T] \times T' \xrightarrow{eval} T}$$

$$\frac{P \mid A, x{:}\tau' \vdash E : \tau}{P \mid A \vdash \lambda x.E : \tau' \to \tau} \qquad \frac{\mathcal{E}P \times (A \times T') \xrightarrow{E} T}{\mathcal{E}P \times A \xrightarrow{\lambda(E \cdot s)} [T' \to T]}$$

where $s{:}(A \times B) \times C \cong A \times (B \times C)$

$$\frac{P \mid A \vdash E : Q \Rightarrow \rho \quad P \Vdash e{:}Q}{P \mid A \vdash Ee : \rho} \qquad \frac{\mathcal{E}P \times A \xrightarrow{E} [\mathcal{E}Q \to R] \quad P \xrightarrow{e} Q}{\mathcal{E}P \times A \xrightarrow{\langle E, \mathcal{E}e \cdot fst \rangle} [\mathcal{E}Q \to R] \times \mathcal{E}Q \xrightarrow{eval} R}$$

$$\frac{P, v{:}Q \mid A \vdash E : \rho}{P \mid A \vdash \lambda v.E : Q \Rightarrow \rho} \qquad \frac{\mathcal{E}(P,Q) \times A \xrightarrow{E} R}{\mathcal{E}P \times A \xrightarrow{\lambda(E \cdot r)} [\mathcal{E}Q \to R]}$$

where $r{:}(\mathcal{E}P \times A) \times \mathcal{E}Q \cong \mathcal{E}(P,Q) \times A$

Figure 9.2: Categorical semantics for qualified types

```
mapTree                 :: (a -> b) -> (Tree a -> Tree b)
mapTree f (Leaf x)      = Leaf (f x)
mapTree f (l :^: r)     = mapTree f l :^: mapTree f r
```

The `mapTree` function has a similar type to that of `map` and also satisfies the functor laws given above. With this in mind, it seems a shame that we have to use different names for each of these variants. A more attractive solution would allow the use of a single name, relying on the types of the objects involved to determine which particular version of `map` is required in any given situation.

It is rather difficult to give a satisfactory definition of `map` using the system of type classes. A much better approach is to notice that each of the types for which the `map` function is required is of the form `(a -> b) -> (f a -> f b)` where `a` and `b` are arbitrary types and `f` ranges over a set of type constructors that includes the list constructor (writing `List a` as an abbreviation for `[a]`) and `Tree`:

```
class Functor f where map :: (a -> b) -> (f a -> f b)

instance Functor List where
    map f []     = []
    map f (x:xs) = f x : map f xs

instance Functor Tree where
    map f (Leaf x)  = Leaf (f x)
    map f (l :^: r) = map f l :^: map f r
```

`Functor` is a simple example of a constructor class. One of the most important properties that we need to guarantee is that all of the instances of a particular class have the same kind. We formalise this idea, writing $*$ for the kind of all types and $\kappa_1 \to \kappa_2$ for the kind of a function that takes something of kind κ_1 and returns something of kind κ_2. Similar systems of kinds have been used in other applications – for example in (Bruce et al. 1990) and (Barendregt, 1991). Note that our system includes Haskell type classes as a special case; a type class is simply a constructor class for which each instance has kind $*$.

The elements of each constructor class are written using constructor expressions of the form:

$$\begin{array}{rcll} C & ::= & \chi & \textit{constants} \\ & | & a & \textit{variables} \\ & | & C\ C' & \textit{applications} \end{array}$$

Note that this does not include a `List` and `Tree` have kind $* \to *$. The kinds of constructor applications can be obtained using the rule:

$$\frac{C :: \kappa' \to \kappa \qquad C' :: \kappa'}{C\ C' :: \kappa}$$

The task of checking that a given type expression is well-formed can now be reformulated as the task of checking that a given constructor expression is well-kinded with kind $*$. Standard techniques can be used to implement *kind inference* so that there is no need for the programmer to specify the kinds of constructor variables.

The type inference algorithm, existence of principal types and coherence criteria in Chapter 5 can be extended to deal with a system of constructor classes based on the ideas outlined here. Constructor classes appear to have many applications, including a flexible treatment of monadic programming as described by Wadler (1992) based on the use of overloading. A preliminary version of this framework has been implemented as an extension of the Gofer system, including the first concrete implementation of monad comprehensions (Wadler, 1990) known to us at the time of writing. Further details may be found in (Jones, 1992b) and we hope to expand on this work in a subsequent paper.

9.3 Reasoning in the presence of overloading

One of the most attractive features of purely functional programming languages is the opportunity to use equational reasoning in program development and transformation (Bird and Wadler, 1989). Equational reasoning in the presence of overloading is much more difficult since it may not always be clear which particular definition of a symbol is intended in a given situation. For example, in a system of type classes, it is not possible to place any semantic restriction on the definitions given in any particular instance other than ensuring that they yield values of the correct types. Furthermore, in the development of a large program, the instance declarations used to construct the definition of a single overloaded operator may be distributed across a number of separate program modules. This makes it very difficult for a programmer to know what properties can be assumed about overloaded functions.

Following suggestions made in (Wadler and Blott, 1989), one approach to this problem is to adopt a programming methodology in which:

- Each class declaration is accompanied by a number of algebraic laws constraining the values of its member functions.
- Each instance declaration is accompanied by a proof of the laws in the particular instance being defined.

Such laws can of course be written as program comments, but it might be preferable to extend the syntax of the language with a concrete syntax for laws:

- Programmers would be encouraged to state laws formally using a uniform syntax, rather than a variety of ad-hoc annotations.
- The type checker can be used to ensure that the laws given are type correct, and hence detect some meaningless or erroneous laws.
- It is unlikely that the proofs for each law could be constructed automatically for each instance declaration. On the other hand, machine readable laws in a given program might well be used in conjunction with an automated proof checker or with machine assisted tools for program derivation and proof.

The following example illustrates one possible syntax for writing the functor laws mentioned in the previous section:

$$\begin{array}{lcl} MapCompose & :: & Functor\ f \Rightarrow (b \rightarrow c) \rightarrow (a \rightarrow b) \rightarrow Law\ (f\ a \rightarrow f\ c) \\ MapCompose\ f\ g & \Rightarrow & map\ f\ .\ map\ g = map\ (f\ .\ g) \end{array}$$

$$\begin{array}{lcl} MapId & :: & Functor\ f \Rightarrow Law\ (f\ a \rightarrow f\ a) \\ MapId & \Rightarrow & map\ id = id \end{array}$$

This notation is particularly attractive since it allows each law to be named (for reference in a proof), enables us to specify the free variables explicitly and to indicate the expected type for each variable and for the values on either side of the law. In practice, it should be possible to obtain appropriate typings using the type inference mechanism, without requiring explicit declarations.

Unfortunately, the task of choosing an appropriate collection of laws may not always be so easy. For example, the law:

$$\begin{array}{lcl} EqReflexive & :: & Eq\ a \Rightarrow a \rightarrow Law\ Bool \\ EqReflexive\ x & \Rightarrow & (x == x) = True \end{array}$$

Chapter 10

Epilogue

One of the main goals in preparing this book for publication was to preserve the thesis, as much as possible, in the form that it was originally submitted. With this in mind, we have restricted ourselves to making only very minor changes to the body of the thesis, for example, correcting typographical errors.

On the other hand, we have continued to work with the ideas presented here, to find new applications and to investigate some of the areas identified as topics for further research. In this short chapter, we comment briefly on some examples of this, illustrating both the progress that has been made and some of the new opportunities for further work that have been exposed.

We should emphasize once again that this is the only chapter that was not included as part of the original thesis.

10.1 Constructor classes

The initial ideas for a system of constructor classes as sketched in Section 9.2 have been developed in (Jones, 1993b), and full support for these ideas is now included in the standard Gofer distribution (versions 2.28 and later). The two main technical extensions in the system of constructor classes to the work described here are:

- The use of kind inference to determine suitable kinds for all the user-defined type constructors appearing in a given program.
- The extension of the unification algorithm to ensure that it calculates only *kind-preserving substitutions*. This is necessary to ensure soundness and is dealt with by ensuring that constructor variables are only ever bound to constructors of the corresponding kind. Fortunately, this has a very simple and efficient implementation.

From a practical point of view, the inclusion of constructor classes in Gofer has proved to be quite popular. In addition, constructor classes have provided a useful tool for other work, for example, in the investigation of monad composition (Jones and Duponcheel, 1993).

One weakness of the current system is its inability to deal with subkinds. For example, a `Set` datatype, implemented using lists of elements with no repeated members, might be assigned a kind indicating that it can only be applied to types on which an equality has been defined. This is necessary, for example, to define a satisfactory instance of the `Functor` class for the `Set` constructor. Predicates provide an obvious way to capture this restriction, assigning `Set` a *qualified kind* of the form $\forall\kappa.(Eq\ \kappa) \Rightarrow \kappa \rightarrow *$. Note that $Eq\ \kappa$ is interpreted as meaning that $\kappa \subseteq Eq$, in contrast with a predicate of the form $Eq\ \tau$ in a type expression, indicating that $\tau \in Eq$. However, it is clear that the introduction of polymorphic kinds and subkinding adds a significant amount of complexity to the kind system, and we do not know what effect this might have on its theoretical properties, or on the performance of concrete implementations.

10.2 Template based implementations

In Section 6.1.5, we outlined an implementation of qualified type overloading that avoids passing evidence parameters at run-time by generating multiple versions of overloaded functions, each specialized for particular evidence values. While promising, we also noted some potential problems with this approach, such as the risk of code-explosion. In addition, the creation of different versions of overloaded functions was described by extending and complicating the type inference algorithm. This would also have required a reworking of some of the important results in the thesis.

Subsequently, it was realized that the same basic idea could be described more elegantly by combining the standard type checking algorithm with a *partial evaluator*. Broadly speaking, a partial evaluator attempts to produce an optimized version of a program by distinguishing static data (known at compile-time) from dynamic data (which is not known until run-time). This process is often split into two stages:

- **Binding-time analysis**: to find (a safe approximation of) the set of expressions in a program that can be calculated at compile-time, and add suitable annotations to the source program.
- **Specialization**: to calculate a specialized version of the program using the binding-time annotations as a guide.

For the purposes of a template-based implementation, all of the the binding-time information that is needed can be obtained from the translation of an input term. Specifically, evidence abstractions and applications should be reduced at compile-time, while standard value abstractions and applications are delayed until run-time. In fact, using a general partial evaluation system, we could use this information as a supplement to the results of a standard binding-time analysis to obtain some of the other benefits of partial evaluation. Thus the combination of the standard type inference algorithm and a general partial evaluator is both more modular and more powerful than our original treatment of template-based implementations.

To experiment with these techniques in a concrete setting, we have modified a version of the Gofer compiler to include a very simple partial evaluator that uses specialization to avoid the use of dictionary values at run-time. This is described more fully in (Jones, 1993a). To our surprise, we found that, rather than a code-explosion, this simple form of specialization actually reduces the size of compiled programs for all of the cases that we tried, including some fairly large examples! The main reason for this appears to be that it is much easier to identify redundant program code and dictionary components in the specialized version of a program. Eliminating these items can significantly reduce the size of compiled programs.

One remaining problem with this approach is the interaction between full separate compilation and specialization; the demand for a specialized version of a function may not appear in the same program module as the definition of that function. The same problem occurs more generally with partial evaluation across module boundaries, and we can expect to see more work in this area in the future.

10.3 Making use of satisfiability

In Section 6.2, we hinted at the possible uses of information about satisfiability of predicate sets to improve the accuracy of inferred types. In recent work (Jones, 1994b), we have investigated one particular approach to this based on the use of a rule for *improvement* of inferred types:

$$\frac{Q \mid TA \overset{W}{\vdash} E : \nu \quad T' = \mathit{impr}\ Q}{T'Q \mid T'TA \overset{W}{\vdash} E : T'\nu}$$

We refer to the function *impr* used here as an *improving* function. The most important property of any improving function is that, if $T' = \mathit{impr}\ Q$, then the set of satisfiable instances of Q must be the same as the set of satisfiable instances of $T'Q$. It is always possible to define an improving function by returning the identity substitution *id* for any given predicate set Q. Clearly, this gives exactly the same results as the version of the type inference algorithm described in Chapter 3. More interesting results can be obtained by using an improving function that satisfies, for example, the following equations:

$$\begin{array}{lcll} \mathit{impr}\ \{\, r\ \mathsf{has}\ l\!:a,\ r\ \mathsf{has}\ l\!:b\,\} & = & [a/b] & \\ \mathit{impr}\ \{\, \mathit{Comp}\ \mathit{Bool}\ a\,\} & = & [\mathit{Bool}/a] & \\ \mathit{impr}\ \{\, a \subseteq (b \to c)\,\} & = & [(d \to e)/a], & d \text{ and } e \text{ new.} \end{array}$$

Note that the first two equations here provide a satisfactory solution to the two problems described in Section 6.2. Combined with the simplification rule described in Section 6.1.1, the use of improving functions seems like a promising way to obtain more accurate and informative inferred types.

It is also worth mentioning that improving functions can be used to capture the essence of the system of parametric type classes described in (Chen, Hudak and Odersky, 1992). For example, if we use a predicate of the form $a \in \mathit{Collect}(b)$ to indicate that values of type a can be used to represent collections of values of type b, then we might use an improving function satisfying:

$$\begin{array}{lcl} \mathit{impr}\ \{\, a \in \mathit{Collect}(b),\ a \in \mathit{Collect}(c)\,\} & = & [c/b] \\ \mathit{impr}\ \{\, [a] \in \mathit{Collect}(b)\,\} & = & [a/b] \end{array}$$

The first of these expresses our intention that, if values of type a represent collections both of type b and of type c, then these two types must in fact be equal. The second is almost a special case, assuming that we have previously defined an instance for $[a] \in \mathit{Collect}(a)$, in which case, if $[a] \in \mathit{Collect}(b)$, then we must have $b = c$.

Up to this point, we have only considered situations where the improving function is built in to a particular application of qualified types. It may also be possible to allow the definition of the improving function to be extended directly by the programmer, although this would have to be very carefully controlled to maintain decidability of type inference.

10.4 ML typing, explicit polymorphism and qualified types

The ML type system was originally introduced as a means of identifying a class of terms in a simple untyped language, often referred to as core-ML, whose evaluation could be guaranteed not to "go wrong". In subsequent work, the terms of core-ML have also been viewed as a 'convenient shorthand' for programs in typed languages. For example, Harper and Mitchell (Harper and Mitchell, 1993) have presented a semantics for ML polymorphism using core-XML, an explicitly typed version of core-ML that includes constructs for type abstraction and application, similar to those in the polymorphic λ-calculus.

In fact, it turns out that the view of core-ML as a shorthand for core-XML does not quite work out because a single core-ML may have semantically distinct translations. Of course, this is just the issue of coherence, dealt with in Chapter 5! Motivated by this insight, we have used a system of qualified types to study the relationship between core-ML and core-XML (Jones, 1994a). For this particular application, we use types themselves as predicates with a definition of entailment corresponding to the usual rules for the construction of well-formed type expressions. As a result, we have been able to use the coherence properties developed in this thesis to establish coherence conditions for the translation from core-ML to core-XML.

By viewing this translation as an application of qualified types we have been able to combine the results of previous work in each of these areas, recognizing related concepts such as the importance of coherence, and also the similarity between Leroy's proposals for polymorphism by name (Leroy, 1993), Wright's value restriction (Wright, 1993) and the monomorphism restriction in Haskell. We expect that the same unified view will also bring several other benefits and useful insights in future work.

10.5 The use of subsumption

At the time this thesis was written, it was assumed that a full treatment of subtyping with implicit coercions could only be obtained by extending the framework for qualified types to include the rule of *subsumption* (see Section 6.3):

$$\frac{P\,|\,A \vdash E : \tau' \quad P \Vdash \tau' \subseteq \tau}{P\,|\,A \vdash E : \tau}$$

Without doubt, this requires substantial changes to the results presented in the thesis, not least because it adds significant complexity to the treatment of syntax-directed typing rules.

In fact, it has now been realized that implicit coercions can be handled in the current framework by preprocessing input terms for the type inference algorithm and inserting calls to a predefined generic coercion function:

$$coerce :: \forall a.\forall b.a \subseteq b \Rightarrow a \to b.$$

For example, writing $[E]$ for the translation of a term E that is produced by the preprocessor, one simple approach would be to define:

$$\begin{array}{lcl} [x] & = & coerce\ x \\ [E\ E'] & = & (coerce\ [E])\ (coerce\ [E']) \\ & \vdots & \end{array}$$

The effect of this is to allow implicit coercions to be applied independently to each subterm in a given program; of course this is exactly what the rule of subsumption allows us to do. In fact, there are other ways to define the action of the preprocessor to reduce the use of coercions. For example:

$$[E\ E'] \quad = \quad coerce\ [E]\ [E']$$

This is possible because the coercion of the argument E' can be incorporated with the coercion of the function E. As a more complicated example, we can omit the coercion of the variable x in an abstraction $\lambda x.E$ if x has at most one occurrence in E, since a suitable coercion can be used when the abstraction is applied to a particular argument. This would be particularly useful in an expression of the form **let** $f = \lambda x.E$ **in** F since it would avoid the need for an unnecessary evidence parameter in the corresponding translation as described in Section 6.1.

Finally, we should mention that, although this approach allows us to use to the framework developed in this thesis for a system with implicit coercions, this does not eliminate the most difficult task in dealing with such a system—the task of simplifying a predicate set to detect unsatisfiable constraints and to minimize the use of coercions. For these problems we must still draw on the work of other researchers cited in Section 6.3.

Appendix A

Proofs

his appendix contains detailed proofs for many of the results given in the body of this thesis, particularly for those in Chapter 5. Most of these are direct extensions of the results described in Chapter 3 and proofs for the latter may be obtained from the proofs given here by ignoring the use of translations, equalities between terms and conversions. For convenience, we repeat the statement of each result in a box at the beginning of the corresponding proof.

> **Proposition 3.4** *Suppose that $\sigma = \forall\alpha_i.Q \Rightarrow \nu$, $\sigma' = \forall\beta_j.Q' \Rightarrow \nu'$ and that none of the variables β_j appears free in σ, P or P'. Then $(P' \mid \sigma') \leq (P \mid \sigma)$ if and only if there are types τ_i such that:*
>
> $$\nu' = [\tau_i/\alpha_i]\nu \quad \textit{and} \quad P', Q' \Vdash P, [\tau_i/\alpha_i]Q.$$

Suppose that $(P' \mid \sigma') \leq (P \mid \sigma)$. Clearly $(Q' \Rightarrow \nu') \leq \sigma'$ and hence $(P', Q' \Rightarrow \nu') \leq (P \mid \sigma)$ by transitivity of $\leq$. It follows that there are types τ_i such that:

$$\nu' = [\tau_i/\alpha_i]\nu \quad \text{and} \quad P', Q' \Vdash P, [\tau_i/\alpha_i]Q.$$

For the converse, suppose that $\nu' = [\tau_i/\alpha_i]\nu$, $P', Q' \Vdash P, [\tau_i/\alpha_i]Q$ and $R \Rightarrow \mu \leq (P' \mid \sigma')$. Then there are types τ_j' such that

$$\mu = [\tau_j'/\beta_j]\nu' \quad \text{and} \quad R \Vdash P', [\tau_j'/\alpha_j']Q'$$

and hence:

$$\mu = [\tau_j'/\beta_j]\nu' = [\tau_j'/\beta_j]([\tau_i/\alpha_i]\nu) = [\nu_i/\alpha_i]\nu$$

where $\nu_i = [\tau_j'/\beta_j]\tau_i$ and the last step above is justified by the hypothesis that none of β_j is free in σ.

In a similar way, using the transitivity of $\Vdash$:

$$\begin{array}{rlll} R & \Vdash & P', [\tau_j'/\beta_j]Q' & \\ & = & [\tau_j'/\beta_j](P', Q') & \text{(none of } \beta_j \text{ free in } P'\text{)} \\ & \Vdash & [\tau_j'/\beta_j](P, [\tau_i/\alpha_i]Q) & \text{(closure property)} \\ & = & P, [\tau_j'/\beta_j]([\tau_i/\alpha_i]Q) & \text{(none of } \beta_j \text{ free in } P\text{)} \\ & = & P, [\nu_i/\alpha_i]Q & \text{(none of } \beta_j \text{ free in } Q\text{)} \end{array}$$

It follows that $R \Rightarrow \mu \leq (P \,|\, \sigma)$ and hence (since $R \Rightarrow \mu$ was arbitrary) that $(P' \,|\, \sigma') \leq (P \,|\, \sigma)$. □

Proposition 5.6 *Suppose that σ, σ' and σ'' are type schemes. Then:*

1. *$id : \sigma \geq \sigma$ where $id = \lambda x.x$ is the identity term.*
2. *If $C : \sigma \geq \sigma'$ and $C' : \sigma' \geq \sigma''$, then $C' \circ C : \sigma \geq \sigma''$ where $C' \circ C = \lambda x.C'(Cx)$.*
3. *If σ is a type scheme and τ is a type, then $id : \forall t.\sigma \geq [\tau/t]\sigma$. In particular, $id : Gen(A, \rho) \geq \rho$.*

The first and second parts are straightforward (the second being a special case of Proposition 5.13) and we omit their proofs here.
For the third part, suppose that $\sigma = \forall \alpha_i.Q \Rightarrow \nu$. If $t \notin TV(\sigma)$, then $\forall t.\sigma = \sigma = [\tau/t]\sigma$ and the result is immediate from the first part. We can therefore assume that $t \in TV(\sigma)$ (and hence that $t \notin \{\alpha_i\}$). Pick new variables β_i and let $S = [\beta_i/\alpha_i]$. Then

$$[\tau/t]\sigma = [\tau/t](\forall \alpha_i.Q \Rightarrow \nu) = [\tau/t](\forall \beta_i.SQ \Rightarrow S\nu) = \forall \beta_i.(S'Q \Rightarrow S'\nu)$$

where $S' = S[\tau/t] = [\tau/t, \beta_i/\alpha_i]$. Clearly none of β_i appear free in $\forall t.\sigma$ and the entailment $w : S'Q \Vdash w : S'Q$ follows by (id). Hence $\lambda x.\lambda w.xw$ is a conversion for $\forall t.\sigma \geq [\tau/t]\sigma$ which, using (η_e), is equivalent to $id = \lambda x.x$. □

Proposition 5.7 *Suppose that P and P' are predicate sets such that $v' : P' \Vdash e : P$. Then:*

$$(\lambda x.\lambda v'.xe) : Gen(A, P \Rightarrow \tau) \geq Gen(A, P' \Rightarrow \tau)$$

for any type assignment A and type τ.

Write $Gen(A, P \Rightarrow \tau) = (\forall \alpha_i.P \Rightarrow \tau)$ and $Gen(A, P' \Rightarrow \tau) = (\forall \beta_j.P' \Rightarrow \tau')$ where $\{\alpha_i\} = TV(P \Rightarrow \tau) \setminus TV(A)$ and $\{\beta_j\} = TV(P' \Rightarrow \tau) \setminus TV(A)$. Clearly none of β_j appears free in $Gen(A, P \Rightarrow \tau)$. Furthermore:

$$\tau = [\alpha_i/\alpha_i]\tau \quad \text{and} \quad v' : P' \Vdash e' : [\alpha_i/\alpha_i]P'$$

and hence

$$(\lambda x.\lambda v'.xe) : Gen(A, P \Rightarrow \tau) \geq Gen(A, P' \Rightarrow \tau)$$

as required. □

Proposition 5.8 *If A is a type assignment, ρ is a qualified type and S is a substitution, then:*

$$id : SGen(A, \rho) \geq Gen(SA, S\rho).$$

Furthermore, there is a substitution R such that:

$$RA = SA \quad \text{and} \quad SGen(A, \rho) = Gen(RA, R\rho).$$

First part: Let S be a substitution, $\{\alpha_i\} = TV(\rho) \setminus TV(A)$ and choose new variables γ_i not involved in S so that:

$$SGen(A, \rho) = \forall \gamma_i . S[\gamma_i/\alpha_i](\rho) = \forall \gamma_i . R\rho$$

where $R = S[\gamma_i/\alpha_i]$. Similarly, writing $\{\beta_j\} = TV(S\rho) \setminus TV(SA)$ we have:

$$Gen(SA, S\rho) = \forall \beta_j . S\rho.$$

To begin with, note that none of the variables β_j appears free in $SGen(A, \rho)$. To see this, suppose that $\beta \in TV(SGen(A, \rho))$. Then $\beta \in TV(S\delta)$ for some $\delta \in TV(\rho) \setminus \{\alpha_i\}$. This in turn implies that $\delta \in TV(A)$ and hence that $\beta \in TV(S\delta) \subseteq TV(SA)$. It follows that $\beta \notin \{\beta_j\} = TV(S\rho) \setminus TV(SA)$.

Suppose that $\rho = (P \Rightarrow \tau)$ and note that:

$$\begin{array}{rcll} S\tau & = & [S\alpha_i/\gamma_i](R\tau) & \\ v : SP & \Vdash & v : SP & \text{(using } (id)\text{)} \\ & = & v : [S\alpha_i/\gamma_i]RP & \end{array}$$

Thus $(\lambda x.\lambda v.xv) : SGen(A, \rho) \geq Gen(SA, S\rho)$ which (by (η_e)) is equivalent to id.

Second part: From above $SGen(A, \rho) = \forall \gamma_i . R\rho$ and by definition, none of α_i appears free in A so $RA = S[\gamma_i/\alpha_i]A = SA$.

We claim that $Gen(RA, R\rho) = SGen(A, \rho)$ and clearly it suffices to show that $\{\gamma_i\} = TV(R\rho) \setminus TV(SA)$:

- To show $\{\gamma_i\} \subseteq TV(R\rho) \setminus TV(SA)$: For each $\alpha_i \in TV(\rho)$ we have $R\alpha_i = \gamma_i$ and hence $\gamma_i \in TV(R\rho)$. Furthermore, since γ_i is a new variable not involved in S, $\gamma_i \notin TV(SA)$.

- To show $TV(R\rho) \setminus TV(SA) \subseteq \{\gamma_i\}$: Suppose $\gamma \in TV(R\rho) \setminus TV(SA)$. Then $\gamma \in TV(R\alpha)$ for some $\alpha \in TV(\rho)$. Note that $\alpha \notin TV(A)$ (otherwise $R\alpha = S\alpha$ and so $\gamma \in TV(R\alpha) = TV(S\alpha) \subseteq TV(SA)$, contradicting the hypothesis that $\gamma \notin TV(SA)$). It follows that $\alpha \in TV(\rho) \setminus TV(A) = \{\alpha_i\}$ and hence $\gamma \in TV(R\alpha_i) = \{R\alpha_i\} = \{\gamma_i\}$.

This establishes the claim above and completes the proof of the proposition. □

Proposition 5.10 *For any qualified type ρ and predicate assignments $v : P$ and $w : Q$ there are conversions:*

$$\begin{array}{lcl} id & : & (P, Q \mid \rho) \geq (P \mid Q \Rightarrow \rho) \\ id & : & (P \mid Q \Rightarrow \rho) \geq (P, Q \mid \rho). \end{array}$$

In particular, taking $P = \emptyset$, there are conversions:

$$id : (P \mid \rho) \geq P \Rightarrow \rho \quad \textit{and} \quad id : (P \Rightarrow \rho) \geq (P \mid \rho).$$

Let $\rho = Q' \Rightarrow \tau$ and pick evidence variables w' for Q', disjoint from v and w. By (id) we have:

$$v : P, w : Q, w' : Q \Vdash v : P, w : Q, w' : Q$$

Thus $\lambda x.\lambda v.\lambda w.\lambda w'.xvww'$ is a conversion for both cases and, using (η_e), is equivalent to $id = \lambda x.x$. □

Proposition 5.11 *If $C : (R \mid \sigma) \geq (R' \mid \sigma')$ and $v' : P' \Vdash e : P$, then there is a conversion:*

$$\lambda x.\lambda v'.C(xe) : (P, R \mid \sigma) \geq (P', R' \mid \sigma').$$

In particular, taking $R = \emptyset = R'$, if $C : \sigma \geq \sigma'$ and $v' : P' \Vdash e : P$, then:

$$\lambda x.\lambda v'.C(xe) : (P \mid \sigma) \geq (P' \mid \sigma').$$

Suppose that $\sigma = \forall \alpha_i.Q \Rightarrow \nu$ and $\sigma' = \forall \alpha'_j.Q' \Rightarrow \nu'$ where the variables α'_j appear only in $Q' \Rightarrow \nu'$. Taking the hypothesis $C : (R \mid \sigma) \geq (R' \mid \sigma')$ it follows from the definition of conversions that $\nu' = [\tau_i/\alpha_i]\nu$, $u' : R', w' : Q' \Vdash f : R, g : [\tau_i/\alpha_i]Q$ and

$$\vdash C = \lambda x.\lambda u'.\lambda w'.xfg$$

for some τ_i, f, g and w', u' (disjoint from v'). Furthermore, $v' : P' \Vdash e : P$ and hence by $(dist)$:

$$v' : P', u' : R', w' : Q' \Vdash e : P, f : R, g : [\tau_i/\alpha_i]Q.$$

Finally, note that:

$$\vdash C(xe) = \lambda u'.\lambda w'.xefg$$

and hence:

$$\vdash \lambda x.\lambda v'.C(xe) = \lambda x.\lambda v'.\lambda u'.\lambda w'.xefg$$

gives the required conversion. □

Proposition 5.12 *Suppose that P and P' are predicate assignments, σ and σ' are type schemes and that $C\!:\!(P\,|\,\sigma) \geq (P'\,|\,\sigma')$. Then:*

$$C\!:\!S(P\,|\,\sigma) \geq S(P'\,|\,\sigma')$$

for any substitution S of types for type variables.

Suppose that $\sigma = \forall\alpha_i.Q \Rightarrow \nu$ and $\sigma' = \forall\alpha'_j.Q' \Rightarrow \nu'$ where none of the variables α'_j appears free in σ, P or P' and none of α_i or α'_j is involved in S. Hence:

$$\begin{array}{rcl} S(P\,|\,\sigma) & = & (SP\,|\,\forall\alpha_i.SQ \Rightarrow S\nu) \\ S(P'\,|\,\sigma') & = & (SP'\,|\,\forall\alpha'_j.SQ' \Rightarrow S\nu') \end{array}$$

Given that $C\!:\!(P\,|\,\sigma) \geq (P'\,|\,\sigma')$, there are types τ_i such that:

$$\nu' = [\tau_i/\alpha_i]\nu \quad \text{and} \quad v'\!:\!P', w'\!:\!Q' \Vdash e\!:\!P, f\!:\![\tau_i/\alpha_i]Q$$

and such that $\vdash C = \lambda x.\lambda v'.\lambda w'.xef$. Applying S to the above we obtain:

$$\begin{array}{rcll} S\nu' & = & S([\tau_i/\alpha_i]\nu) & \\ & = & [S\tau_i/\alpha_i](S\nu) & \text{(none of } \alpha_i \text{ involved in } S) \\ v'\!:\!SP', w'\!:\!SQ' & = & S(v'\!:\!P', w'\!:\!Q') & \\ & \Vdash & S(e\!:\!P, f\!:\![\tau_i/\alpha_i]Q) & \text{(closure property)} \\ & = & e\!:\!SP, f\!:\![S\tau_i/\alpha_i](SQ) & \text{(none of } \alpha_i \text{ involved in } S) \end{array}$$

Hence $C\!:\!S(P\,|\,\sigma) \geq S(P'\,|\,\sigma')$ as required. □

Proposition 5.13 *For any type scheme σ and predicates P there is a conversion:*

$$id\!:\!(P\,|\,\sigma) \geq (P\,|\,\sigma).$$

Furthermore, if $C\!:\!(P\,|\,\sigma) \geq (P'\,|\,\sigma')$ and $C'\!:\!(P'\,|\,\sigma') \geq (P''\,|\,\sigma'')$, then:

$$(C' \circ C)\!:\!(P\,|\,\sigma) \geq (P''\,|\,\sigma'').$$

For the first part note that $id\!:\!\sigma \geq \sigma$ by Proposition 5.6(1) and $v\!:\!P \Vdash v\!:\!P$ by (id). The result follows from Proposition 5.11 since $\vdash \lambda x.\lambda v.id(xv) = id$.

Now suppose that:

$$\sigma = \forall\alpha_i.Q \Rightarrow \nu, \quad \sigma' = \forall\alpha'_j.Q' \Rightarrow \nu' \quad \text{and} \quad \sigma'' = \forall\alpha''_k.Q'' \Rightarrow \nu''$$

where the variables α'_j appear only in $Q' \Rightarrow \nu'$ and the variables α''_k appear only in $Q'' \Rightarrow \nu''$. By definition of conversions:

$$\nu' = [\tau_i/\alpha_i]\nu \quad \text{and} \quad v'\!:\!P', w'\!:\!Q' \Vdash e\!:\!P, f\!:\![\tau_i/\alpha_i]Q$$

for some τ_i, e and w' (disjoint from v) such that $\vdash C = \lambda x.\lambda v'.\lambda w'.xef$. In a similar way,

$$\nu'' = [\tau'_j/\alpha'_j]\nu' \quad \text{and} \quad v'': P'', w'': Q'' \Vdash e': P', f': [\tau'_j/\alpha'_j]Q'$$

for some τ'_j, e' and w'' (disjoint from v) such that $\vdash C' = \lambda x.\lambda v''.\lambda w''.xe'f'$.
Since none of α'_j appear free in ν:

$$\nu'' = [\tau'_j/\alpha'_j]\nu' = [\tau'_j/\alpha'_j]([\tau_i/\alpha_i]\nu) = [\tau''_i/\alpha_i]\nu$$

where $\tau''_i = [\tau'_j/\alpha'_j]\tau_i$. In a similar way, applying $[\tau'_j/\alpha'_j]$ to first of the predicate entailments above and noting that none of α'_j appear in P, P' or Q we obtain:

$$v': P', w': [\tau'_j/\alpha'_j]Q' \Vdash e: P, f: [\tau''_i/\alpha_i]Q.$$

Hence (by transitivity) we have:

$$v'': P'', w'': Q'' \Vdash [e'/v', f'/w'](e: P, f: [\tau''_i/\alpha_i]Q).$$

To complete the proof, notice that:

$$\begin{array}{rcll} \vdash \lambda x.C'(Cx) & = & \lambda x.\lambda v''.\lambda w''.(Cx)e'f' & \text{(property of } C') \\ & = & \lambda x.\lambda v''.\lambda w''.(\lambda v'.\lambda w'.xef)e'f' & \text{(property of } C) \\ & = & \lambda x.\lambda v''.\lambda w''.[e'/v', f'/w'](xef) & \text{(by } (\beta_e)) \end{array}$$

which is the required conversion. □

Proposition 5.14 *For any type scheme σ and predicate assignment $v : P$ there is a conversion:*

$$(\lambda x.\lambda v.x) : \sigma \geq (P \mid \sigma).$$

Furthermore, if $C : \sigma \geq (P \mid \sigma')$ and $C' : \sigma' \geq (P \mid \sigma'')$, then:

$$(\lambda x.\lambda v.C'(Cxv)v) : (P \mid \sigma) \geq (P'' \mid \sigma'').$$

For the first part note that $id : \sigma \geq \sigma$ by Proposition 5.6(1) and $v : P \Vdash \emptyset$ by (*term*). The result follows from Proposition 5.11 since $\vdash \lambda x.\lambda v.id(x) = \lambda x.\lambda v.x$.
Now suppose that:

$$\sigma = \forall \alpha_i.Q \Rightarrow \nu, \quad \sigma' = \forall \alpha'_j.Q' \Rightarrow \nu' \quad \text{and} \quad \sigma'' = \forall \alpha''_k.Q'' \Rightarrow \nu''$$

where the variables α'_j appear only in $Q' \Rightarrow \nu'$ and the variables α''_k appear only in $Q'' \Rightarrow \nu''$. By definition of conversions:

$$\nu' = [\tau_i/\alpha_i]\nu \quad \text{and} \quad v: P, w': Q' \Vdash e: [\tau_i/\alpha_i]Q$$

for some τ_i, e and w' (disjoint from v) such that $\vdash C = \lambda x.\lambda v.\lambda w'.xe$. In a similar way,

$$\nu'' = [\tau'_j/\alpha'_j]\nu' \quad \text{and} \quad v: P, w'': Q'' \Vdash e': [\tau'_j/\alpha'_j]Q'$$

for some τ'_j, e' and w'' (disjoint from v) such that $\vdash C' = \lambda x.\lambda v.\lambda w''.xe'$.
Since none of α'_j appear free in ν:

$$\nu'' = [\tau'_j/\alpha'_j]\nu' = [\tau'_j/\alpha'_j]([\tau_i/\alpha_i]\nu) = [\tau''_i/\alpha_i]\nu$$

where $\tau''_i = [\tau'_j/\alpha'_j]\tau_i$. In a similar way, applying $[\tau'_j/\alpha'_j]$ to first of the predicate entailments above and noting that none of α'_j appear in P, P or Q we obtain:

$$v:P, w':[\tau'_j/\alpha'_j]Q' \Vdash e:[\tau''_i/\alpha_i]Q.$$

From the second entailment (using $v:P \Vdash v:P$ and combining using (*univ*)):

$$v:P, w'':Q'' \Vdash v:P, e':[\tau'_j/\alpha'_j]Q'.$$

Hence by transitivity we obtain:

$$v:P, w'':Q'' \Vdash [e'/w']e:[\tau''_i/\alpha_i]Q).$$

To complete the proof, notice that:

$$\begin{array}{rcll}\vdash \lambda x.\lambda v.C'(Cxv) & = & \lambda x.\lambda v.\lambda w''.(Cxv)e' & \text{(property of } C')\\ & = & \lambda x.\lambda v.\lambda w''.(\lambda w'.xe)e' & \text{(property of } C)\\ & = & \lambda x.\lambda v.\lambda w''.[e'/w']xe & \text{(by } (\beta_e))\end{array}$$

which is the required conversion. □

Theorem 5.18 *If $P \,|\, A \overset{s}{\vdash} E \leadsto E' : \tau$, then $P \,|\, A \vdash E \leadsto E' : \tau$.*

By induction on the structure of $P \,|\, A \overset{s}{\vdash} E \leadsto E' : \tau$. The proofs for the cases where the last rule in the derivation is $(\to E)^s$ or $(\to I)^s$ are straightforward. The remaining cases are:

Case $(var)^s$: We have a derivation of the form:

$$\frac{(x:(\forall \alpha_i.Q \Rightarrow \nu)) \in A \quad P \Vdash e:[\tau_i/\alpha_i]Q}{P \,|\, A \overset{s}{\vdash} x \leadsto xe : [\tau_i/\alpha_i]\nu}$$

Hence we can construct the required derivation:

$$\cfrac{\cfrac{\cfrac{(x:(\forall \alpha_i.Q \Rightarrow \nu)) \in A}{P \,|\, A \vdash x \leadsto x : \forall \alpha_i.Q \Rightarrow \nu}\,(var)}{P \,|\, A \vdash x \leadsto x : [\tau_i/\alpha_i]Q \Rightarrow [\tau_i/\alpha_i]\nu}\,(\forall E) \qquad P \Vdash e:[\tau_i/\alpha_i]Q}{P \,|\, A \vdash x \leadsto xe : [\tau_i/\alpha_i]\nu}\,(\Rightarrow E)$$

Case $(let)^s$**:** We have a derivation of the form:

$$\frac{v' : P' \,|\, A \overset{s}{\vdash} E \leadsto E' : \tau' \quad P \,|\, A_x, x : \sigma' \overset{s}{\vdash} F \leadsto F' : \tau}{P \,|\, A \overset{s}{\vdash} (\mathbf{let}\ x = E\ \mathbf{in}\ F) \leadsto (\mathbf{let}\ x = \lambda v'.E'\ \mathbf{in}\ F') : \tau}$$

where $\sigma' = Gen(A, P' \Rightarrow \tau')$. Hence we can construct the derivation:

$$\dfrac{\dfrac{\dfrac{\dfrac{v' : P' \,|\, A \overset{s}{\vdash} E \leadsto E' : \tau'}{v' : P' \,|\, A \vdash E \leadsto E' : \tau'}\ \text{induction}}{\emptyset \,|\, A \vdash E \leadsto \lambda v'.E' : P' \Rightarrow \tau'}\ (\Rightarrow I)}{\emptyset \,|\, A \vdash E \leadsto \lambda v'.E' : \sigma'}\ (\forall I) \qquad \dfrac{P \,|\, A_x, x : \sigma' \overset{s}{\vdash} F \leadsto F' : \tau}{P \,|\, A_x, x : \sigma' \vdash F \leadsto F' : \tau}\ \text{induction}}{P \,|\, A \vdash (\mathbf{let}\ x = E\ \mathbf{in}\ F) \leadsto (\mathbf{let}\ x = \lambda v'.E'\ \mathbf{in}\ F') : \tau}\ (let)$$

This completes the proof. □

Proposition 5.19 *If* $P \,|\, A \overset{s}{\vdash} E \leadsto E' : \tau$*, then* $EV(E') \subseteq dom\ P$*.*

By induction on the structure of $P \,|\, A \overset{s}{\vdash} E \leadsto E' : \tau$. The proofs for the cases where the last rule in the derivation is $(\rightarrow E)^s$ or $(\rightarrow I)^s$ are straightforward and the proof for the case $(var)^s$ follows directly from $(evars)$.
In the remaining case we have a derivation of the form:

$$\frac{v' : P' \,|\, A \overset{s}{\vdash} E \leadsto E' : \tau' \quad P \,|\, A_x, x : \sigma' \overset{s}{\vdash} F \leadsto F' : \tau}{P \,|\, A \overset{s}{\vdash} (\mathbf{let}\ x = E\ \mathbf{in}\ F) \leadsto (\mathbf{let}\ x = \lambda v'.E'\ \mathbf{in}\ F') : \tau}$$

where $\sigma' = Gen(A, P' \Rightarrow \tau')$. By induction $EV(F') \subseteq dom\ P$ and $EV(E') \subseteq v'$ and hence $EV(\lambda v'.E') = \emptyset$. It follows that:

$$EV(\mathbf{let}\ x = \lambda v'.E'\ \mathbf{in}\ F') = EV(F') \subseteq dom\ P$$

which completes the proof. □

Proposition 5.20 *If* $P \,|\, A \overset{s}{\vdash} E \leadsto E' : \tau$ *and* S *is an arbitrary substitution of types for type variables, then* $SP \,|\, SA \overset{s}{\vdash} E \leadsto E' : S\tau$*.*

By induction on the structure of $P \,|\, A \overset{s}{\vdash} E \leadsto E' : \tau$. The proofs for the cases where the last rule in the derivation is $(\rightarrow E)^s$ and $(\rightarrow I)^s$ are straightforward. The remaining cases are:

Case $(var)^s$**:** We have a derivation of the form:

$$\frac{(x : (\forall \alpha. Q \Rightarrow \nu)) \in A \quad P \Vdash e : [\tau/\alpha]Q}{P \,|\, A \overset{s}{\vdash} x \leadsto xe : [\tau/\alpha]\nu}$$

Pick new variables β not involved in S so that:

$$\begin{array}{rcl} S(\forall\alpha.Q \Rightarrow \nu) & = & S(\forall\alpha.Q \Rightarrow \nu) \\ & = & S(\forall\beta.[\beta/\alpha](Q \Rightarrow \nu)) \\ & = & \forall\beta.S[\beta/\alpha](Q \Rightarrow \nu) \end{array}$$

and hence $(x : (\forall\beta.S[\beta/\alpha](Q \Rightarrow \nu))) \in SA$. Note also that:

$$\begin{array}{rcll} SP & \Vdash & e : S([\tau/\alpha]Q) & \text{(by } (\mathit{close})\text{)} \\ & = & e : S[S\tau/\alpha]Q & \\ & = & e : [S\tau/\beta](S[\beta/\alpha]Q) & \end{array}$$

Hence, by $(\mathit{var})^s$:

$$SP \,|\, SA \overset{s}{\vdash} x \leadsto xe : [S\tau/\beta](S[\beta/\alpha]\nu)$$

which is the derivation required since $S[\tau/\beta](S[\beta/\alpha]\nu) = S([\tau/\alpha]\nu)$.

Case $(\mathit{let})^s$: We have a derivation of the form:

$$\frac{v' : P' \,|\, A \overset{s}{\vdash} E \leadsto E' : \tau' \qquad P \,|\, A_x, x : \sigma' \overset{s}{\vdash} F \leadsto F' : \tau}{P \,|\, A \overset{s}{\vdash} (\mathbf{let}\ x = E\ \mathbf{in}\ F) \leadsto (\mathbf{let}\ x = \lambda v'.E'\ \mathbf{in}\ F') : \tau}$$

where $\sigma' = \mathit{Gen}(A, P' \Rightarrow \tau')$. By Proposition 5.8 there is a substitution R such that:

$$RA = SA \quad \text{and} \quad \mathit{Gen}(SA, RP' \Rightarrow R\tau') = S\mathit{Gen}(A, P' \Rightarrow \tau').$$

Write $\sigma = \mathit{Gen}(SA, RP' \Rightarrow R\tau') = S\sigma'$. The required derivation can now be constructed:

$$\dfrac{\dfrac{\dfrac{v' : P' \,|\, A \overset{s}{\vdash} E \leadsto E' : \tau'}{v' : RP' \,|\, RA \overset{s}{\vdash} E \leadsto E' : R\tau'}\,(\text{a})}{v' : RP' \,|\, SA \overset{s}{\vdash} E \leadsto E' : R\tau'}\,(\text{c}) \qquad \dfrac{\dfrac{P \,|\, A_x, x : \sigma' \overset{s}{\vdash} F \leadsto F' : \tau}{SP \,|\, SA_x, x : S\sigma' \overset{s}{\vdash} F \leadsto F' : S\tau}\,(\text{b})}{SP \,|\, SA_x, x : \sigma \overset{s}{\vdash} F \leadsto F' : S\tau}\,(\text{d})}{SP \,|\, SA \overset{s}{\vdash} (\mathbf{let}\ x = E\ \mathbf{in}\ F) \leadsto (\mathbf{let}\ x = \lambda v'.E'\ \mathbf{in}\ F') : S\tau'}\,(\mathit{let})^s$$

(Steps (a) and (b) are obtained by induction whilst (c) and (d) are justified by the equalities $SA = RA$ and $\sigma = S\sigma'$ respectively.)

This completes the proof. □

Proposition 5.21 *If* $v : P \,|\, A \overset{s}{\vdash} E \leadsto E' : \tau$ *and* $Q \Vdash e : P$ *then* $Q \,|\, A \overset{s}{\vdash} E \leadsto [e/v]E' : \tau$.

By induction on the structure of $v : P \,|\, A \overset{s}{\vdash} E \leadsto E' : \tau$. The proofs for the cases where the last rule in the derivation is $(\rightarrow E)^s$ and $(\rightarrow I)^s$ are straightforward. The remaining cases are:

Case $(var)^s$: We have a derivation of the form:

$$\frac{(x:(\forall\alpha.P' \Rightarrow \tau')) \in A \quad v:P \Vdash e':[\tau/\alpha]P'}{v:P\,|\,A \overset{s}{\vdash} x \rightsquigarrow xe' : [\tau/\alpha]\tau'}$$

By transitivity of $\Vdash$ we have $Q \Vdash [e/v]e' : [\tau/\alpha]P'$ and hence there is a derivation $Q\,|\,A \overset{s}{\vdash} x \rightsquigarrow x([e/v]e') : [\tau/\alpha]\tau'$. The result follows since $x([e/v]e') \equiv [e/v](xe')$.

Case $(let)^s$: We have a derivation of the form:

$$\frac{v':P'\,|\,A \overset{s}{\vdash} E \rightsquigarrow E' : \tau' \quad v:P\,|\,A_x, x:\sigma' \overset{s}{\vdash} F \rightsquigarrow F' : \tau}{P\,|\,A \overset{s}{\vdash} (\textbf{let } x = E \textbf{ in } F) \rightsquigarrow (\textbf{let } x = \lambda v'.E' \textbf{ in } F') : \tau}$$

where $\sigma' = Gen(A, P' \Rightarrow \tau')$. By induction, $Q\,|\,A_x, x:\sigma' \overset{s}{\vdash} F \rightsquigarrow [e/v]F' : \tau$ and hence:

$$Q\,|\,A \overset{s}{\vdash} (\textbf{let } x = E \textbf{ in } F) \rightsquigarrow (\textbf{let } x = \lambda v'.E' \textbf{ in } [e/v]F') : \tau.$$

By Proposition 5.19, $EV(E') \subseteq v'$ (i.e. $EV(\lambda v'.E') = \emptyset$) and so:

$$\begin{aligned} [e/v](\textbf{let } x = \lambda v'.E' \textbf{ in } F') &\equiv \textbf{let } x = [e/v](\lambda v'.E') \textbf{ in } [e/v]F' \\ &\equiv \textbf{let } x = \lambda v'.E' \textbf{ in } [e/v]F' \end{aligned}$$

as required.

This completes the proof. □

> **Lemma 5.23** *Suppose that A and A' are type assignments, P and Q are predicate sets and that $v : P \mid A \overset{s}{\vdash} E \rightsquigarrow E' : \tau$ for some type τ. Then $v:P'\,|\,A \overset{s}{\vdash} E \rightsquigarrow E' : \tau'$ for some P' and τ' (instances of P and τ respectively under a single substitution) and*
>
> $$id: Gen(A', Q, P' \Rightarrow \tau') \geq (Q\,|\,Gen(A, P \Rightarrow \tau)).$$

Let $\rho = (P \Rightarrow \tau)$, $\{\alpha_i\} = TV(\rho) \setminus TV(A)$ and $S = [\beta_i/\alpha_i]$ where β_i are new variables. By Proposition 5.20, $v:SP\,|\,SA \overset{s}{\vdash} E \rightsquigarrow E' : S\tau$, but none of α_i appear free in A and hence this derivation is

$$v:P'\,|\,A \overset{s}{\vdash} E \rightsquigarrow E' : \tau'$$

where $P' = SP$ and $\tau' = S\tau$. Note that $Gen(A,\rho) = (\forall\alpha_i.\rho) = (\forall\beta_i.S\rho)$ and that $Gen(A', Q, P' \Rightarrow \tau') = \forall\gamma_j.\forall\beta_i.Q, S\rho$ for some variables γ_j since each variable β_i appears free in $S\rho$ but not in A'. It follows from the trivial observations:

$$\begin{aligned} w:Q, v:SP &\Vdash [\beta_i/\beta_i, \gamma_j/\gamma_j](w:Q, v:SP) \\ \tau' &= [\beta_i/\beta_i, \gamma_j/\gamma_j](S\tau') \end{aligned}$$

that $Gen(A', Q, P' \Rightarrow \tau') \geq (Q\,|\,Gen(A, P \Rightarrow \tau))$ with conversion $\lambda x.\lambda v.\lambda x.xwv$ which, by (η_e), is equivalent to $id = \lambda x.x$. □

Proposition 5.22 *If* $v\!:\!P\,|\,A' \overset{s}{\vdash} E \leadsto E' : \tau$ *and* $C\!:\!A \geq (v\!:\!P\,|\,A')$, *then* $v\!:\!P\,|\,A \overset{s}{\vdash} E \leadsto E'' : \tau$ *with* $v\!:\!P\,|\,A \vdash CE' = E'' : \tau$.

By induction on the structure of $v : P \mid A' \overset{s}{\vdash} E \leadsto E' : \tau$. For convenience, we write $v\!:\!P\,|\,A \overset{s}{\vdash} E \leadsto E'' = CE' : \tau$ as an abbreviation for the two judgements in the conclusion of the proposition.

Case $(var)^s$**:** We have a derivation of the form:

$$\frac{(x\!:\!(\forall\alpha'_j.Q' \Rightarrow \nu')) \in A' \quad v\!:\!P \Vdash e'\!:\![\tau'_j/\alpha'_j]Q'}{v\!:\!P\,|\,A' \overset{s}{\vdash} x \leadsto xe' : [\tau'_j/\alpha'_j]\nu'}$$

Suppose $A(x) = \forall\alpha_i.Q \Rightarrow \nu$. By hypothesis, $C\!:\!A \geq (v\!:\!P\,|\,A')$ and so

$$(\lambda x.\lambda v.Cx)\!:\!(\forall\alpha_i.Q \Rightarrow \nu) \geq (P\,|\,\forall\alpha'_j.Q' \Rightarrow \nu').$$

By Proposition 5.6(3) we have:

$$id\!:\!(\forall\alpha'_j.Q' \Rightarrow \nu') \geq [\tau'_j/\alpha'_j](Q' \Rightarrow \nu')$$

and so by Proposition 5.11:

$$id\!:\!(P\,|\,\forall\alpha'_j.Q' \Rightarrow \nu') \geq (P\,|\,[\tau'_j/\alpha'_j](Q' \Rightarrow \nu')).$$

Composing with $\lambda x.\lambda v.Cx$ gives:

$$(\lambda x.\lambda v.Cx)\!:\!(\forall\alpha_i.Q \Rightarrow \nu) \geq (P\,|\,[\tau'_j/\alpha'_j](Q' \Rightarrow \nu')).$$

Hence there are types τ_i, evidence variables v' and evidence expressions e such that:

$$v\!:\!P, v'\!:\![\tau'_j/\alpha'_j]Q' \Vdash e\!:\![\tau_i/\alpha_i]Q,$$

$$[\tau'_j/\alpha'_j]\nu' = [\tau_i/\alpha_i]\nu$$

$$\text{and } \vdash Cx = \lambda v'.xe.$$

By hypothesis, $v\!:\!P \Vdash e'\!:\![\tau'_j/\alpha'_j]Q'$ and hence $v\!:\!P \Vdash [e'/v']e\!:\![\tau_i/\alpha_i]Q$ using (cut). By $(var)^s$, $v : P \mid A \overset{s}{\vdash} x \leadsto x([e'/v']e) : [\tau_i/\alpha_i]\nu$ but $[\tau'_j/\alpha'_j]\nu' = [\tau_i/\alpha_i]\nu$ and so this derivation is:

$$v\!:\!P\,|\,A \overset{s}{\vdash} x \leadsto x([e'/v']e) : [\tau'_j/\alpha'_j]\nu'.$$

Finally, note that:

$$\begin{array}{rcll} v\!:\!P\,|\,A \vdash C(xe') & = & (Cx)e' & \text{(substitution)} \\ & = & (\lambda v'.xe)e' & (\vdash Cx = \lambda v'.xe) \\ & = & [e'/v'](xe) & (\beta_e) \\ & = & x([e'/v']e) : [\tau'_j/\alpha'_j]\nu' & \text{(substitution)} \end{array}$$

which establishes the required equality.

Case $(\rightarrow E)^s$: We have a derivation of the form:

$$\frac{v\!:\!P\,|\,A' \overset{s}{\vdash} E \leadsto E' : \tau' \rightarrow \tau \quad v\!:\!P\,|\,A' \overset{s}{\vdash} F \leadsto F' : \tau'}{v\!:\!P\,|\,A' \overset{s}{\vdash} EF \leadsto E'F' : \tau}$$

By induction there are derivations:

$$\begin{array}{c} v\!:\!P\,|\,A \overset{s}{\vdash} E \leadsto E'' = CE' : \tau' \rightarrow \tau \\ v\!:\!P\,|\,A \overset{s}{\vdash} F \leadsto F'' = CF' : \tau'. \end{array}$$

Using $(\rightarrow E)^s$ we obtain:

$$v\!:\!P\,|\,A \overset{s}{\vdash} EF \leadsto E''F'' : \tau$$

and $v\!:\!P\,|\,A \vdash C(E'F') = (CE')(CF') = E''F'' : \tau$.

Case $(\rightarrow I)^s$: We have a derivation of the form:

$$\frac{v\!:\!P\,|\,A'_x, x\!:\!\tau' \overset{s}{\vdash} E \leadsto E' : \tau}{v\!:\!P\,|\,A' \overset{s}{\vdash} \lambda x.E \leadsto \lambda x.E' : \tau' \rightarrow \tau}$$

By hypothesis, $C\!:\!A \geq (v\!:\!P\,|\,A')$ and hence by Proposition 5.16(3):

$$C_x\!:\!(A_x, x\!:\!\tau') \geq (v\!:\!P\,|\,A'_x, x\!:\!\tau').$$

By induction, $v\!:\!P\,|\,A_x, x\!:\!\tau' \overset{s}{\vdash} E \leadsto E'' = C_xE' : \tau$ and hence:

$$v\!:\!P\,|\,A' \overset{s}{\vdash} \lambda x.E \leadsto \lambda x.E' : \tau' \rightarrow \tau$$

with:

$$\begin{array}{rcll} v\!:\!P\,|\,A \vdash C(\lambda x.E') & = & \lambda x.C_xE' & \text{(Proposition 5.16(1))} \\ & = & \lambda x.E'' : \tau' \rightarrow \tau & (\vdash C_xE' = E''). \end{array}$$

Case $(let)^s$: We have a derivation of the form:

$$\frac{v'\!:\!P'\,|\,A' \overset{s}{\vdash} E \leadsto E' : \tau' \quad P\,|\,A'_x, x\!:\!\sigma' \overset{s}{\vdash} F \leadsto F' : \tau}{P\,|\,A' \overset{s}{\vdash} (\textbf{let } x = E \textbf{ in } F) \leadsto (\textbf{let } x = \lambda v'.E' \textbf{ in } F') : \tau}$$

where $\sigma' = Gen(A, P' \Rightarrow \tau')$. By Lemma 5.23, $v' : P''\,|\,A' \overset{s}{\vdash} E \leadsto E' : \tau''$ for some P'' and τ'' and $id : \sigma \geq (P\,|\,\sigma')$ where $\sigma = Gen(A', P, P'' \Rightarrow \tau'')$. We also have $id\!:\!(P|\sigma') \geq (P\,|\,(P' \Rightarrow \tau'))$ (Proposition 5.6(3) and Proposition 5.11) and hence:

$$id\!:\!\sigma \geq (P\,|\,P' \Rightarrow \tau').$$

Note that $v\!:\!P, v'\!:\!P'' \Vdash v'\!:\!P''$ and that $C\!:\!A \geq (v\!:\!P, v'\!:\!P''\,|\,A')$ and so there is a derivation:

$$\cfrac{\cfrac{v'\!:\!P''\,|\,A' \overset{s}{\vdash} E \leadsto E' : \tau''}{v\!:\!P, v'\!:\!P''\,|\,A' \overset{s}{\vdash} E \leadsto E' : \tau''}\ \text{Proposition 5.21}}{v\!:\!P, v'\!:\!P''\,|\,A \overset{s}{\vdash} E \leadsto E'' = CE' : \tau''}\ \text{induction}$$

It follows that $\emptyset \,|\, A \vdash \lambda v.\lambda v'.CE' = \lambda v.\lambda v'.E'' : \sigma$. Next we consider the derivation:

$$v : P \,|\, A'_x, x : \sigma' \overset{s}{\vdash} F \rightsquigarrow F' : \tau.$$

Note that $C[xv/x] : (A_x, x : \sigma) \geq (v : P \,|\, A'_x, x : \sigma')$ and hence by induction $v : P \,|\, A_x, x : \sigma \overset{s}{\vdash} F \rightsquigarrow F'' : \tau$ with $v : P \,|\, A_x, x : \sigma \vdash (C[xv/x]F') = F'' : \tau$. It follows from $(let)^s$ that:

$$v : P \,|\, A \overset{s}{\vdash} (\mathbf{let}\ x = E\ \mathbf{in}\ F) \rightsquigarrow (\mathbf{let}\ x = \lambda v.\lambda v'.E''\ \mathbf{in}\ F'') : \tau$$

Finally, we have:

$$\begin{array}{rcll} v : P \,|\, A & \vdash & C(\mathbf{let}\ x = \lambda v'.E'\ \mathbf{in}\ F') & \\ & = & \mathbf{let}\ x = \lambda v'.CE'\ \mathbf{in}\ C_x F' & \text{(Prop. 5.16(2))} \\ & = & \mathbf{let}\ x = (\lambda v.\lambda v'.CE')v\ \mathbf{in}\ C_x F' & (\beta_e) \\ & = & \mathbf{let}\ x = (\lambda v.\lambda v'.E'')v\ \mathbf{in}\ C_x F' & \\ & = & \mathbf{let}\ x = [\lambda v.\lambda v'.E''/x](xv)\ \mathbf{in}\ C_x F' & \text{(substitution)} \\ & = & \mathbf{let}\ x = \lambda v.\lambda v'.E''\ \mathbf{in}\ [xv/x](C_x F') & \text{(Prop. 5.4(1))} \\ & = & \mathbf{let}\ x = \lambda v.\lambda v'.E''\ \mathbf{in}\ C[xv/x]F' & \text{(Prop. 5.16(4))} \\ & = & \mathbf{let}\ x = \lambda v.\lambda v'.E''\ \mathbf{in}\ F''. & \end{array}$$

This completes the proof. □

Theorem 5.25 *If $v : P \,|\, A \vdash E \rightsquigarrow E' : \sigma$, then there is a predicate assignment $v' : P'$, a type τ' and a term E'' such that $v' : P' \,|\, A \overset{s}{\vdash} E \rightsquigarrow E'' : \tau'$ and $v : P \,|\, A \vdash C(\lambda v'.E'')v = E' : \sigma$ where $C : Gen(A, P' \Rightarrow \tau') \geq (P \,|\, \sigma)$.*

By induction on the structure of $v : P \,|\, A \vdash E \rightsquigarrow E' : \sigma$.

Case (var): We have a derivation of the form:

$$\frac{(x : \sigma) \in A}{v : P \,|\, A \vdash x \rightsquigarrow x : \sigma}$$

Write $\sigma = \forall \alpha_i.\forall \beta_j.\rho$ where $\rho = (Q \Rightarrow \nu)$, $\{\alpha_i\} \subseteq TV(\rho)$ and none of the variables β_j appears free in ρ. Pick new variables γ_i, δ_j and let S denote the substitution $[\gamma_i/\alpha_i, \delta_j/\beta_j]$. By (id), $v' : SQ \Vdash v' : SQ$ and so:

$$v' : SQ \,|\, A \overset{s}{\vdash} x \rightsquigarrow xv' : S\nu.$$

Note that $(x : \sigma) \in A$, so $TV(\sigma) \subseteq TV(A)$ and $TV(S\rho) \setminus TV(A) = \gamma_i$. Thus:

$$\begin{array}{rcll} Gen(A, SQ \Rightarrow S\nu) & = & Gen(A, S\rho) & \\ & = & \forall \gamma_i.S\rho & \\ & = & \forall \gamma_i.[\gamma_i/\alpha_i]\rho & \text{(none of } \beta_j \text{ free in } \rho) \\ & = & \forall \alpha_i.\rho & \text{(renaming bound variables)} \\ & = & \forall \alpha_i.\forall \beta_j.\rho & \text{(none of } \beta_j \text{ free in } \rho) \\ & = & \sigma. & \end{array}$$

Note that $(\lambda x.\lambda v.x) : \sigma \geq (P \mid \sigma)$ and hence:

$$(\lambda x.\lambda v.x) : (SQ \Rightarrow S\nu) \geq (P \mid \sigma).$$

which satisfies the theorem since $v : P \mid A \vdash (\lambda x.\lambda v.x)(\lambda v'.xv')v = x : \sigma$ using (β), (β_e) and (η_e).

Case $(\rightarrow E)$: We have a derivation of the form:

$$\frac{v : P \mid A \vdash E \leadsto E' : \tau' \rightarrow \tau \quad v : P \mid A \vdash F \leadsto F' : \tau'}{v : P \mid A \vdash EF \leadsto E'F' : \tau}$$

By induction, $v' : P' \mid A \overset{s}{\vdash} E \leadsto E'' : \nu'$ and $C : Gen(A, P' \Rightarrow \nu') \geq (v : P \mid \tau' \rightarrow \tau)$ such that $v : P \mid A \vdash C(\lambda v'.E'')v = E' : \tau' \rightarrow \tau$. Writing $Gen(A, P' \Rightarrow \nu') = \forall \alpha_i.P' \Rightarrow \nu'$, it follows that there are types τ_i such that:

$$v : P \Vdash e' : [\tau_i/\alpha_i]P', \quad \tau' \rightarrow \tau = [\tau_i/\alpha_i]\nu' \quad \text{and} \quad \vdash C = \lambda x.\lambda v.xe'.$$

Applying the substitution $[\tau_i/\alpha_i]$ to the syntax-directed derivation for E gives:

$$v' : [\tau_i/\alpha_i]P' \mid [\tau_i/\alpha_i]A \overset{s}{\vdash} E \leadsto E'' : [\tau_i/\alpha_i]\nu'$$

None of α_i appears free in A and hence this is equivalent to:

$$v' : [\tau_i/\alpha_i]P' \mid A \overset{s}{\vdash} E \leadsto E'' : \tau' \rightarrow \tau.$$

Note also that:

$$v : P \mid A \vdash E' = C(\lambda v'.E'')v = (\lambda x.\lambda v.xe')(\lambda v'.E'')v = [e'/v']E'' : \tau' \rightarrow \tau.$$

By a similar argument, $v'' : [\nu_j/\beta_j]P'' \mid A \overset{s}{\vdash} F \leadsto F'' : \tau'$ for some β_j, ν_j, P'', F'', e'' and v'' (disjoint from v'), such that:

$$v : P \Vdash e'' : [\nu_j/\beta_j]P'' \quad \text{and} \quad v : P \mid A \vdash F' = [e''/v'']F'' : \tau'.$$

Let $Z = (v' : X, v'' : Y)$ where $X = [\tau_i/\alpha_i]P'$ and $Y = [\nu_j/\beta_j]P''$ and hence $Z \Vdash v' : X$ and $Z \Vdash v'' : Y$. By Proposition 5.21 we can construct the following derivation:

$$\frac{\dfrac{v' : X \mid A \overset{s}{\vdash} E \leadsto E'' : \tau' \rightarrow \tau}{Z \mid A \overset{s}{\vdash} E \leadsto E'' : \tau' \rightarrow \tau} \quad \dfrac{v'' : Y \mid A \overset{s}{\vdash} F \leadsto F'' : \tau'}{Z \mid A \overset{s}{\vdash} F \leadsto F'' : \tau'}}{Z \mid A \overset{s}{\vdash} EF \leadsto E''F'' : \tau} (\rightarrow E)^s$$

Furthermore, $v : P \Vdash e' : X, e'' : Y$ and so:

$$(\lambda x.\lambda v.xe'e'') : Gen(A, (X, Y) \Rightarrow \tau) \geq Gen(A, P \Rightarrow \tau)$$

by Proposition 5.7. Note that $id : Gen(A, P \Rightarrow \tau) \geq (P \mid \tau)$ and hence:

$$(\lambda x.\lambda v.xe'e'') : Gen(A, (X, Y) \Rightarrow \tau) \geq (v : P \mid \tau)$$

Finally, we have:

$$\begin{array}{rcll} v\!:\!P\,|\,A & \vdash & (\lambda x.\lambda v.xe'e'')(\lambda v'.\lambda v''.E''F'')v & \\ & = & (\lambda v'.\lambda v''.E''F'')e'e'' & (\beta) \\ & = & [e'/v', e''/v''](E''F'') & (\beta_e) \\ & = & ([e'/v']E'')([e''/v'']F'') & \\ & = & E'F' : \tau. & \end{array}$$

which establishes the required equality, the penultimate step being justified by the observation that $EV(E'') \subseteq v'$ and $EV(F'') \subseteq v''$.

Case ($\rightarrow I$): We have a derivation of the form:

$$\frac{v\!:\!P\,|\,A_x, x\!:\!\tau' \vdash E \leadsto E' : \tau}{v\!:\!P\,|\,A \vdash \lambda x.E \leadsto \lambda x.E' : \tau' \rightarrow \tau}$$

By induction, $v' : P' \,|\, A_x, x : \tau' \overset{s}{\vdash} E \leadsto E'' : \nu$ and $C : Gen(A, P' \Rightarrow \nu) \geq (P \,|\, \tau)$ such that $v\!:\!P\,|\,A_x, x\!:\!\tau' \vdash C(\lambda v'.E'')v = E' : \tau$. Writing $Gen(A, P' \Rightarrow \nu) = \forall\alpha_i.P' \Rightarrow \nu$ it follows that there are types τ_i such that:

$$v\!:\!P \Vdash e'\!:\![\tau_i/\alpha_i]P', \quad \tau = [\tau_i/\alpha_i]\nu \quad \text{and} \quad \vdash C = \lambda x.\lambda v.xe'.$$

Note that

$$\begin{array}{rcl} v\!:\!P\,|\,A_x, x\!:\!\tau' \vdash E' & = & C(\lambda v'.E'')v \\ & = & (\lambda x.\lambda v.xe')(\lambda v'.E'')v \\ & = & [e'/v']E'' : \tau \end{array}$$

and hence $P\,|\,A \vdash \lambda x.[e'/v']E'' = \lambda x.E' : \tau' \rightarrow \tau$.

Applying $[\tau_i/\alpha_i]$ to the (syntax-directed) derivation for E above and noting that none of the variables α_i appear free in A we obtain $v' : [\tau_i/\alpha_i]P' \,|\, A_x, x : \tau' \overset{s}{\vdash} E \leadsto E'' : \tau$. Hence by $(\rightarrow I)^s$:

$$v'\!:\![\tau_i/\alpha_i]P'\,|\,A \overset{s}{\vdash} \lambda x.E \leadsto \lambda x.E'' : \tau' \rightarrow \tau.$$

Composing the conversions:

$$\begin{array}{llcll} C: & Gen(A, [\tau_i/\alpha_i]P' \Rightarrow \tau' \rightarrow \tau) & \geq & Gen(A, P \Rightarrow (\tau' \rightarrow \tau)) & \text{(Prop. 5.7)} \\ id: & Gen(A, P \Rightarrow (\tau' \rightarrow \tau)) & \geq & P \Rightarrow (\tau' \rightarrow \tau) & \text{(Prop. 5.6)} \\ id: & P \Rightarrow (\tau' \rightarrow \tau) & \geq & (P\,|\,\tau' \rightarrow \tau) & \text{(Prop. 5.10)} \end{array}$$

we obtain:

$$C\!: Gen(A, [\tau_i/\alpha_i]P' \Rightarrow \tau' \rightarrow \tau) \geq (P\,|\,\tau' \rightarrow \tau).$$

This conversion satisfies the theorem since:

$$\begin{array}{rcll} v\!:\!P\,|\,A \vdash C(\lambda v'.\lambda x.E'')v & = & (\lambda x.\lambda v.xe')(\lambda v'.\lambda x.E'')v & \\ & = & (\lambda v'.\lambda x.E'')e' & \text{(by } (\beta), (\beta_e)) \\ & = & [e'/v'](\lambda x.E'') & \text{(by } (\beta_e)) \\ & = & \lambda x.[e'/v']E'' & \text{(substitution)} \\ & = & \lambda x.E' : \tau' \rightarrow \tau. & \end{array}$$

Case (*let*): We have a derivation of the form:

$$\frac{v\!:\!P\,|\,A \vdash E \leadsto E' : \sigma \quad w\!:\!Q\,|\,A_x, x\!:\!\sigma \vdash F \leadsto F' : \tau}{v\!:\!P, w\!:\!Q\,|\,A \vdash (\mathbf{let}\ x = E\ \mathbf{in}\ F) \leadsto (\mathbf{let}\ x = E'\ \mathbf{in}\ F') : \tau}$$

By induction, $v' : P' \,|\, A \overset{s}{\vdash} E \leadsto E'' : \nu'$ and $v : P \,|\, A \vdash C'(\lambda v'.E'')v = E' : \sigma$ where $C'\!:\!\sigma' \geq (P\,|\,\sigma)$ and $\sigma' = Gen(A, P' \Rightarrow \nu')$.

Similarly, $w' : Q' \,|\, A_x, x\!:\!\sigma \overset{s}{\vdash} F \leadsto F'' : \tau'$ and $w : Q \,|\, A_x, x\!:\!\sigma \vdash C(\lambda w'.F'')v = F' : \tau'$ where $C\!:Gen((A_x, x\!:\!\sigma), Q' \Rightarrow \tau') \geq (Q\,|\,\tau)$.

By Lemma 5.23, $w'\!: Q''\,|\,A_x, x\!:\!\sigma \overset{s}{\vdash} F \leadsto F'' : \tau''$ where:

$$id\!: Gen(A, P, Q'' \Rightarrow \tau'') \geq (P\,|\,Gen((A_x, x\!:\!\sigma), Q' \Rightarrow \tau')).$$

We can now construct the following derivation:

$$\dfrac{v'\!:P'\,|\,A \overset{s}{\vdash} E \leadsto E'' : \nu' \qquad \dfrac{\dfrac{w'\!: Q''\,|\,A_x, x\!:\!\sigma \overset{s}{\vdash} F \leadsto F'' : \tau''}{v\!:P, w'\!: Q''\,|\,A_x, x\!:\!\sigma \overset{s}{\vdash} F \leadsto F'' : \tau''}\,(a)}{v\!:P, w'\!: Q''\,|\,A_x, x\!:\!\sigma' \overset{s}{\vdash} F \leadsto F''' : \tau''}\,(b)}{v\!:P, w'\!: Q''\,|\,A \vdash (\mathbf{let}\ x = E\ \mathbf{in}\ F) \leadsto (\mathbf{let}\ x = \lambda v'.E''\ \mathbf{in}\ F''') : \tau''}\,(let)^s$$

The step labelled (a) is justified using Proposition 5.21. The step labelled (b) is justified by Proposition 5.22 using the observation that:

$$[C'xv/x]\!: A_x, x\!:\!\sigma' \geq (v\!:P\,|\,A_x, x\!:\!\sigma).$$

The term F''' which appears as a result of this step is related to the term F'' by the equality $v\!:P\,|\,A \vdash [C'xv/x]F'' = F''' : \tau''$.

The process of establishing the necessary conversion for this derivation is straightforward but requires several steps.

By Proposition 5.10 $id\!:(Q\,|\,\tau) \geq (Q \Rightarrow \tau)$ and composing with C we obtain:

$$C\!: Gen((A_x, x\!:\!\sigma), Q' \Rightarrow \tau') \geq (Q \Rightarrow \tau).$$

Noting that $v\!:P \Vdash v\!:P$ we can extend this to:

$$\lambda x.\lambda v.C(xv)\!:(P\,|\,Gen((A_x, x\!:\!\sigma), Q' \Rightarrow \tau')) \geq (P\,|\,Q \Rightarrow \tau)$$

and then compose this with the conversion id above to give:

$$\lambda x.\lambda v.C(xv)\!: Gen(A, P, Q'' \Rightarrow \tau'') \geq (P\,|\,Q \Rightarrow \tau).$$

By Proposition 5.10:

$$id\!:(P\,|\,Q \Rightarrow \tau) \geq (P, Q\,|\,\tau)$$

and composing these last two we obtain the required conversion:

$$\lambda x.\lambda v.C(xv)\!: Gen(A, P, Q'' \Rightarrow \tau'') \geq (P, Q\,|\,\tau).$$

It remains to show that this conversion relates the translation of **let** $x = E$ **in** F in the original derivation to that in the (syntax-directed) derivation given above:

$$\begin{aligned}
v\!:\!P, w\!:\!Q \,|\, A \;\vdash\; & (\lambda x.\lambda v.C(xv))(\lambda v.\lambda w'.\mathbf{let}\ x = \lambda v'.E''\ \mathbf{in}\ F''')vw \\
& \quad \text{(by } (\beta) \text{ and } (\beta_e)) \\
= \; & C(\lambda w'.\mathbf{let}\ x = \lambda v'.E''\ \mathbf{in}\ F''')w \\
& \quad \text{(Proposition 5.4, parts (2), (3) and (4))} \\
= \; & \mathbf{let}\ x = \lambda v'.E''\ \mathbf{in}\ C(\lambda w'.F''')w \\
& \quad (\text{using} \vdash [C'xv/x]F'' = F''') \\
= \; & \mathbf{let}\ x = \lambda v'.E''\ \mathbf{in}\ C(\lambda w'.[C'xv/x]F'')w \\
& \quad (x \notin FV(C) = \emptyset) \\
= \; & \mathbf{let}\ x = \lambda v'.E''\ \mathbf{in}\ [C'xv/x](C(\lambda w'.F'')w) \\
& \quad \text{(Proposition 5.4(1))} \\
= \; & \mathbf{let}\ x = [\lambda v'.E''/x](C'xv)\ \mathbf{in}\ C(\lambda w'.F'')w \\
& \quad \text{(substitution)} \\
= \; & \mathbf{let}\ x = C'(\lambda v'.E'')v\ \mathbf{in}\ C(\lambda w'.F'')w \\
& \quad (\text{using} \vdash C'(\lambda v'.E'')v = E') \\
= \; & \mathbf{let}\ x = E'\ \mathbf{in}\ C(\lambda w'.F'')w \\
& \quad (\text{using} \vdash C(\lambda w'.F'')v = F') \\
= \; & \mathbf{let}\ x = E'\ \mathbf{in}\ F' : \tau
\end{aligned}$$

Case ($\Rightarrow E$): We have a derivation of the form:

$$\frac{v\!:\!P \,|\, A \vdash E \leadsto E' : \pi \Rightarrow \rho \qquad v\!:\!P \Vdash e\!:\!\pi}{v\!:\!P \,|\, A \vdash E \leadsto E'e : \rho}$$

By induction, $v'\!:\!P' \,|\, A \overset{s}{\vdash} E \leadsto E'' : \nu'$ and $v\!:\!P \,|\, A \vdash C(\lambda v'.E'')v = E' : \pi \Rightarrow \rho$ where $C\!:\!Gen(A, P' \Rightarrow \nu') \geq (P \,|\, \pi \Rightarrow \rho)$. By Proposition 5.10:

$$id\!:\!(P \,|\, \pi \Rightarrow \rho) \geq (P, \pi \,|\, \rho)$$

and by Proposition 5.11 (using $v\!:\!P \Vdash v\!:\!P, e\!:\!\pi$):

$$(\lambda x.\lambda v.xve)\!:\!(P, \pi \,|\, \rho) \geq (P \,|\, \rho).$$

Composing these two conversions with C gives:

$$(\lambda x.\lambda v.Cxve)\!:\!Gen(A, P' \Rightarrow \nu') \geq (P \,|\, \rho)$$

which yields the required equality:

$$v\!:\!P \,|\, A \vdash (\lambda x.\lambda v.Cxve)(\lambda v'.E'')v = C(\lambda v'.E'')ve = E'e : \rho.$$

Case ($\Rightarrow I$)**:** We have a derivation of the form:

$$\frac{v\!:\!P, w\!:\!\pi, u\!:\!P' \,|\, A \vdash E \leadsto E' : \rho}{v\!:\!P, u\!:\!P' \,|\, A \vdash E \leadsto \lambda w.E' : \pi \Rightarrow \rho}$$

By induction, $v'\!:\!P' \,|\, A \overset{s}{\vdash} E \leadsto E'' : \nu'$ and $v\!:\!P, w\!:\!\pi, u\!:\!P' \,|\, A \vdash C(\lambda v'.E'')vwu = E' : \rho$ where $C\!:\!Gen(A, P' \Rightarrow \nu') \geq (P, \pi, P' \,|\, \rho)$. It is straightforward to show that:

$$(\lambda x.\lambda v.\lambda u.\lambda w.xvwu)\!:\!(P, \pi, P' \,|\, \rho) \geq (P, P' \,|\, \pi \Rightarrow \rho)$$

which, composing with C, gives $C' = \lambda x.\lambda v.\lambda u.\lambda w.Cxvwu$ such that:

$$C'\!:\!Gen(A, P' \Rightarrow \nu') \geq (P, P' \,|\, \pi \Rightarrow \rho).$$

To complete the proof for this case, note that:

$$v\!:\!P \,|\, A \vdash C'(\lambda v'.E'')vu = \lambda w.C(\lambda v'.E'')vwu = \lambda w.E' : \pi \Rightarrow \rho$$

using (β) and (β_e).

Case ($\forall E$)**:** We have a derivation of the form:

$$\frac{v\!:\!P \,|\, A \vdash E \leadsto E' : \forall t.\sigma}{v\!:\!P \,|\, A \vdash E \leadsto E' : [\tau/t]\sigma}$$

By induction, $v'\!:\!P' \,|\, A \overset{s}{\vdash} E \leadsto E'' : \nu'$ and $v\!:\!P \,|\, A \vdash C(\lambda v'.E'')v = E' : \forall t.\sigma$ where $C\!:\!Gen(A, P' \Rightarrow \nu') \geq (v\!:\!P \,|\, \forall t.\sigma)$. By Proposition 5.6, $id\!:\!\forall t.\sigma \geq [\tau/t]\sigma$ and hence by Proposition 5.11, $id\!:\!(P \,|\, \forall t.\sigma) \geq (P \,|\, [\tau/t]\sigma)$. Composing with C we obtain:

$$C\!:\!Gen(A, P' \Rightarrow \nu') \geq (P \,|\, [\tau/t]\sigma)$$

and the result follows since, using the equality given above:

$$v\!:\!P \,|\, A \vdash C(\lambda v'.E'')v = E' : [\tau/t]\sigma.$$

Case ($\forall I$)**:** We have a derivation of the form:

$$\frac{v\!:\!P \,|\, A \vdash E \leadsto E' : \sigma}{v\!:\!P \,|\, A \vdash E \leadsto E' : \forall t.\sigma}$$

where $t \notin TV(A)$ and $t \notin TV(P)$. By induction, $v' : P' \,|\, A \overset{s}{\vdash} E \leadsto E'' : \nu'$ and $v\!:\!P \,|\, A \vdash C(\lambda v'.E'')v = E' : \sigma$ where $C\!:\!Gen(A, P' \Rightarrow \nu') \geq (P \,|\, \sigma)$.

Write $Gen(A, P' \Rightarrow \nu') = (\forall \alpha_i.P' \Rightarrow \nu')$ and suppose that $\sigma = (\forall \beta_j.Q \Rightarrow \nu)$ where none of β_j appears free in $Gen(A, P' \Rightarrow \nu')$. Note that if $t \notin TV(\sigma)$, then $\forall t.\sigma = \sigma$ and the result is immediate. We can therefore assume that $t \in TV(\sigma)$ and hence that $t \notin \{\alpha_i\}$.

Since $C\!:\!Gen(A, P' \Rightarrow \nu') \geq (P \,|\, \sigma)$, there are types τ_i such that:

$$\nu = [\tau_i/\alpha_i]\nu', \quad v\!:\!P, w\!:\!Q \Vdash e : [\tau_i/\alpha_i]P' \quad \text{and} \quad \vdash C = \lambda x.\lambda v.\lambda w.xe.$$

Note that $[\tau_i/\alpha_i] = [\tau_i/\alpha_i, t/t]$ (because $t \notin \{\alpha_i\}$) and that t does not appear free in P by hypothesis. Furthermore, t does not appear free in $Gen(A, P' \Rightarrow \nu')$ since that would contradict the hypothesis that $t \notin TV(A)$. These observations are exactly what is needed to show that:

$$C : Gen(A, P' \Rightarrow \nu') \geq (v : P \,|\, \forall t.\sigma),$$

and the equality $v : P \,|\, A \vdash c(\lambda v'.E'')v = E' : \forall t.\sigma$ needed to complete the proof follows directly from above.

This completes the proof. □

Theorem 5.26 *If $P \,|\, TA \stackrel{W}{\vdash} E \leadsto E' : \tau$, then $P \,|\, TA \stackrel{s}{\vdash} E \leadsto E' : \tau$.*

By induction on the structure of $P \,|\, TA \stackrel{W}{\vdash} E \leadsto E' : \tau$. The proofs for the cases where the last rule in the derivation is $(var)^W$ or $(\to I)^W$ are straightforward. The remaining cases are:

Case $(\to E)^W$: We have a derivation of the form:

$$\frac{P \,|\, TA \stackrel{W}{\vdash} E \leadsto E' : \tau \quad Q \,|\, T'TA \stackrel{W}{\vdash} F \leadsto F' : \tau' \quad T'\tau \stackrel{U}{\sim} \tau' \to \alpha}{U(T'P, Q) \,|\, UT'TA \stackrel{W}{\vdash} EF \leadsto E'F' : U\alpha}$$

where α is a new variable. By induction, $P \,|\, TA \stackrel{s}{\vdash} E \leadsto E' : \tau$ and hence $UT'P, UQ \,|\, UT'TA \stackrel{s}{\vdash} E \leadsto E' : UT'\tau$ by Proposition 5.19 (applying the substitution UT') and by Proposition 5.21 (using the entailment $UT'P, UQ \Vdash UT'P$). Note that $UT'\tau = U\tau' \to U\alpha$ by definition of U and hence we have $UT'P, UQ \,|\, UT'TA \stackrel{s}{\vdash} E \leadsto E' : U\tau' \to U\alpha$.

By a similar argument, $UT'P, UQ \,|\, UT'TA \stackrel{s}{\vdash} F \leadsto F' : U\tau'$ and hence by $(\to E)^s$ we obtain $UT'P, UQ \,|\, UT'TA \stackrel{s}{\vdash} EF \leadsto E'F' : U\alpha$.

Case $(let)^W$: We have a derivation of the form:

$$\frac{v : P \,|\, TA \stackrel{W}{\vdash} E \leadsto E' : \tau \quad P' \,|\, T'(TA_x, x : \sigma) \stackrel{W}{\vdash} F \leadsto F' : \tau'}{P' \,|\, T'TA \stackrel{W}{\vdash} (\mathbf{let}\ x = E\ \mathbf{in}\ F) \leadsto (\mathbf{let}\ x = \lambda v.E'\ \mathbf{in}\ F) : \tau'}$$

where $\sigma = Gen(TA, P \Rightarrow \tau)$. By Proposition 5.8, there is a substitution R such that $RTA = T'TA$ and $Gen(T'TA, R(P \Rightarrow \tau)) = T'Gen(TA, P \Rightarrow \tau)$. Write $\sigma' = Gen(T'TA, R(P \Rightarrow \tau)) = T'\sigma$. The required derivation can now be constructed:

$$\frac{\dfrac{\dfrac{v : P \,|\, TA \stackrel{W}{\vdash} E \leadsto E' : \tau}{v : P \,|\, TA \stackrel{s}{\vdash} E \leadsto E' : \tau}\,(a)}{v : RP \,|\, T'TA \stackrel{s}{\vdash} E \leadsto E' : R\tau} \quad \dfrac{\dfrac{P' \,|\, T'(TA_x, x : \sigma) \stackrel{W}{\vdash} F \leadsto F' : \tau'}{P' \,|\, T'TA_x, x : T'\sigma \stackrel{s}{\vdash} F \leadsto F' : \tau'}\,(b)}{P' \,|\, T'TA_x, x : \sigma' \stackrel{s}{\vdash} F \leadsto F' : \tau'}\,(c)}{P' \,|\, T'TA \stackrel{s}{\vdash} (\mathbf{let}\ x = E\ \mathbf{in}\ F) \leadsto (\mathbf{let}\ x = \lambda v.E'\ \mathbf{in}\ F) : \tau'}\,(let)^s$$

where (a) and (b) are justified by induction and (c) follows from $T'\sigma = \sigma'$.

This completes the proof. □

> **Theorem 5.28** *Suppose that* $v{:}P\,|\,SA \overset{s}{\vdash} E \leadsto E' : \tau$. *Then* $w{:}Q\,|\,TA \overset{W}{\vdash} E \leadsto E'' : \nu$ *and there is a substitution* R *such that* $S \approx RT$, $\tau = R\nu$, $v{:}P \Vdash e : RQ$ *and* $v{:}P\,|\,SA \vdash E' = [e/w]E'' : \tau$.

By induction on the structure of $v{:}P\,|\,SA \overset{s}{\vdash} E \leadsto E' : \tau$.

Case $(var)^s$: Suppose that $(x:\sigma) \in A$ where $\sigma = (\forall \alpha_i . Q \Rightarrow \nu)$. Pick new variables β_i so that $S\sigma = \forall \beta_i . S[\beta_i/\alpha_i](Q \Rightarrow \nu)$. We therefore have a derivation of the form:

$$\frac{(x : S\sigma) \in SA \quad v{:}P \Vdash e : [\tau_i/\beta_i](S[\beta_i/\alpha_i]Q)}{v{:}P\,|\,SA \overset{s}{\vdash} x \leadsto xe : [\tau_i/\beta_i](S[\beta_i/\alpha_i]\nu)}$$

Since $(x : (\forall \alpha_i . Q \Rightarrow \nu)) \in A$ and β_i are new variables we have a derivation:

$$v' : [\beta_i/\alpha_i]Q\,|\,A \overset{W}{\vdash} x \leadsto xv : [\beta_i/\alpha_i]\nu.$$

Let $R = S[\tau_i/\beta_i]$ and note that $R \approx S$. Furthermore:

$$[\tau_i/\beta_i](S[\beta_i/\alpha_i]\nu) = S[\tau_i/\alpha_i]\nu = S[\tau_i/\beta_i]([\beta_i/\alpha_i]\nu) = R([\beta_i/\alpha_i]\nu)$$

and, in a similar way:

$$v{:}P \Vdash e : [\tau_i/\beta_i](S[\beta_i/\alpha_i]Q) = e : R([\beta_i/\alpha_i]Q).$$

Finally note that $[e/v](xv) \equiv xe$ which gives the required equality.

Case $(\to E)^s$: We have a derivation of the form:

$$\frac{v{:}P\,|\,SA \overset{s}{\vdash} E \leadsto E' : \tau' \to \tau \quad v{:}P\,|\,SA \overset{s}{\vdash} F \leadsto F' : \tau'}{v{:}P\,|\,SA \overset{s}{\vdash} EF \leadsto E'F' : \tau}$$

By induction, $v' : P'\,|\,TA \overset{W}{\vdash} E \leadsto E'' : \nu'$ and there is a substitution R such that $S \approx RT$, $\tau' \to \tau = R\nu'$, $v{:}P \Vdash e' : RP'$ and:

$$v{:}P\,|\,SA \vdash E' = [e'/v']E'' : \tau' \Rightarrow \tau.$$

Writing $SA = R(TA)$ we have $v : P\,|\,R(TA) \overset{s}{\vdash} F \leadsto F' : \tau'$ and hence by induction $v'' : P''\,|\,T'(TA) \overset{W}{\vdash} F \leadsto F'' : \nu''$ and there is a substitution R' such that $R \approx R'T'$, $\tau' = R'\nu''$, $v{:}P \Vdash e'' : R'P''$ and:

$$v{:}P\,|\,SA \vdash F' = [e''/v'']F'' : \tau'.$$

Note that (without loss of generality) we can assume that the evidence variables v, v' and v'' are pairwise disjoint.

Pick a new variable α and let $R'' = R'[\tau/\alpha]$. Note that:

$$\begin{array}{rcl} R''(T'\nu') & = & R''T'\nu' \\ & = & R'T'\nu' \\ & = & R\nu' \\ & = & \tau' \rightarrow \tau \\ & = & R'\nu'' \rightarrow R''\alpha \\ & = & R''(\nu'' \rightarrow \alpha) \end{array}$$

and hence R'' is a unifier of $T'\nu'$ and $\nu'' \rightarrow \alpha$. It follows that $T'\nu' \overset{U}{\sim} (\nu'' \rightarrow \alpha)$ for some most general unifier U such that $R'' = U'U$ for some U'.

By $(\rightarrow E)^{\mathrm{W}}$, there is a derivation:

$$U(v' : T'P', v'' : P'') \,|\, UT'TA \overset{\mathrm{W}}{\vdash} EF \leadsto E''F'' : U\alpha.$$

Note that $S \approx RT \approx R'T'T \approx U'(UT'T)$, $U'(U\alpha) = R''\alpha = \tau$ and:

$$\begin{array}{rcll} v : P & \Vdash & e' : RP', e'' : R'P'' & (\text{by } (dist)) \\ & = & e' : R'T'P', e'' : R'P'' & (R \approx R'T') \\ & = & R''(e' : T'P', e'' : P'') & (R'' \approx R') \\ & = & U'U(e' : T'P', e'' : P'') & (R'' = U'U) \end{array}$$

Finally, the required equality can be established using:

$$v : P \,|\, A \vdash [e'/v', e''/v''](E''F'') = ([e'/v']E'')([e''/v'']F'') = E'F' : \tau.$$

Case $(\rightarrow I)^s$: We have a derivation of the form:

$$\frac{v : P \,|\, SA_x, x : \tau' \overset{s}{\vdash} E \leadsto E' : \tau}{P \,|\, SA \overset{s}{\vdash} \lambda x.E \leadsto \lambda x.E' : \tau' \rightarrow \tau}$$

Let α be a new variable and set $S' = S[\tau'/\alpha]$ so that the derivation for E can be written as $v : P \,|\, S'(A_x, x : \alpha) \overset{s}{\vdash} E \leadsto E' : \tau$. By induction, $v' : P' \,|\, T(A_x, x : \alpha) \overset{\mathrm{W}}{\vdash} E \leadsto E'' : \nu$ and there is a substitution R such that $S' \approx RT$, $\tau = T\nu$, $v : P \Vdash e' : RP'$ and:

$$v : P \,|\, SA_x, x : \tau' \vdash E' = [e'/v']E'' : \tau$$

from which it follows that:

$$v : P \,|\, SA \vdash [e'/v'](\lambda x.E'') = \lambda x.[e'/v']E'' = \lambda x.E' : \tau' \rightarrow \tau.$$

By $(\rightarrow I)^{\mathrm{W}}$, there is a derivation $v' : P' \,|\, TA \overset{\mathrm{W}}{\vdash} \lambda x.E \leadsto \lambda x.E'' : T\alpha \rightarrow \nu$. Note that $S \approx S' \approx RT$, $v : P \Vdash e' : RP'$ and:

$$R(T\alpha \rightarrow \nu) = RT\alpha \rightarrow R\nu = \tau' \rightarrow \tau.$$

Case $(let)^s$: We have a derivation of the form:

$$\frac{w : Q \,|\, SA \overset{s}{\vdash} E \leadsto E' : \nu \quad v : P \,|\, SA_x, x : \sigma \overset{s}{\vdash} F \leadsto F' : \tau}{v : P \,|\, SA \overset{s}{\vdash} (\textbf{let } x = E \textbf{ in } F) \leadsto (\textbf{let } x = \lambda w.E' \textbf{ in } F') : \tau}$$

where $\sigma = Gen(SA, Q \Rightarrow \nu)$. By induction, $w' : Q' \mid TA \vdash^{W} E \rightsquigarrow E'' : \nu'$ and there is a substitution R such that $S \approx RT$, $\nu = R\nu'$, $w : Q \Vdash f' : RQ'$ and $w : Q \mid SA \vdash E' = [f'/w']E'' : \nu$.

Writing $\eta = Gen(TA, Q' \Rightarrow \nu')$ we have:

$$\begin{array}{rcll} R\eta & = & RGen(TA, Q' \Rightarrow \nu') & \\ & \geq & Gen(RTA, RQ' \Rightarrow R\nu') & \text{(Proposition 5.8, conversion } id\text{)} \\ & = & Gen(SA, RQ' \Rightarrow R\nu') & (S \approx RT) \\ & = & Gen(SA, RQ' \Rightarrow \nu) & (\nu = R\nu') \\ & \geq & Gen(SA, Q \Rightarrow \nu) & \text{(Proposition 5.7, conversion } \lambda x.\lambda w.xf'\text{)} \\ & = & \sigma. & \end{array}$$

Composing these conversions we obtain $(\lambda x.\lambda w.xf') : R\eta \geq \sigma$ and hence:

$$R(TA_x, x : \eta) = (RTA_x, x : R\eta) = (SA_x, x : R\eta) \geq (SA_x, x : \sigma)$$

with conversion substitution $[\lambda w.xf'/x]$. It follows from Corollary 5.24 that:

$$v : P \mid R(TA_x, x : \eta) \vdash^{s} F \rightsquigarrow F'' : \tau$$

where $v : P \mid SA_x, x : \sigma \vdash [\lambda w.xf'/x]F' = F'' : \tau$.

By induction, $v' : P' \mid T'(TA_x, x : \eta) \vdash^{W} F \rightsquigarrow F''' : \tau'$ and there is a substitution R' such that $R \approx R'T'$, $\tau = R'\tau'$, $v : P \Vdash e' : R'P'$ and $v : P \mid SA_x, x : \sigma \vdash F'' = [e'/v']F''' : \tau$. By $(let)^{W}$ there is a derivation:

$$v' : P' \mid T'TA \vdash^{W} (\textbf{let } x = E \textbf{ in } F) \rightsquigarrow (\textbf{let } x = \lambda w'.E'' \textbf{ in } F''') : \tau'.$$

Note that R' satisfies $S \approx RT \approx R'(T'T)$, $\tau = R'\tau'$ and $v : P \Vdash e' : R'P'$. Finally, we consider:

$$\begin{array}{rcll} v : P \mid A & \vdash & [e'/v'](\textbf{let } x = \lambda w'.E'' \textbf{ in } F''') & \\ & = & \textbf{let } x = \lambda w'.E'' \textbf{ in } [e'/v']F''' & (v' \notin EV(\lambda w'.E'') = \emptyset) \\ & = & \textbf{let } x = \lambda w'.E'' \textbf{ in } F'' & (\vdash F'' = [e'/v']F''') \\ & = & \textbf{let } x = \lambda w'.E'' \textbf{ in } [\lambda w.xf'/x]F' & (\vdash [\lambda w.xf'/x]F' = F'') \\ & = & \textbf{let } x = [\lambda w'.E''/x](\lambda w.xf') \textbf{ in } F' & \text{(Proposition 5.4(1))} \\ & = & \textbf{let } x = \lambda w.(\lambda w'.E'')f' \textbf{ in } F' & \text{(substitution)} \\ & = & \textbf{let } x = \lambda w.[f'/w']E'' \textbf{ in } F' & (\beta_e) \\ & = & \textbf{let } x = E' \textbf{ in } F' & (\vdash E' = [f'/w']E'') \end{array}$$

which establishes the required equality.

This completes the proof. □

References

A. Aho, R. Sethi and J. Ullman (1986). *Compilers, principles, techniques and tools.* Addison Wesley.

A. Appel (1992). *Compiling with continuations.* Cambridge University Press.

L. Augustsson (1984). A compiler for lazy ML. In *ACM Symposium on Lisp and Functional Programming Languages.* Austin, Texas. ACM Press.

L. Augustsson (1991). Haskell B. user's manual. Draft notes included as part of the distribution for Haskell B. and LML. December 1991.

H. Barendregt (1991). Introduction to generalised type systems. *Journal of functional programming,* volume 1, part 2. Cambridge University Press, April 1991.

R.S. Bird and P. Wadler (1989). *Introduction to functional programming.* Prentice Hall International, 1989.

S.M. Blott (1991). An approach to overloading with polymorphism. Ph.D. thesis, Department of computing science, University of Glasgow, July 1991 (draft version).

V. Breazu-Tannen, T. Coquand, C.A. Gunter and A. Scedrov (1989). Inheritance and coercion. In *IEEE Symposium on Logic in Computer Science,* Asilomar, California, June 1989.

K.B. Bruce, A.R. Meyer and J.C. Mitchell (1990). The semantics of second order lambda calculus. In G. Huet (ed.), *Logical Foundations of Functional Programming,* Addison Wesley, 1990.

L. Cardelli (1988). A semantics of multiple inheritance. *Information and Computation,* 76.

L. Cardelli and J.C. Mitchell (1990). Operations on records. In *Fifth International Conference on Mathematical Foundations of Programming Language Semantics.* Lecture notes in computer science 442, Springer Verlag, 1990. (An earlier version appeared as Technical report 48, Digitial Equipment Corporation, Systems Research Center, August 1989.)

K. Chen, P. Hudak and M. Odersky (1992). Parametric type classes (extended abstract). In *ACM Conference on LISP and functional programming* San Francisco, California, June 1992.

D. Clément, J. Despeyroux, T. Despeyroux and G. Kahn (1986). A simple applicative language: Mini-ML. In *ACM symposium on LISP and functional programming*, Cambridge, Massachusetts, August 1986.

P.-L. Curien and G. Ghelli (1990). Coherence of subsumption. In *Fifteenth Colloquium on Trees in Algebra and Programming.* Lecture notes in computer science 431, Springer Verlag.

H.B. Curry and R. Feys (1958). *Combinatory logic.* North Holland, Amsterdam.

L. Damas (1985). Type assignment in programming languages. PhD thesis, University of Edinburgh, CST-33-85.

L. Damas and R. Milner (1982). Principal type schemes for functional programs. In *8th Annual ACM Symposium on Principles of Programming languages*, Albuquerque, New Mexico, January 1982.

J. Fairbairn, and S. Wray (1987). Tim: a simple, lazy abstract machine to execute supercombinators. In *Functional Programming Languages and Computer Architecture.* Lecture notes in computer science 274, Springer Verlag.

Y.-C. Fuh and P. Mishra (1989). Polymorphic subtype inference: Closing the theory-practice gap. Lecture notes in computer science 352, Springer Verlag.

Y.-C. Fuh and P. Mishra (1990). Type inference with subtypes. *Theoretical computer science*, 73.

J.-Y. Girard (1971). Une extension de l'interprétation de Gödel à l'analyse et son application à l'élimination des coupures dans l'analyse et la théorie de types. Fenstad (ed.), Proceedings of the Scandanavian logic symposium. North Holland.

J.-Y. Girard, P. Taylor and Y. Lafont (1989). *Proofs and types.* Cambridge tracts in theoretical computer science. Cambridge University Press.

K. Hammond and S. Blott (1989). Implementing Haskell type classes. *Proceedings of the 1989 Glasgow Workshop on Functional Programming*, Fraserburgh, Scotland. Workshops in computing series, Springer Verlag.

R.W. Harper and B.C. Pierce (1990). Extensible records without subsumption. Technical report CMU-CS-90-102, Carnegie Mellon University, School of computer science, February 1990.

R. Harper and J.C. Mitchell (1993). On the type structure of Standard ML. *ACM Transactions on Programming Languages and Systems*, 15, 2, April 1993.

B. Hilken and D. Rydeheard (1991). Towards a categorical semantics of type classes. In *Mathematical Foundations of Computer Science.* Lecture notes in computer science 520, Springer Verlag.

J.R. Hindley (1969). The principal type-scheme of an object in combinatory logic. *Transactions of the American Mathematical Society*, 146, December 1969.

J.R. Hindley and J.P. Seldin (1986) *Introduction to combinators and λ-calculus.* London mathematical society student texts 1. Cambridge University Press.

C.K. Holst (1990). Improving full laziness. *Proceedings of the 1990 Glasgow Workshop on Functional Programming,* Ullapool, Scotland. Workshops in computing series, Springer Verlag.

W.A. Howard (1980). The formulae-as-types notion of construction. In Seldin, J.P. and Hindley, J.R. (eds), *To H.B. Curry: Essays on combinatory logic, lambda calculus and formalism.* Academic Press.

P. Hudak, S.L. Peyton Jones and P. Wadler (eds.) (1992). Report on the programming language Haskell, version 1.2. *ACM SIGPLAN notices,* 27, 5, May 1992.

L.A. Jategaonkar and J.C. Mitchell (1988). ML with extended pattern matching and subtypes (preliminary version). In *ACM conference on LISP and Functional Programming,* Snowbird, Utah, July 1988.

T. Johnsson (1984). Efficient compilation of lazy evaluation. In *SIGPLAN '84 symposium on compiler construction.* Montreal, Canada.

T. Johnsson (1987). Compiling lazy functional languages. PhD thesis, Programming methodology group, Chalmers University, Göteborg, Sweden.

M.P. Jones (1990). Computing with lattices: An application of type classes. Technical report PRG-TR-11-90, Programming Research Group, Oxford University Computing Laboratory, June 1990. Revised version appears in *Journal of Functional Programming,* volume 2, part 4, October 1992.

M.P. Jones (1991a). Towards a theory of qualified types. Technical report PRG-TR-6-91, Programming Research Group, Oxford University Computing Laboratory, April 1991.

M.P. Jones (1991b). Type inference for qualified types. Technical report PRG-TR-10-91, Programming Research Group, Oxford University Computing Laboratory, June 1991.

M.P. Jones (1991c). An introduction to Gofer. Included as part of the distribution for Gofer version 2.21. November 1991.

M.P. Jones (1992a). A theory of qualified types. In *European symposium on programming,* Rennes, France, February 1992. Lecture notes in computer science 582, Springer Verlag.

M.P. Jones (1992b). Programming with constructor classes (preliminary summary). In *Draft Proceedings of the Fifth Annual Glasgow Workshop on Functional Programming,* Ayr, Scotland, July 1992.

M.P. Jones (1993a). Partial evaluation for dictionary-free overloading. Yale University, Department of Computer Science, Research Report YALEU/DCS/RR-959, April 1993. Revised version appears in *ACM SIGPLAN Workshop on Partial Evaluation and Semantics-Based Program Manipulation,* Orlando, Florida, June 1994.

M.P. Jones (1993b). A system of constructor classes: overloading and implicit higher-order polymorphism. In *Proceedings of the 6th ACM conference on Functional Programming Languages and Computer Architecture*, Copenhagen, Denmark, ACM Press, June 1993. Expanded version to appear in the *Journal of functional programming.*

M.P. Jones and L. Duponcheel (1993). Composing Monads. Yale University, Department of Computer Science, Research Report YALEU/DCS/RR-1004, December 1993.

M.P. Jones (1994a). ML typing, explicit polymorphism and qualified types. In *TACS '94: Conference on theoretical aspects of computer software*, Sendai, Japan, April 1994. Lecture notes in computer science, Springer Verlag.

M.P. Jones (1994b). Improving and simplifying qualified types. Yale University, Department of Computer Science, Research Report, May 1994.

S. Kaes (1988). Parametric overloading in polymorphic programming languages. In *European symposium on programming*, Nancy, France. Lecture notes in computer science 300, Springer Verlag.

S. Kaes (1992). Type inference in the presence of overloading, subtyping and recursive types. In *ACM Conference on LISP and functional programming* San Francisco, California, June 1992.

X. Leroy and P. Weis (1991). Polymorphic type inference and assignment. In *18th Annual ACM Symposium on Principles of Programming languages*, Orlando, Florida, January 1991.

X. Leroy (1993). Polymorphism by name for references and continuations. In *20th Annual Symposium on Principles of Programming Languages*, Charleston, South Carolina, January 1993.

S. MacLane (1971). *Categories for the working mathematician.* Graduate texts in mathematics, 5. Springer Verlag.

R. Milner (1978). A theory of type polymorphism in programming. *Journal of Computer and System Sciences*, 17, 3.

J.C. Mitchell (1984). Coercion and type inference (summary). In *11th Annual ACM symposium on Principles of Programming Languages.* Salt Lake City, Utah, January 1984.

J.C. Mitchell (1988). Polymorphic type inference and containment. *Information and computation*, 76, 1988. Included, with corrections, in G. Huet (ed.), *Logical Foundations of Functional Programming*, Addison Wesley, 1990.

J.C. Mitchell (1990). A type-inference approach to reduction properties and semantics of polymorphic expressions. In G. Huet (ed.), *Logical Foundations of Functional Programming*, Addison Wesley, 1990.

J.C. Mitchell (1991). Type inference with simple subtypes. *Journal of functional programming*, volume 1, part 3. Cambridge University Press, July 1991.

T. Nipkow and G. Snelting (1991). Type classes and overloading resolution via order-sorted unification. In *5th ACM conference on Functional Programming Languages and Computer Architecture*, Cambridge, MA, August 1991. Lecture notes in computer science 523, Springer Verlag.

M. Odersky (1992). Observers for linear types. In *European symposium on programming*, Rennes, France, February 1992. Lecture notes in computer science 582, Springer Verlag.

A. Ohori and P. Buneman (1988). Type inference in a database programming language. In *ACM conference on LISP and Functional Programming*, Snowbird, Utah, July 1988.

A. Ohori (1989). A simple semantics for ML polymorphism. In *4th International Conference on Functional Programming Languages and Computer Architecture*, Imperial College, London, September 1989. ACM Press.

A. Ohori and P. Buneman (1989). Static type inference for parametric classes. In *Proceedings OOPSLA '89*, ACM SIGPLAN notices, October 1991.

A. Ohori (1992). A compilation method for ML-style polymorphic record calculi. In *19th Annual Symposium on Principles of Programming Languages*, Santa Fe, New Mexico, January 1992.

S.L. Peyton Jones (1987). *The implementation of functional programming languages.* Prentice Hall International.

S.L. Peyton Jones and D. Lester (1991). A modular fully-lazy lambda lifter in Haskell. *Software – Practice and Experience*, **21**(5).

S.L. Peyton Jones and P. Wadler (1992). A static semantics for Haskell (draft). Manuscript, Department of Computing Science, University of Glasgow, February 1992.

S.L. Peyton Jones (1992). Implementing lazy functional languages on stock hardware: the spineless tagless G-machine. *Journal of functional programming* (to appear). Cambridge University Press.

D. Rémy (1989). Typechecking records and variants in a natural extension of ML. In *Sixteenth Annual ACM Symposium on Principles of Programming Languages.* Austin, Texas, January 1989.

D. Rémy (1992). Efficient representation of extensible records. In *ACM SIGPLAN workshop on ML and its applications.* San Francisco, June 1992 (To appear).

J.C. Reynolds (1974). Towards a theory of type structure. *Paris colloquium on programming.* Lecture notes in computer science 19, Springer-Verlag.

J.C. Reynolds (1991). The coherence of languages with intersection types. In *Theoretical aspects of computer software.* Lecture notes in computer science 526, Springer Verlag.

J.G. Riecke (1990). A complete and decidable proof system for call-by-value equalities (preliminary report). In *17th International Colloquium on Automata, Languages and Programming*, Warwick University, England, July 1990. Lecture notes in computer science 443, Springer Verlag.

J.A. Robinson (1965). A machine-oriented logic based on the resolution principle. *Journal of the Association for Computing Machinery*, 12, 1965.

G. Smith (1991). Polymorphic type inference for languages with overloading and subtyping. PhD thesis, Department of Computer Science, Cornell University, Ithaca, New York. August 1991.

R. Stansifer (1988). Type inference with subtypes. In *Fifteenth Annual ACM Symposium on Principles of Programming Languages.* San Diego, California, January 1988.

C. Strachey (1967). *Fundamental concepts in programming languages.* International summer school in computer programming, Copenhagen.

S. Thatte (1990). Type inference and implicit scaling. In *European Symposium on Programming.* Lecture notes in computer science 432, Springer Verlag.

S. Thatte (1991). Coercive type isomorphism. In *5th ACM Conference on Functional Programming Languages and Computer Architecture*, Cambridge, MA, August 1991. Lecture notes in computer science 523, Springer Verlag.

S. Thatte (1992). Typechecking with ad hoc polymorphism (preliminary report). Manuscript, Department of mathematics and computer science, Clarkson University, Potsdam, NY. May 1992.

J. Tiuryn (1990). Type inference problems: A survey. In *Mathematical Foundations of Computer Science.* Lecture notes in computer science 452, Springer Verlag.

D. Volpano and G. Smith (1991). On the complexity of ML typability with overloading. In *5th ACM conference on Functional Programming Languages and Computer Architecture.* Lecture notes in computer science 523. Springer Verlag.

P. Wadler and S. Blott (1989). How to make ad-hoc polymorphism less ad-hoc. In *Sixteenth Annual ACM Symposium on Principles of Programming Languages.* Austin, Texas, January 1989. ACM Press.

P. Wadler (1989). Theorems for free! In *Fourth ACM conference on Functional Programming Languages and Computer Architecture.* London, September 1989. Addison Wesley.

P. Wadler (1990). Comprehending monads. In *ACM conference on LISP and Functional Programming*, Nice, France, June 1990.

P. Wadler (1991). Simplified overloading for Haskell 2. Distributed to the Haskell mailing list, April 1991.

P. Wadler (1992). The essence of functional programming. In *19th Annual Symposium on Principles of Programming Languages*, Santa Fe, New Mexico, January 1992.

M. Wand (1987). Complete type inference for simple objects. In *IEEE Symposium on Logic in Computer Science.* Ithaca, New York, June 1987.

A.K. Wright (1992). Typing references by effect inference. In *European symposium on programming*, Rennes, France, February 1992. Lecture notes in computer science 582, Springer Verlag.

A.K. Wright (1993). Polymorphism for imperative languages without imperative types. Rice University Technical Report TR93-200, February 1993.

Index